Colin White & Laurie Boucke

The UnDutchables®

an observation of the netherlands:
its culture and its inhabitants

Illustrated by Rusty Haller

Photographs by
Colin White, Laurie Boucke

**WHITE
BOUCKE**
PUBLISHING

LAFAYETTE, COLORADO

UnDutchables is a registered trademark of White-Boucke Publishing, Inc.

First Published December 1989 (0-9625006-0-7)
Second Edition February 1991 (0-9625006-1-5)
Third Edition February 1993 (0-9625006-3-1)
Fourth Edition October 2001 (1-888580-22-4)
Fifth Edition January 2006 (1-888580-32-1)
Sixth Edition March 2010 (1-888580-44-5)
Seventh Edition August 2013 (1-888580-47-X)

Printed in USA
ISBN: 978-1-888580-47-1

LIBRARY OF CONGRESS CATALOGING-IN-PUBLICATION DATA
White, Colin, 1949-
The UnDutchables : an observation of the Netherlands: its culture and its inhabitants / Colin White & Laurie Boucke ; illustrated by Rusty Haller ; photographs by Colin White, Laurie Boucke. -- 7th edition.
p cm
Includes index.
ISBN 978-1-888580-47-1 (trade pbk.)
1. Netherlands--Social life and customs--20th century. 2. Netherlands--Social life and customs--21st century. 3. Netherlands--Description and travel. 4. Netherlands--Guidebooks. 5. Dutch--Social life and customs. I. Boucke, Laurie. II. Haller, Rusty, illustrator. III. Title.

DJ290.W45 2013
949.207--dc23   2013018797

WHITE BOUCKE PUBLISHING
PO BOX 400, LAFAYETTE, CO 80026, USA

Hearty thanks to all those who have provided ideas, suggestions, anecdotes and artwork for this and earlier editions, with special mention to:

Brendan Bartram, Tom Bijvoet, Brian Bramson, Paul Claassen, John Elston, Eva Goetschel, the late Rusty Haller, Bertie Kaal, Lonneke Kersten, Jackie Lubeck, Arjen Meima, Steven Pemberton, Wim Stortenbeek, Gerben van den Bergh, Anton van Hooff, Jacob Vossestein, & Walter Wynbelt.

TABLE OF CONTENTS

PREFACE

This is the seventh edition and 24th year in publication of *The UnDutchables: an observation of the Netherlands, its culture and its inhabitants*. When first published in 1989, we declared the book to be an impressionistic view of a certain side of the Dutch as it is often perceived by visitors to Holland. In the ensuing years it has brought much laughter to its readers and enabled many to vent their frustrations through joking. This is thus not a dry, scholarly offering. Rather, it is offered as a pro-Dutch, fun yet irreverent exposé. Thanks to their spirit of openness, the humour has resonated well with most Netherlanders.

It is not possible to cover every province, town, custom and aspect of life in a short work—such information is available elsewhere. We have avoided such an approach as it would have stifled the character of this book. Some readers may resent what they perceive to be stereotypic images, but all people form such images (to some extent) when they travel or reside abroad. Fortunately, most readers have been able to appreciate the humour without feeling offended.

Although much of the book clearly concerns contemporary Dutch life, certain national traits have been around for centuries. These have been commented upon in works dating back to the 1600s. We believe the Dutch will still be renowned for certain classic characteristics for many generations to come.

Similarly, the book is biased towards the urban environment, especially Amsterdam. However, in travelling through the countryside, one finds many of the same things, perhaps in a more peaceful setting and at a slower pace, but fundamentally the same traits: commercial cunning; cosy homes; coffee rituals; money worshipping; moralizing; criticizing; obsession with weather; humanitarianism; compromise and consensus; straightforwardness; and so forth.

Many readers view this book as a psychological survival kit for expats—the lowdown on Holland, so to speak. This being the case, we feel that our efforts have been more than worthwhile.

Colin White & Laurie Boucke
Colorado USA, August 2013

A WORD OF WARNING

Yes, we, the Dutch, are a funny lot, but we are much too straight to notice that ourselves.

Being a kind of outsider as a little boy, I noticed that something was warped, especially when I made friends in other countries, but I could not put my finger on it. Part of me, a defining part, was out of sync with the rest of the world. I wanted to know what it was, for, being a child of the Sixties, I wanted to know myself. That's when I started collecting books about the Dutch, written by foreigners. I still do, but they were stiff and academic and did not tell me much . . . until May 1990, when I stumbled upon *The UnDutchables*. This sloppy bundle of photocopied leaflets, filled with wisecracks about the Dutch, made me laugh so hard, that I stepped outside myself and had my first really good look at that side of the Dutch that is hidden from themselves by themselves.

At the time I wrote a daily column for *Het Parool*, and I immediately attested to the importance of this humorous and truthful masterpiece, for it showed so painfully where we had stumbled from what we thought was the sublime into the ridiculous.

I ended my review with the words "**Een werkje dat nog jaren meekan, dus.**" ("So a booklet that will go far"). And that it did.

As it so eminently deserved, a Dutch translation was made, and it was at least as popular as the original. They both went through several

INTRODUCTION
the way the textbooks sell it

THERE . . .

The Netherlands: A country (often called Holland) in Western Europe bordering on the North Sea, with Belgium on its southern frontier and Germany on its eastern flank; total area 41,526 km² (16,485 sq miles) approximately, of which 18.41 percent is water; divided into 12 provinces—plus three Caribbean islands—which in turn are divided into municipalities; official language, Dutch; capital, Amsterdam; seat of government, The Hague; population nearly 17 million and counting (2013).

"Holland" is an informal, cosy name for the country,[1] but officially it defines the dominant provinces of North Holland and South Holland. Originally heavily forested, these provinces were referred to as "Holt Land" (lit. "wood land"), from which the word "Holland" derives.

THEM . . .

The area was occupied by Celts and Frisians who came under Roman rule from the 1st century BC until the 4th century AD and was then overrun by German tribes, with the Franks establishing an ascendancy during the 5th–8th centuries. During the Middle Ages, it was divided between numerous principalities. The northern

(Dutch) swamp (part of the Habsburg Empire) revolted in the 16th century against Spanish attempts to crush the Protestant faith and won independence in a series of wars lasting into the 17th century, becoming a Protestant republic. The southern part was absorbed into the Spanish Habsburgs and then in 1713 into the Austrian Habsburgs. Prior to wars with England and France, the country enjoyed great prosperity and became a centre of art and scholarship as well as a leading maritime power, building up a vast commercial empire in the East Indies, South Africa and Brazil. In the 18th century, it sharply declined as a European power. In 1814, north and south were united, but by 1840 the southern and eastern extremities of the Netherlands had become the independent nations of Belgium and Luxembourg. The Dutch managed to maintain their neutrality in World War I, but were occupied by Germany in World War II.

The post-war period has seen the country turn away from its traditional dependence on agriculture, although farming is still an important part of the economy. In 1960, large quantities of natural gas were discovered in the north; the ensuing wealth helped the Dutch mould their country into a "super" welfare state and emerge as a key figure (while struggling to maintain its individuality) in the increasingly oppressive European Union.

1. Although "the Netherlands" and "Holland" are used interchangeably in much of the world and in this book, fringe areas of the country (particularly Limburg and Friesland) consider themselves very different to true "Hollanders" and are often insulted by the connection.

> "Never in my long and adventurous life have I known a people so riddled with paradoxes as the **Dutch.**"
>
> *Duke de Baena, The Dutch Puzzle, 1966*
>
> "We have to be clear about what makes this land so great: the freedom to be yourself."
>
> *Lodewijk Asscher, Social Affairs Minister*

GETTING ACQUAINTED

THERE . . .

Do not be surprised if one of your first impressions is of being in doll-house country. Everything is small, crowded and cramped: houses, streets, shops, supermarkets, parks, woods, cars—horizontally, vertically, diagonally, upside-down and inside-out. Holland is by far the most densely populated country in the Western European Union. With an average of 484 people per square kilometre of soggy land, its inhabitants have mastered the art of using the centimetre to the fullest.

This ability and talent has arisen, of course, from the fact that around 60 percent of the country consists of land reclaimed from the sea. And the reclaiming continues even today.

On an international flight, when the pilot announces that you are flying over Holland, don't blink! You'll miss it—it's that small. You can, in fact, cross the whole nation by car in three hours.

For those of you arriving by plane from distant lands, a word of advice. Having entered the country and adjusted to the barometric pressure prevalent below sea-level (jet lag withstanding), you'll undoubtedly want to view the windmills, tulips, cheese markets and canals. Water and horizontal hills abound. So do sex shops. And, yes, you'll see your share of wooden shoes and Frisian cows. Tourist attractions can be exhausted within a few days, so ration yourself carefully.

If you expect to find delicious national food or the exotic, forget it. If you like wide, open spaces or a little solitude in nature, this is not the country for you. There are no large forests or wide expanses of land. When walking in the woods, dunes or on the beach, you have the feeling that millions have trod wherever you place your feet. They have. Can this be the stuff that inspired Rembrandt and Van Gogh?

THEM . . .

The inhabitants of this small chunk of ex-seabed are not lacking in self-esteem, as reflected in literary titles such as *And the Dutch Created the Netherlands* and a KLM advertising poster that claimed: "*Most people only get to visit great works of art—the Dutch get to live in one.*"

They are bursting with dikes, liberalism, independence, equality and global beliefs. Some Dutchmen even go so far as to seriously believe that they should have the right to vote in US presidential elections. Why? "*Considering the amount of business that Holland does with America, it's just not democratic that we can't vote there!*" They brag about their freedom yet are caught in a self-imposed web of restrictions in the form of ever-increasing regulations and laws.

The Dutch appear a friendly lot: kind, polite and helpful to tourists. They love to talk about their country and to provide any directions or information you may require. Their fascination with things foreign— products, attitudes, ideas, customs, languages, etc.—is impressive and flattering. The Dutch reputation for tolerance is all too apparent to the overseas visitor. You get a strong message that: "*You can do whatever you want . . . as long as it doesn't interfere with me.*" But do not let this image fool you—it changes drastically if you stay long enough to be regarded as "part of the scene."

The longer you stay, the deeper you sink into it. The dark cloud of disapproval descends as your Dutch comrades constantly criticize what they consider to be unfavourable situations beyond their borders. There is no relief from this moralizing, despite the fact that similar or even worse situations often exist within their own kingdom. Do not take the onslaught personally. You will soon discover that the Dutch reprimand is not reserved for foreigners alone. The natives thrive on shaking their fingers at and scolding each other. One household in ten actually relocates to get away from the dancing digits of neighbours.

They also seem to be caught up in a cycle of endless envy. They cannot free themselves from feelings such as, "*If you are sitting, then I should be sitting too!*" They are extremely jealous of each other's possessions and keep a constantly updated mental inventory of what their neighbours, relatives and colleagues have and have not. But they are also a very giving people when it comes to charities and crises. They are world famous for their universal humanitarianism, and exercising this particular type of generosity gives them much satisfaction. The key to getting cash from cloggies is that they must feel that they WANT to give and not that they HAVE to give.

They always speak their mind and ask what most foreigners consider to be probing questions about one's personal life. Their directness gives many the impression that they are rude and crude— attributes they prefer to call "openness." You can put it to the test by discussing intimate and shocking topics with them that you would never dare speak about with persons of any other nationality. What may strike you as being blatantly blunt topics and comments are no more embarrassing or unusual to the Dutch than discussing the weather.

This frankness is linked to their reputation for being opinionated and obstinate. When they believe in something, they will stubbornly adhere to their principles through thick and thin, unless and until they are ready to change their mind of their own accord. It is easy for newcomers to view the Netherlands as a country full of pontificating alpha-cloggies battling for leadership of the herd.

A typical Dutchman stands some 18 hands high, the equivalent of 1.88 metres (6 feet 2 inches)—noticeably taller than the global average. In the event of a natural disaster, these lanky lowlanders can act as human periscopes and view their country as it was before man despoiled it. Yet this overwhelming advantage has become a cause for complaint about things not fitting them. Over a million men are too tall for their cars, tall women "bitch" about clothing being too short and the two genders combine to moan about ducking through doors, having to lay diagonally in hotel beds, sitting upright in bathtubs and crouching to see their faces in bathroom mirrors. The lanky look may now be on the way out as many are now increasing in girth. Over half of the population is overweight, with kids expanding the fastest.

Over the centuries, Dutchies have developed and refined a sort of sand psychology which manifests itself in many walks of life. Since most of the country is built on sand, the use of lego-roads is widespread. Streets are paved with bricks which are merely pounded into place.

Rusty Haller

The brick surface has no graded foundation layers. This construction method, combined with the Northern European climate, guarantees maximum inconvenience for motorists, cyclists and pedestrians: dips in the roads, sinking tramlines and a multitude of closed roads while re-flattening/re-tiling operations are in progress.

The Dutch proudly defend the character of their roads. Workmen need only lift up the requisite amount of bricks to reach the work area. One wonders if they would need to lift up any bricks at all if they constructed the roads properly in the first place.

A cloggy's prize possession is the Bicycle. It may be a multi-speed, ultra-light, racing model or a rusty old third-generation job, honourably handed down through the family. The country is infested with the contraptions, and the emotional attachment to them is great.

The Dutch are masters of innovation, although some visitors may never identify or appreciate the results. Innovation and experimentation

Laurie Boucke

Laying lengths of lowlands lego lanes

are constantly applied to a revolving process of refinement of social issues, agriculture, industry and urban/rural development. Sometimes the experiments are a success; sometimes they fail. Either way, new adventures in trial and error will rapidly replace the gains/losses. These progressive pursuits are announced and reported in the media with much pride and enthusiasm on an almost daily basis.

Hollanders enjoy one of the highest standards of living and rank among the leaders in longevity. Their quality of life is excellent, although this fact is often disguised by constant complaining about the same. But should a terminally ill Netherlander decide to shorten his life, he has the right to do so.

They are supreme masters of things connected with water: bridges, dikes, canals, rain, etc. They have constantly defended their sand against natural elements with an elaborate survival system, as they will not hesitate to tell you. After centuries of fighting the water and successfully reclaiming the land (***polders***), there is now a growing movement to reverse course and "cooperate with the water" by reflooding the sand-land (***ontpoldering***), effectively starting the whole man-vs-mud thing over again.

They have been a seafaring people for centuries on end. Along with this comes their love of travel, foreign cultures and bartering. There is nothing more exciting or satisfying for a Dutch person than to make a good deal. They have all the patience and time one can imagine if it means earning or saving a fraction of a €uro. They are also world trade experts, often ranking first place (worldwide) in tonnage at Rotterdam and first place in dairy and poultry export, while their agricultural export value ranks second in the world. Rotterdam also boasts of being the world's first fully automated container port.

Many of them are pathologically obsessed with a form of cleanliness which has little logical connection with practical hygiene. This is especially true of the older generation. It seems the older they grow, the cleaner everything must be. Perhaps it's the age-old connection between water and cleansing/purification that drives them to it.

As old age approaches, the Dutch(wo)man's ferocity of frankness dilutes. Although they are still in full possession of their Dutchness, it does not manifest itself as intensely as with the younger generations. Perhaps after decades of defiance and belligerence, they are finally prepared to "chill out," hand the baton to their heirs and adopt the philosophy:

We must view the world with
a more worldly view.

BECOMING THEM . . .

For readers who are going to sink in deeper and stay longer than the allotted tourist time (whether you want to, have to, or have to want to), you will likely need to prove yourself worthy of "clog(wo)manship" by completing a social integration course or *inburgeringscursus*. The Netherlands was the first country to require assimilation classes for immigrants, having introduced the practice back in 1996.

For some people, the course must be taken in advance of moving to Holland. For others, it is taken within the country (to gain/maintain residency or to continue existing welfare benefits). And for the lucky minority, it's never taken at all.

So far, there appears to be no established structure or content to the course. However, the following characteristics seem to prevail:

1. The course has three parts: culture, work and language.

2. The subject matter and presentation is largely dependent upon the mood, politics, sexual orientation, or other interests of the teacher.

The programme clearly needs some fine-tuning. Here is what some graduates learned in their classes:

"We learned all the major Dutch swear words and how to employ them against our neighbours."

"Dutch men are egotistically bloated, socially apathetic, and intimately inadequate."

"Dutch women are angry, shrill, domineering, and impaired in their ability to adequately nurture their families."

"For the cultural part, our class went to the Groningen museum and also took the canal boat ride through the city."

And here is how others reflect on their instructors/instruction:

"I didn't really hear Dutch as spoken by natives for the entire first eight months of lessons!"

"We students took it in turns for two weeks because there was no money for a teacher."

"The course book seemed to be trying to prepare foreigners for a dreary, low-satisfaction, creativity-impaired life here in Nederland . . . and trying to make us all go away."

By 2004 the attempt to make everyone in the Netherlands transparently Dutch came under threat from none other than then Minister for Integration and Immigration Maria Cornelia Frederika "Rita" Verdonk herself, who reportedly announced that:

"It is in the urgent interest of society to distinguish between naturalized Dutch and indigenous Dutch people. . . . It is not in contravention of the principle of equal treatment to treat unequal cases unequally."

THE POLITIC/ OF THEM . . .

The Netherlands is a parliamentary democratic constitutional monarchy where the main political parties (identified by their predominant initials—CDA, PvdA, VVD, etc.) duke it out in the upper and lower chambers (**Eerste Kamer** and **Tweede Kamer**) of the Binnenhof in The Hague.

Most Dutch are either disinterested or disgusted with politics/politicians. Some are both. Even though there are different national, provincial and local parties, only 300,000 people are registered members of a political party. Those who occasionally feel a spark of interest tend to form their own party based on the trends, issues, feelings and complaints *du jour*. The result is over 200 political parties, some with such diverse names as "Pirates Party," "Party for the Ice Skating Rink," "No Windmills," "A Computer for Everyone," "Better Neighbours" and "Islam Democrats." Here is one Dutchman's description of how the system works:

> *"Starting at the bottom of the pole we have our municipal governments. Anyone can start a political organization and take part in local (municipal) elections. All it needs is a fixed number of signatures, and presto, you have a new party. The problem is this: The same holds true for provincial and national elections, except for the required number of signatures. In essence this means anyone can grab a piece of the electoral pie if he can convince enough people to get his name on the list of candidates (**kieslijst**). And we certainly have enough of them to go around. Provincial government has an added bonus for those who get the job: It is the provincial government that chooses the **Eerste Kamer**. Thus part of our legislative system is undemocratic: The **Eerste Kamer** has to approve of the laws agreed upon in the **Tweede Kamer**. Since I cannot directly vote for those who are appointed to the **Eerste Kamer**, laws proposed by those whom I can vote for can be overturned by people who are only marginally a product of democracy in action.*
> *National elections are farcical. Since a majority in the **Tweede Kamer** is needed to form a government, and no party has a chance of winning 76 seats, a consensus is needed between a number of parties in order to get those 76 seats. There is simply no way to get your vote to do what you want it to do."*

Paul Claassen

PUBLIC TRANSPORT

n addition to the national train service, Holland (like most countries) utilizes regional bus companies to provide for local transportation of people. Larger urban areas also have tram systems, and Amsterdam and Rotterdam have metro train services. The public transport system (***openbaar vervoer*** or ***ov***) used to be excellent (efficient, modern and comfortable), but has been downgraded to "relatively good" (reasonably efficient, modern-ish and comfortable when not overcrowded). There are also ample taxis which can be costly, especially over longer distances. The domestic air network is understandably sparse. All forms of public transport are fairly reasonably priced if you know the rules of the game. If you don't, look forward to a frustrating and expensive experience.

OV-KAARTOLOGY . . .

For thirty-odd years the Netherlands employed a revolutionary ticketing system for public transportation whereby the country was divided into 2,226 individually numbered travel zones represented by individual strips on a multi-strip ticket (***strippenkaart***) which could be used on any bus, tram or metro in the country.

Eventually Dutch residents were in danger of understanding the strip/zone system, and travel books provided useful warnings and tips for visitors. It was time to change everything. Having been overwhelmingly impressed by the concept of the "paperless office," and with the entire nation obsessed with microchipping everything, Dutch transport experts spent 18 years developing a system that would weld the two concepts into the "paperless national transport ticket" and named it the *ov-chipkaart*.

Passengers pay per actual kilometre travelled, although the kilometre charge may differ with municipality. This is claimed to be "more fair" to the consumer than the old flat "per zone" charge. There is a family of cards, each of which serves a specific traveller demographic:

PERSONAL (*persoonlijke ov-chipkaart*). The personal card is styled much like a PIN card and includes a bad passport photo of the bearer. It can be automatically recharged with travel-€uros straight from your bank or giro account when necessary. It is ideal for the regular, seasoned traveller, as it qualifies the owner for discounts and other travel perks. It has built-in pickpocket protection (can be electronically invalidated). This card is only issued after providing the authorities with your personal life history.

ANONYMOUS (*anonieme ov-chipkaart*). The ideal choice for privacy freaks and less frequent travellers. This card can be borrowed (or stolen), but it cannot apply most discounts and cannot be automatically reloaded. It's the perfect card for tourists who want to pretend that they are Dutch.

DISPOSABLE (*wegwerpkaart*). This type of card has limited validity (number of hours, days or trips) and is supposedly available from tobacconists (if you can find one), news-agents, supermarkets, vending machines and similar locations. Short-duraton tickets can be bought on trams and buses. This is the most expensive way to use public transport, and therefore touted as the standard tourist card.

The system, where operational, functions through transponder-like sensors that read the cards and deduct the trip charges at vehicle/ station entry and exit points. Non-passengers are able to visit station platforms free of charge—providing they do not linger too long—but it is not yet clear if additional sensors will be installed in station toilets to replace the miserable little ladies who currently impose the pee fee. A highly stylized pink logo resembling two people engaging in oral sex announces where, in theory, *kaartjes* can be *koop*'ed. In reality, *kaartjes* often cannot be *koop*'ed from the *kaartjes koop*'ing machines since there is a fair chance that the damned thing will not spit out tickets (which is not surprising since the machines are made in France and the *kaartjes* come from Britain).

OFF THE RAILS . . .

The national train service (*Nederlandse Spoorwegen*) uses a more conventional system whereby you purchase a ticket at the point of departure (kiosk/*servicebalie* or ticket machine/*kaartautomaat*) or over the Internet. To take the boredom out of this mundane task, a range of ticket categories has been introduced which will defy the most adept financial wizard. In fact, the matter is so complex that *Nederlandse Spoorwegen* publishes an annual travel/price guide to give the potential traveller a fighting chance at getting a fair deal on the journey cost. As an example, these are the class options that the class-loathing cloggies employ:

FIRST CLASS (*eerste klas*). Maximum comfort and minimum congestion at premium prices. Some trains have electronics charging points installed.

SECOND CLASS (*tweede klas*). This accounts for most of the overall train accommodation. Some seats are marked as quiet zones (for passengers who want to stop being Dutch for a while).

BIKE CLASS. You have to buy a special ticket (*Dagkaart fiets*) in order to sit on a buttock-bruising pull-down seat near the door alongside your Bike. Also, forget about going green at the most crucial times, as Bikes are not allowed on trains during rush hour.

For Internet addicts, the whole database is available online. To use the website database, you enter the starting point and destination, and the date and time of travel, and it will display your ticket options (with fares). Supplementary information includes:

secure Bicycle storage	Bicycle rental
Bicycle lockers/depot	taxi stand
paid parking	green wheels
ticket locket	baggage facilities
elevator installed	food services (defined)
NS service point	currency exchange
shops/flower vendors	newsagent
wheelchair ramps	Wi-Fi

Thus if you are touring the country, a laptop computer, tablet and/ or smartphone will serve you well as an addition to the other items you will need (see "What to Take," this chapter)—all for a country where you can easily travel the full perimeter in 24 hours.

We encourage visitors to experience the ticket *loket* queue while you still can. You will notice a curious sight: After purchasing a ticket, the average cloggy takes one sidestep (usually to the left) and spends a few moments fiddling before departing with a satisfied look. Foreigners might think the sidestep is part of the ticket purchasing process. Wrong. These Netherlanders (male or female) are merely organizing their plastic bags, taking an inventory of their coin purses and putting their tickets into their handbags or rucksacks.

KAARTJE/COP/ . . .

Long before the *ov-chipkaart* revolution, transportation authorities trusted passengers to purchase tickets. When it became obvious that the honour system had failed, ticket inspection squads were formed. At first, the controllers frequently dressed in plain clothes. This "uniform" was soon eliminated by the democratic Dutch who complained that a *zwart* (fare-evading, lit. black) passenger should have a fair chance to escape. Eventually controller-teams evolved into groups of conflicted cloggies dressed in a manner that could almost pass as uniforms.

*Kaartjes*cops are rarely lenient with offenders. Do not be surprised to witness the team frantically tackling a would-be escapee trying to sneak out of a bus or tram when it reaches a stop. If the *zwartrijder* tries to escape from their grasp, the vehicle will be delayed for the duration of the struggle. When the *zwartrijder* finally admits guilt, the dastard pays an on-the-spot fine that can be appealed later and then continues with the journey.

Transport companies originally hoped that nationwide adoption of the *ov-chipkaart* would render *zwartrijden* almost extinct, but the ease at which entry-exit readers can be tricked and the *chipkaart* can be hacked/ghosted has kept the game in play. Meanwhile, *Veolia Transport Nederland* started to tool-up with test tubes in order to collect passenger saliva, mucus and other bodily emissions spat and blown on the clothing and faces of their inspectors and conductors . . . for DNA testing. To even the score, *zwart*-techies have taken to Twitter to report recent *kaartjes*cop sightings, using the OV's own Wi-Fi system to distribute the info.

WHAT TO TAKE . . .

All nationalities have their habits and traits when it comes to public transport, especially on longer journeys. The Russians may take vodka or a chess set. Some nationalities will take their livestock to market on a bus. Instead of taking sheep, chickens and goats with them on public transport, the Dutch like to take their Bicycles, reading matter, mobile telephones and at least one very large bunch of flowers for everyone to admire. Reading matter, phones and flowers go free of charge since:

- They bring so much joy to the passengers.
- They are an excellent conversation piece.

The Dutch delight in taking dogs on all forms of public transport. Dog tickets are on sale if the dog is too large to fit in your shopping bag or prefers to sit on its own seat.

One last item that has become absolutely essential for **trein** travel is a plastic container . . . preferably sealable. For reasons of "economy" and "safety," many existing trains and stations had their toilet parts decommissioned, and new-build Sprinter Lighttrain units are loo*loos*. **Nederlandse Spoorwegen** claims that the space wasted by the on-board toilet compartment, which (unbelievably) is half the size of the standard home installation (see Chapter 5 – A Dutch Home), can be used to seat four additional passengers.

WAITING GAMES . . .

Whether you're waiting for the bus, tram, metro or train:

1. Form a compact mass with the others who are waiting, and do so as soon as the vehicle appears in the distance. When it arrives, block the doors so the exiting passengers cannot leave. Above all, do not move out of the way when the doors open and people attempt to get out, as this might speed things up. After all, you wouldn't want anyone to get ahead of you in the mob. If, however, you are a passenger waiting to exit, then you have the right to curse the idiots blocking your way. In some areas, you can only enter the vehicle through assigned doors where sentries are posted. Unfortunately, you cannot exit through these entry doors. In solving

the problem previously described, this solution has merely widened the snarl-up zone to include both the outside and inside, as passengers frantically try to reach the appropriate door before the vehicle departs.

2. In rush hour, there will be enough of you to form an additional blockade. Stand or slowly stroll so as to prevent those who have managed to exit from hurrying to the stairs or escalator, or to a connecting bus or tram. In this pinball game, you score points each time someone bumps into you or is otherwise inconvenienced and frustrated by you.

When it comes to service failures, the rules of the waiting game change dramatically:

- **MECHANICAL BREAKDOWNS.** Seasonal factors can seriously affect transportation. In wintertime, points (rail switches) sometimes freeze; in warm summers, air conditioning failures and heatwaves can result in suspension of services.

- **STRIKES.** If advance warning is given to the public, workers are delighted to hear the good news that they can *lekker thuis blijven*—spend a nice (paid) day at home—and are sympathetic to the strike. If no advance warning is given and they experience inconvenience, they do not support the strike and consider it to be "antisocial" or "sick."
  Reasons for strikes sometimes go beyond pay disputes. A common cause is protest against harassment by non-paying passengers (conductors are fed up with passenger aggression), but by striking, they only cause more of the same.

- **PERSONNEL TANTRUMS.** Overcrowding sometimes causes frustrated conductors and/or engineers to disrupt services. A typical tantrum unfolds like this: The conductor announces, *"We're not doing this anymore. Everyone out!"* and the engineer refuses to move the train.

Happy travelling!

ON-BOARD ACTIVITIE/ . . .

If you want to blend into the local colour, be sure to passionately discuss the favourite topic of the country: *geld*.

It is compulsory for Dutch nationals to complain, whine and express disapproval of subsidy levels, welfare benefits, food prices and the economy in general. However, it is highly inadvisable for non-Dutch to air negative views on Dutch ways.

If the train is waiting at a station and it is quiet in the compartment, the mere rattling of a bag is enough to draw the attention of all those within earshot. They'll immediately stop all present activities in order to try and see what you're going to pull out of the bag (and probably read whatever is written on the back of the bag).

Select your reading material to impress your fellow passengers. It is obligatory that the person(s) sitting near you spend a considerable part of the journey studying your reading matter. Depending on their mood, they may do this while holding up their newspaper as if they are reading it, by casually glancing up from their book or by just blatantly staring. It keeps them happy—they are studying free of charge. If you choose to write, "text," or otherwise tap your tablet, their curiosity will double.

If you hear music, it's likely to be either a fellow passenger's listening apparatus or a "looney tunes" ringtone played by a mobile phone. Dutch passengers seem to derive much pleasure from eavesdropping on telephone conversations, except perhaps in the case of youths blabbing away about nothing (people who do not speak Dutch are naturally denied this particular pleasure). If you are hoping for a tranquil train journey, don't bother about a designated *stiltezone* (quiet area, where loud talking, mobile phones, MP3 players, etc. are forbidden, indicated by the letter "S" on windows): you'll get a headache from the racket.

Above all, you must learn to multitask. While you are heavily engaged in all this posing and nosing and reading and phoning (or watching others doing it), keep a vigilant eye on your belongings— particularly on routes to and from airports and main railway stations. Thieves have been known to snatch everything from a laptop computer to an in-use mobile phone before you can say *doei*. There is so much thievery on the rail route between Schiphol airport and Amsterdam CS that platform cleaners have to contend with waste bins full of "liberated" wallets, purses and other bags every day.

BEHAVIOUR . . .

Rules of behaviour on public transport are deeply ingrained in the Dutch. If you do not want to offend them, please observe the following:

1. If you are one of the first to enter the vehicle, spread your belongings out across the adjoining seat(s). Then stretch your legs out to block access to vacant seats. The rule is to sit in the aisle seat whenever the window seat is not occupied. If someone comes along looking for a place to sit, ignore him/her by looking away, reading a newspaper, texting or pretending to be asleep. Another ploy is to remove one shoe and rest your stinky foot on the facing seat.

   It is allowed to vacate seats for elderly/handicapped/ pregnant people, but only to the extent that it remains the exception to the rule.

2. If the vehicle is full, you must stand inside the compartment where you are sure to block traffic when others want to pass through.

3. As the train approaches your destination, you must begin to fidget. If possible, stand up and fidget with your belongings.

4. Those in the back of the compartment must push, shove and/or stampede to the front of the car. (It is tempting to say "queue" since the way in which they stand vaguely resembles a queue; this is only because you must stand single file in the narrow compartment.)

Dutch law of motion:
"Exit time is inversely proportional to distance from door."

In other words, those who sit nearest the door leave last. If you are in a hurry to get off the train, you must sit as far from the door as possible.

5. Once you manage to exit the train, brace yourself for panicked people racing past or bumping into you as they rush to blockade their train. You may also witness frustrated folks attacking or cursing at defective ticket vending machines. Your best defence is to focus intensely on the floor as you work your way towards the exit (or toilet, if the station has one). Continue this practice when you exit the station—it will reduce the risk of (dog) *shit*-surfing along the streets of inner cities.

Take no offence to our use of the word *shit*. The Dutch have adopted it as an everyday, non-vulgar word in their vocabulary.

TAXI$ . . .

Dutch cities support an abundance of taxis. Their drivers are highly skilled in manœuvring through narrow side streets, ranks of pedestrians, herds of cyclists and other hazards while jabbering on their plastic communicators. They are impervious to rules and masters of the spoken obscenity—an instant introduction to local colour.

City taxis have their busiest moments at night. Taxis are traditionally dispatched to callers through a coordinating centre for local operations (*taxicentrale*). On a wet, cold winter's night, when public transport has stopped and you are stranded far from home, dial the *taxicentrale* and expect the following relief:

- A recorded message advising, *Er zijn nog vijftien wachtenden voor u* (There are fifteen calls ahead of you).
- Allow the recording to count down to one call ahead of you.
- When you are greeted by a human operator (usually with a curt *TAXI!*), tell him/her where you are and where you want to go.
- The operator recites the number of the local *centrale* for your district.
- Dial the local *centrale* and expect no answer.
- Redial the original *taxicentrale* number and start again. There is no guarantee that a repeat effort will be more successful, but at least it stops you from falling asleep.

Independent taxi services—those not operated through the *taxicentrale*—are also available, including the train taxi (*treintaxi*). As exotic as this may sound, it is no more than a plain old shuttle bus or shared taxi (*deeltaxi*). Travellers with a valid train ticket can take a *treintaxi* from any location in town to the train station (and, upon return, from the station to any location in town) for a modest price.

The two camps occasionally feud over the rights and wrongs of each other's practices and territories. When civil-taxi-war and anarchy strike, the biggest casualty is the paying passenger. Typically, government bodies write a few rules to right a few wrongs and meter them out to the owners and operators. This (of course) only makes things worse, with the result that many customers regard the cabbies as taxi tyrants and avoid the service whenever possible, prompting the question: Why aren't there more Bikes in Holland?

AIR DO'ſ . . .

Amsterdam's Schiphol airport is the pride of the country's air travel industry, and deservedly so. It has been under almost perpetual modernization, innovation and expansion, and, in general, the process has been carried out at "reasonable inconvenience" to the public. It is regarded by many to be the most impressive international airport in the whole of Europe. Schiphol is not only an airport, it is an indoor shopping centre, a major freight terminal, hotel complex and focal point for all forms of ground transportation. What's more, it is tourist-friendly and comfortable (except for the predictable waits at toilet facilities). The immigration and customs officials are, for the most part, polite and understanding when compared with other EU countries. Lesser airports serve Eindhoven, Enschede, Groningen, Lelystad, Maastricht and Rotterdam.

The majority of passenger services are provided by the French-owned Dutch national airline, KLM—***Koninklijke Luchtvaart Maatschappij*** or "Royal Dutch Airlines" for the millions of air travellers who are familiar with the initials but never considered what they might stand for.

The distinctive bright blue uniforms and blonde hair of the predominantly female personnel give a traveller a sense of efficiency and safety. KLM (pronounced "cah-el-em") has not experienced a major disaster since the unfortunate runway-sharing accident at Tenerife in 1977. The occasional minor disaster and PR nightmare still happens, such as the time the royal airline minced 440 Chinese squirrels that had been smuggled into the country. The ensuing public outcry and fines led the airline to create better and more humane rules for handling illegal live cargo.

Not long thereafter, KLM became the world premier in offering in-flight safety instructions in Braille and large-print text on their flights, which is significant to blind and short-sighted people, but of little consolation to the Chinese rodents.

Dutch airline staff can be downright rude and cold. Passengers who "know their place" and behave properly (translation: are NOT demanding or arrogant) at check-in stand a good chance of being treated fairly and efficiently. But for those in the queue who feel they are "above others," the staff will sense this and soon find a way to deflate them. Sometimes the need to put people in their place transforms a non-judgmental Netherlander into a cliquish cloggy, as per the following outrageous experience:

> "*Some years ago we flew from Amsterdam to Los Angeles on our honeymoon. At the time, KLM upgraded honeymooners, so we sat contentedly in our business-class seats, enjoying a glass of wine. About 1½ hours into the flight, I had the audacity to ask the attendant for a second glass of wine. Two minutes later the purser appeared, not with my wine, but with a computer printout. In her loudest voice she said: 'It states clearly on my list here that you were upgraded. The other people in this cabin paid for sitting here. I do not expect any trouble from you!' It was really embarrassing. Everyone was looking at us.*
> *On the way back, when offered the upgrade again, we declined and sat in economy. A letter of complaint resulted in a standard apology (they must do a lot of those) and a bouquet of wilting flowers.*"
>
> Tom Bijvoet

In order to counteract the effects of these bad-press moments, KLM has turned to technology and good-old environmentalism. In 2011, the airline boasted that most Amsterdam-Paris flights would henceforth be powered by biofuel (**biobrandstof**) made from used cooking oil. In effecting this change, the engines of the **Febo**liners required no modification as the processed chip oil has the same properties as regular aviation fuel. By 2013, Amsterdam-New York services joined what have become known as **patatvluchten** (chip flights). Between these two milestones, the airline experimented with "social seating," a boarding system whereby passengers could choose

Rusty Haller

Upgrading, Dutch style

their seat neighbours according to the latters' Facebook and LinkedIn Internet profiles.

In closing, take note of this valuable tip for travellers hoping to get a tax refund on goods purchased in the European Union. In addition to a tax refund form, you must physically present your purchases to the customs agents. Countless travellers meet with frustration when they are told that they cannot collect their promised tax refund because their guaranteed bargains are now in the inner sanctum of the baggage handlers. No prior notice is made of this and no explanation is offered, other than the nonchalant: *"Ja, I don't make the rules."*

"When I first got [to Holland], I received so many tickets from driving on the A9 that I just considered it a toll road."

Driving Me Crazy, blog-city.com

DRIVING

FREEWHEELING WAYS . . .

A first experience of *rijden* (driving) in Holland can be positively bewildering. But do not be dismayed. You are not an inferior driver. You have simply missed some elementary unwritten rules of the road.

1. Drive as close to the car in front of you as possible.

2. Change lanes constantly while driving. Roads are built from taxpayers' money. If you've paid your taxes, it's your right to use as much of YOUR road as possible.

3. At least two cars should go through each red light. Avoid, at all cost, reducing speed or stopping. Any brake-light indication combined with an amber or recently red traffic signal will subject you to a barrage of stereophonic horn-blasting even though it is considered vulgar to use the car horn except in an emergency. WARNING: Beware of elderly drivers. They stubbornly adhere to the old-fashioned system of preparing to stop when the lights turn amber, and they religiously stop at red lights. These senior citizens are the cause of many collisions.

4. When you witness a motorist driving through a red light, sound your horn violently in tribute while you visually

scold the violator for his flagrant disrespect of the law. Move alongside him and pound your head with your right hand (alternatives: tap forehead repeatedly with index finger or demonstrate your internationalism by raising your middle finger). Appropriate angry facial expressions, bouncing up and down on your seat. Yelling **idioot** (idiot), **godverdomme** (may God damn me) and **klootzak** (scrotum) are beneficial extras. Never mind the fact that you are more of a traffic hazard than he was as you accelerate, slow down and wander across the fast lane, while concentrating on your gesticulating.

5. If you are the first car to stop at a red light, do not expect to be able to see the traffic lights. Thanks to brilliant Dutch engineering, your car will be sitting directly under the lights. Just relax and rely on a honk or two from the car(s) behind you. Horns are guaranteed to sound if you do not react instantly to the green light that you can't see.

   Alternatively, step out of your car until the light changes. This at best is taken as a display of protest by the locals, and at worse is taken as an expression of your individuality. Both earn you much respect.

Clearly, there is a lot of road rage below sea level. Perhaps one cause of the increasing aggression can be found in a statistic from the foundation for Holland's Tall People (**stichting Lange Mensen Nederland**), namely that Hollanders drive around with *"the knees wrapped around the steering wheel and the head nearly touching the roof."*

ROAD RIGHT∫ . . .

Dutch democracy on the road has long been exemplified by inconsistent yield signs, best described by the saying:

Sometimes the small roads have to have the power.

As local respect for speed limits is non-existent, popular means to slow down the traffic in residential areas include one-way streets, *drempels* (berms, speed bumps), the *plateau* (a raised intersection) and other road constrictions.

Frequently changing traffic laws supposedly give drivers more responsibility by reducing the number of rules to be followed. A maxim proclaiming "Give priority to your intellect" possibly explains why:

1. No one gives way in traffic.
2. Many drivers seem confused as to what the rules are.
3. The list of Dutch notables caught committing driving offences includes members of the royal family, a past Prime Minister and members of his Cabinet, and the Chairman of the Council for Traffic Safety.

Holland conforms to the European fender-bender rule of priority to vehicles approaching an intersection from the right. It is imperative for visitors to understand that "vehicles" means Bicycles as well as motorized transport.

TRAFFIC JAM∫ . . .

Traffic jams (*files*) are a frustrating experience in any country. In Holland, the feeling is worse with the realization that a 100-km line of stationary vehicles would span the width of the country.

What is unique is the wealth and extent of studies, proposals and laws generated to reduce them. When it was established that people who enjoy horse riding sometimes cause traffic to slow down, a law was passed requiring the horse (not its rider) to wear licence plates on either side of its head—a sure way to improve traffic flow.

When things got to a ridiculous level, it was time to contemplate the daddy of all solutions, namely *rekeningrijden*: Turn the main arteries and ring roads into toll roads. With people having to PAY to drive anywhere significant, traffic will naturally decrease. This concept predictably brought the Netherlands close to staging the mother of all demonstrations. All the elements of "Dutchdom" (government agencies, pressure groups, citizens-rights outfits, public figures, environmentalists and vegans) gushed forth their studies, theories, complaints, protests, discussions, debates and other passions. After about three years of bickering, it was generally agreed that the toll system would not be a guaranteed success. So they dumped it.

With **rekeningrijden** seemingly put to rest, the next sure-fire proposal was a "per kilometre charge" (**kilometerheffing**) to replace all existing auto/road/fuel taxes with—er—national **rekeningrijden,** but this reeked too much of "Big Brother." Next came **kilometerheffing II**: a phased introduction of custom GPS transmitters that would record length, duration and route of every journey driven, and report this info back to the Ministry of Transport who would combine the data with a base charge (**basistarief**), rush-hour (**spits**) loading, vehicle type/model and fuel type/consumption to generate f'ing **heffing** bills. Naturally, the government claimed that "everyone will benefit" from the system and that "privacy is guaranteed." But all this reassurance guaranteed was a nationwide outcry at the thought of being constantly tracked by black-boxes and **heff**ed-to-death at the end of each journey. So it's back to the drawing board. Again. Maybe.

The multitude of studies, experiments and laws do not appear to have done much to decongest Dutch drivers. As the methodology for calculating jam statistics varies considerably from source to source and year to year, it is nigh impossible to keep tabs on specific trends. However, the following **file** facts are worthy of note:

- The first official Dutch traffic jam occurred in 1955. 50,000 vehicles were stacked behind an intersection near Utrecht, due to the rare "perfect storm" of spring holiday weekend, sunny weather . . . and lots of Germans visiting. Rather than seeing this as a warning of worse things to come, Holland celebrated the event as the country entering the "modern era."

- In 1999 the annual traffic-jam length was calculated to be the equivalent of girdling the earth 2½ times, or making 71 round trips from The Hague to Barcelona.

- At 8:00 am on 26 February 2004, there were 63 traffic jams, involving 760 km of fuming, honking, clogged cloggies.

PUNITIVE PARKING . . .

A perpetual problem in Dutch cities is parking cars. Local authorities are somewhat sympathetic to residents' and visitors' needs, but are naturally more sympathetic to the revenue that parking fees can generate.

Rusty Haller

A drive in the country

In the interests of the Dutch philosophy of "levelling" (see Chapter 7 – The National Passion), we would like to offer readers some proven suggestions as to how parking fines can be protested. (Success rates are based on official statistics—don't blame us if they don't work!):

"The meter was broken." or *"My ticket blew away."* 98%

"This doesn't look like my licence plate number on the ticket" or *"The cop's writing is too messy."* 77%

"I have a parking permit!" (proof required) 49%

The modern-day cultural equivalent of the medieval thumbscrew is the wheel clamp (***wielklem***). ***Wielklem*** barbarity is at its worst when clamping a car that is double-parked, thereby placing at least one innocent parked car in similar jeopardy and prolonging the danger to passing traffic. Dutch wheel clamps are among the most sophisticated available, incorporating transponders and other radio-reporting devices to detect tampering.

Kloggykind developed retaliatory skills to combat wheel clamps. The methods used varied as *klem*-technology improved, but usually consisted of jacking a car off the offending device. Some locals even resorted to installing their own (real or imitation) *wielklem* in the belief that the parking cops (*parkeerpolitie*) would bypass an already *klem*med *wiel*.

In order to preserve Dutch fairness, those responsible for installing these accursed devices have shown no favouritism when it comes to foreign vehicles, to the extent that the *wielklem* became responsible for driving away more tourists than those dreaded mosquitoes that infest Dutch towns and cities in the summer.

Laurie Boucke

When it was realized that the loss in tourist revenue was exceeding *klem* clams, it was time to boot the boot in major city centres (where parking—and visitor—problems are at their worst). In 2007 at the height of the *klem*paign, 22,000 clampings took place in Amsterdam alone. The dreaded device has now found a new, less stressful role as a means of extracting unpaid taxes and overdue parking fines. It is also an effective means of torturing townsfolk who are guilty of sneaking into other people's private parking places. Expect it to make a comeback . . . just as soon as not using them becomes old-fashioned.

GETTING YOUR LICENCE . . .

There are two ways to obtain a Dutch licence (*rijbewijs*): by taking lessons through an authorized driving school (*rijschool*) or by surrendering a valid foreign licence for a Dutch one.

The *rijschool* is rigorous and expensive, with rates around €1,300–1,800 to prepare you for your first driving test, which also costs. (If your timing is right, you can cut the cost by up to 50 percent by taking the lessons during a *rijschool* war.) All manner of interesting and unique equipment is used; some classrooms provide individual steering wheels and gear levers for the simulation phase. Do not be discouraged if you fail several driving tests; each additional course will only cost you roughly half as much again. At least one nationally accredited school has a programme where one can enroll in a short, guaranteed-success driving course. Eligibility is determined by psychological testing. If you pass the psycho-test with flying colours, you get the guarantee at a low-end price, but if you are a slow learner or suffer from exam phobia (*examenvrees*), you pay a high-end price or get rejected. Now there's fairness for you.

Not all foreign licences can be surrendered for a Dutch one. In the past, most foreign licences were acceptable, but the system has been "simplified" such that a selected foreign licence can be exchanged on production of some of the following:

- *Uittreksel*, certificate of fitness, foreign licence (with or without official translation), international licence, passport, a batch of photos, 30 percent tax rule qualification, stool sample or DNA analysis.

- And, of course, some money.

Additionally, the required bureaucratic "formage" varies from *gemeente* to *gemeente* (municipality). If the local office doesn't know what to do, they will refer you to the Department of Transport (*Rijksdienst voor het Wegverkeer*) who may or may not know how to proceed.

Driving licences are regulated by the *Rijksdienst voor het Wegverkeer or RDW*, and the driving test is managed and approved by the *Centraal Bureau Rijvaardigheidsbewijzen or CBR* but issued by the local *gemeente*—so now you know where to go with questions. The formal driving test follows the standard 2-part format (theory then practical). Note that if there is any money left after the *rijschool* costs, it is possible to purchase an interim test-run at the TTT practical test (*tussentijdse toets*) before being skilled enough to actually take it. In addition to driving a vehicle safely, the tests require the applicant to:

- Demonstrate the ability to erect an emergency triangle (even though it is not necessary to carry one).

- Have intimate knowledge of the vehicle and its inner workings (even though the applicant may never see the instructor's make and model again).

- Stay calm and collected when a tester hurls verbal and physical insults.

If an applicant fails the practical driving test four times within a 5-year period, he or she is deemed to have paid enough into the *rij*-coffers, and that person is automatically offered a consolation test (*nader onderzoek)*. The consolation test is held in more peaceful surroundings, the test time is longer, and there is more "personal guidance." In the unhoped-for event that the unlucky testee also fails the consolation test, then the matter is passed on to the Special Driving Test Office (*Bureau Nader Onderzoek Rijvaardigheid*) which offers consolatory consolation tests. And on it goes until a pass is attained.

Another option for first- second- or third-time failures is to declare yourself as stricken with failure phobia (*faalangst*), necessitating the deployment of an examiner who is also a *faalangst* specialist and more time for the test. *Koffiepauzen* can be taken between test phases. This is a faster solution than going the *nader onderzoek* route but has a certain stigma attached (not that many cloggies give a dripping flowerpot about that).

At the end of the day (or decade), the sense of euphoria experienced when you are awarded your *rijbewijs* evaporates into angst as you stuff this latest plastic wafer into your wallet and join over 50 percent of the country's population battling *file* fatigue, tailgaters, and intersection rights.

Finally, there is one very important thing to understand if you want to KEEP that hard-earned *rijbewijs*: The level of intoxication allowed by Dutch law depends upon a driver's drunk-driving experience. For new drivers (licence held for less than 5 years) the max level is 0.2 percent. Those who have held a licence for 5 years or more are allowed an extra couple of beers to bring the level up to 0.5 percent. This goes for cars, motorcycles, motorscooters and mopeds (*bromfietsen*). If you want to drink more, float a boat home (they've got plenty)—you can continue for a few more rounds in order to get the level up to 0.8 percent.

A DUTCH HOME

sk a Dutch person about HOME and you will be told that it is ***gezellig***, a word that they claim has no English equivalent. The dictionary translates it as "cosy." And, in this case, for "cosy" read "cramped."

The soul of the place is reflected through its living inhabitants—plants, pets and people—and the atmosphere (***sfeer***) is created by a widespread proliferation of inanimate objects. All these elements constitute ***thuis*** (home).

URBAN ARCHITECTURE . . .

The classic Dutch look is the responsibility of 17th-century architects whose desire it was to maximize the impression of the height of a house. This, in conjunction with the then-as-now overcrowding in cities, led to the introduction of highly characteristic design elements, many of which survive to this day. The convention that the depth of a house should be greater than its width is a prime example, no doubt popularized by a housing tax which rated a dwelling on its breadth. The tall aspect of the famous canal buildings in Amsterdam is enhanced by the height of the windows being progressively reduced from bottom floor to top (but more about windows later).

A typical old, urban house now provides four separate accommodation units or **flats**. There are two front entrances to the building, commonly one for the ground-floor owner and one for the elevated tenants. The very long and narrow staircase is found in the section leading to the upper floors. Inevitably, one or more Bicycles and a few thick, winter coats hang from the wall above the banister.

This efficient design provides:

- maximum inconvenience to those entering the building

- maximum disturbance to a resident hearing chattering, giggling, stomping, door-slamming locals stampeding through the building

- maximum inconvenience and disturbance to all concerned, by the uninitiated attempting self-disentanglement from the Bicycles (or trying to remove pedals or handlebars from an ear)

A curious architectural characteristic is located just below—or as part of—the famous Dutch gable. A rusty old meat-hook hangs from a wooden or metal arm which extends from the front of the building. This is not a symbolic carry-over from the pacifist nation's barbarous past. The hook supports a pulley which allows large, heavy items of furniture, and other bulky possessions, to be hoisted up from ground level. The windows and their frames are constructed for easy removal, thus allowing the load enough space for entry into the house on any floor. Many a Dutchman fears the public disgrace suffered if the load is allowed to adopt a pendulous motion, entering the building through a neighbouring window. To reduce the possibility of bashing bricks, windows and possessions, buildings are designed to lean forward, although it is not clear why builders cannot agree on a standard angle to apply.

Other notable exterior features (optional) include:

- a short metal tube, extending from the front wall at a 45-degree angle. This is, in fact, a flagpole holder used to support the national flag on patriotic holidays. The ground-floor installations are also used as litter bins and cigarette-butt containers by urban youths.

- the spy mirror (**spionnetje**), mounted on or close to a window frame. It resembles a large automobile wing mirror (probably stolen from a heavy goods vehicle) which older people use to study street life, unobserved.

- a collection of old household junk, typically gardening implements, toilet seat, wash basin or similar gems to add character to the abode.

- a series of tree trunks extending from the nearest kerb to the upper-front wall of the building. These wooden megaliths serve to provide neighbourhood dogs with a natural toilet place, and to inconvenience pedestrians, cyclists and motorists alike. A secondary function is to stop the house from falling down.

- a human window cleaner, present and working at approximately four-weekly intervals—irrespective of weather, time-of-year or window conditions.

Finally, Dutch architects seem to enjoy dicking around with doors, as evidenced in this description from an Eindhoven import:

> *"Like most houses, ours has a front door and a back door. Of course, the front door is at the side and the back door is at the front (this will make more sense when you see it). Some houses have both the back door and the front door in the same wall, even if this is at the side."*
>
> Brian Bramson

ſTAIRſ . . .

This marvelous invention—the Dutch staircase—is called a ***trap***, and it is not uncommon to feel trapped when you climb the staircase. The ***trap*** will be steep and narrow, of meagre depth, and will probably accommodate less than half your foot. In older houses, the staircase evokes images of a warped ladder.

Indeed, you must climb the stairs in the same way you climb a ladder, clinging precariously to the upper steps with your hands or to the banister (if there is one), with one dangerous difference: There is no room for your foot to extend over the steps for balance, as with a ladder. The lofty Dutch accept this ridiculous arrangement as a fact of life; it provides that essential exercise that citizens of other nations obtain from climbing their hills.

As you enter a residential building, the first thing you encounter in the narrow entry corridor is a herd of Bicycles. You may well find more lurking on the walls upstairs. After acquiring a number of pedal scars on your neck, you'll soon become adept at contorting your way around these dangling deathtraps.

Colin White

Subside-ized housing

The staircase covering gives an indication of the status of the residents. Owners' stairs are usually immaculate, with nice, fitted carpeting. Renters' staircases are usually musty, dusty and downright filthy. The steps are either painted or covered with badly worn, stained carpet or linoleum. The exception to the rule is the top-floor flat, whose renters often keep their section in good condition since it is for their exclusive use.

Following the path of the stairs, a rope or heavy cord passes through a series of loops and runs from attic to ground floor, terminating in a series of indescribable knots attaching it to the street door latch. This high-tech device allows residents of all floors to open the street door to visitors without the necessity of negotiating the stairs, which would entail more exercise than is good for a Dutchie (too much stair-exercise causes untold wear on shoes and floor/stair covering, resulting in premature replacement of both). Whatever you do, DO NOT use the rope as a banister when ascending the staircase. You will trip the door mechanism and will be obliged to return to the front door again to close it. Continued misuse will draw you into an almost perpetual-motion situation, cycling between climbing up the stairs, climbing down the stairs, closing the door, climbing up the stairs . . .

FURNISHINGS . . .

The favourite furniture styles are either pseudo-modern (Scandinavian influence) or country/*Riviera Maison* style (French influence), and **stijlmeubelen** (imitation Italian/Spanish renaissance pieces).

Rooms are literally cluttered with the stuff, adding to the sense of claustrophobia already caused by the:

- lack of size of the dwelling
- regulation Dutch colour scheme consisting of light earth tones, particularly insipid shades of curdled cream with excreta brown trim (bright orange fabric blinds are sometimes added for good effect.)
- over-abundance of house plants (see Chapter 9 – A Growing Concern)

One area must be dominated by a desk and cumbersome bookshelves. With these two items present, certain tax advantages can be gained. In addition, the content of the bookshelves displays the image the owner wants to project.

This hotchpotch of styles and colours is magically transformed into a delicious *décor* when the house lights are switched on. Accent lighting, focused spots and strategically placed filler lights bathe the entire dwelling with an intimate atmosphere of *claire-obscure*. To create this effect, the Dutch don't mind forking out a generous part of their income, whatever that level may be.

WINDOW PAINS . . .

Windows (**ramen**) are a focus for Dutch technology. In some respects, the character of a Dutch home is defined by the style of window installed. They are as much a conversation piece as the remainder of the place. The Dutch invest a large portion of their income in embellishing the interiors of their homes—they need to show them off through large windows, yet are obliged to clutter the things up as much as possible to avoid accusations of egotism.

In contemporary homes, panes must be as large as possible and as technologically advanced as possible. When modernizing a house, strive to get the maximum number of "doubles" into your replacement windows:

double size	double locking
double glazing	double impressive (style)
double opening	double curtains (see below)

Be sure not to neglect your windows. They need plenty of cleaning (make sure your neighbours see this happening regularly) and protection (take out adequate window insurance). For the ultimate impression, have your windows professionally cleaned while it is raining.

Curtains (**gordijnen**) are important in Dutch life. Almost every home has a double set of curtains: net curtains (**vitrage**) and heavier, full-length curtains. It is customary to leave the front-room curtains open day and night so everyone can look in and admire the possessions. Even the poorest of the Dutch get their hands on enough money to make their front room a showpiece, to give it their special snug atmosphere they feel is worth displaying to all passers-by. By true Dutch standards (see Chapter 6 – Money), the concept of paying for curtains by the metre and only enjoying a quarter of them is heresy. Upon further reflection, it seems highly likely that the unused width is in fact used to mask the emptiness from thieves, vagabonds and squatters (**krakers**) when the official dwellers are on vacation, or otherwise not **thuis**.

Some claim that the open-curtain convention stems from an old Calvinistic tradition indicating to passers-by that nothing "sinful" is happening. It is debatable in this current era of sexual freedoms that such a pious principle presently persists. The weird thing is that on the one hand, Netherlanders are glad to exhibit their openness via open curtains; yet on the other hand, no self-respecting Dutchie would dare stare into the front window of another. The whole issue becomes moot when you consider that dwellers invariably nix any nosing with view-blockers such as the following:

- a plethora of plants proximate the panes
- embroidered doilies encased in wooden frames
- cloudy strips or stained-glass disks (usually made of plastic).

THE TOILET . . .

Nowhere is the sense of claustrophobia more pronounced than in the water closet. The Dutch have taken the term literally and made that most private of rooms the size of a cupboard. Once you've managed to get inside the thing, you then face the problem of turning around to close the door and adjust your clothing. Before seating yourself, you face the dilemma of deciding whether you want your knees pressed tightly against the door or wall, or rammed under your chin. Any sense of relief on completion of your duties is counteracted by the realization that you must now find a way to manoeuvre yourself up and out again.

By far the most distressing feature of the classic Dutch WC is the toilet itself. The bowl is uniquely shaped to include a plateau, well above the normal water level. Its purpose becomes obvious the first time you see (or use) one. Why the worldly, cultured Dutch have this sadistic desire to study the recent content of their stomach remains a mystery. Perhaps it is not the sight of the deposit fermenting on the "inspection shelf," but the personal aroma that emanates from the depths and lingers in the closet for hours after the offending substance has been launched on its final journey.

The flushing system is a technological wonder—not so much a miracle of hydraulic genius, but more a case of "find the flusher." The Dutch seem to derive some form of hydraulic happiness in constructing the most bewildering launching mechanisms. Be prepared for any of the following:

DEVICE TYPE & LOCATION	SUCCESSFUL FLUSHING TIPS
A linear-motion, vertical-action, flapper-valve actuating device (i.e. knob) that needs pulling upwards.	The device is a sophisticated torture instrument insomuch as it tests the user's acumen with regard to resolving force-over-matter and other scientific equations. When you lift the lever, you expect some semblance of mechanical resistance. There is none. You release it, expecting to try again, and it immediately drops back into the original position, with no discernible results. Once again you pull upwards and a slushy gurgling sound occurs. You think you've succeeded, but your deposit remains intact. After the fake flushing hiss has stopped, you try one more time. (You are almost ready to tip a bucket of water into the bowl as a last resort.) It works. You have absolutely no idea why.
Chain, rope or string reaching down from a high cistern.	Although a comfortable medium for older generations, this classic mechanism is not as foolproof as it seems. Flushing forces and pulling speeds are extremely deceptive, resulting in frequent failed flushes by foreigners. The solution is to first gently pull the chain or rope and then cough (to disguise the failed flush). Allow the tank to refill, inspect the fecal shelf, then pull and cough again as needed.
Conventional button at the top or front of a low cistern.	This is probably the closest you'll get to a proper toilet mechanism. Appreciate it–you might want to note the address and come back.
Lever at the side.	At first glance, its familiar look may put you off guard. Go gently–the Dutch are notorious for varying the flushing force. Too much and you'll break the thing; too little and you'll instigate a series of aborted launches that will be commented on by others.

DEVICE TYPE & LOCATION

SUCCESSFUL FLUSHING TIPS

DEVICE TYPE & LOCATION	SUCCESSFUL FLUSHING TIPS
Large touch panel (stainless steel or white plastic) in wall.	Most foolproof modern model. Works a treat.
Dual touch panels.	Similar to previous device, but the philosophy appears to be that you push the smaller panel to dispose of urine and the other (larger) panel to launch solid (larger) matter. We suppose that if you have diarrhea, you press both panels simultaneously (this theory not yet proven).
Small touch panel on top of a low cistern.	Apply pressure gently at first, then increase the force until flushing is achieved. Remember, "the force is with you."
Button on a pipe leading up to a high cistern.	Lean forward and push VERY hard with thumb, making sure no clothing drapes over the bowl. NOTE: Some people have found that a persistent pumping action works better.
Foot pedal.	Foot pedal flushers have become unfashionable. If you can't get one to work, the best course of action is to embarrass the owner by saying that you are surprised that they still have one.
Fish whose tail needs wagging.	False alarm. Pull away, pardner!
Little boy whose tail needs wagging.	No comment–it's a Dutch thing.
No apparent device?	It's probably an automatic flushing device, but don't bank on it! Sneak away and hope that it will self-flush. If it doesn't, be satisfied that the next user will be blamed.

If you don't find any of these, check for a spring-loaded pipe extending from the bowl to the cistern. If you find one, pump it—don't worry about your hand getting wet; it's all part of the game. If nothing works, return to your host and complain about unhealthy people clogging up the works. Under normal circumstances, it's good sport; however, combined with the aforementioned aromatic horrors of the venue . . . enough said!

Whatever happens, don't pull the pipe extending from the front of a high cistern. This is an overflow pipe which will christen you with a large quantity of unblessed water for the duration of your occupancy. Even if it dripped on you earlier, please don't break it off now.

All good things must end and alas, the Dutch inspection shelf is slowly being replaced by a more modern design sans shelf. The more nostalgic reader might appreciate one Dutchman's defence of the infamous apparatus:

> *"Where I live today we have the same toilet bowl that is standard in Britain and America. Let's call it 'the funnel system.' It does not have a display shelf. (Felt sometimes as a sad miss, but never mind that.) I have known cigarette ends to survive on the surface of the water for days in spite of the turmoil of numerous flushings. I have known a dead leaf, from a house plant of course, to resist evacuation as well. I have also know the waters from the deep to splash up sharply under the impact of receiving a particularly well-constructed delivery from above, such that it actually made contact!*
>
> *Now you must admit that all this is not possible in the inspection-and-display environment. All loose matter is pushed before the advent of the flush and this continues for a couple of litres. Also there is no fear of a splash. Oh, yes. Pretty it may not be, but you see there's magic in the madness."*
>
> Dirk Bosch

The toilet brush is another compulsory component. It is necessitated by the inspection shelf and is included in the full spectrum of Dutch dwellings, both permanent and temporary. After using the toilet, a well-behaved guest will always clean the toilet bowl meticulously with the brush and chemical cleansers provided. From the poorest houseboat to the most exclusive and elegant hotel, the trusty toilet brush will always occupy a meaningful space in the chamber. It is an item accepted by all, mentioned by none, seen to be used by no one . . . yet always wet.

For anyone wanting to really go native, there is a tried and true way to brush off the embarrassment. Before taking your seat, place one or two sheets of toilet paper on the shelf. When flushing, your deposit should slide away on the sheets without leaving any skid marks on the porcelain. Although this uses a little extra toilet paper, the cost is offset by the savings on the toilet cleanser you don't need to use.

Typical WC decor consists of a birthday calendar (***verjaardags-kalender***) pinned to the door or wall; the compulsory plant (heaven help it); reading matter; a can of ineffective air freshener; and an aged, corny sign or cartoon requesting men, pigs or bulls to lift the seat.

Don't think for one minute that Netherlanders aren't aware of the aromatic properties of their toilets. During a visit to a friend one day, our host rose from his chair and announced, with true Dutch chivalry and bluntness, *"I have to **shit**. Do you want to **shit** before me?"*

Rusty Haller

THE KITCHEN . . .

Second place for the smallest-room award goes to the kitchen, if indeed a separate room exists for it. This room, or area, epitomizes the Dutch gift for efficient space utilization. The whole area is cluttered with cooking pots, utensils, house plants and beer crates.

In many homes, an aging, white four-ring gas hob (*gasstel*) sits atop the refrigerator. Some hobs have a hinged lid that should not be used to hide the ugly burners, but must be left open to act as a splash guard to protect the back wall from hot fats and cooking oils. Beside the *gasstel* sits a cracked or chipped saucer containing 2-6 dead matches. The purpose of this eye-catching accessory is nicely described by Dutch reader Dirk Bosch:

> *"Whenever you light a ring for the first time, you strike a new match and immediately extinguish it. You would then put the dead match in the saucer, and you or anyone else after you who wanted to light a second ring would just rekindle the match in the flame of the first one (yes, a pan might be lifted out of the way to enable this) and then the second ring would be lit with that used match. I believe a match might have [as many as] three lives."*

Also prominently featured/displayed: a wide selection of exotic and ethnic herbs and spices (usually supported by wall charts and guide books), even if they are never used.

A small gas water heater (*geiser*) is usually mounted on the wall above the sink and provides hot water for the entire home. This configuration works well, provided only one hot water outlet is used at a time. If you take a shower and the water turns cold, it is probably because someone is pouring a glass of water in the kitchen.

No Dutch kitchen would be complete without the coffee corner, a sacrosanct area displaying a drip-type or *pad*/pod-loading coffee maker (*koffiezetapparaat*), an array of jars and cans, an abundant supply of condensed milk (*koffiemelk*) and a collection of coffee cups, saucers and miscellaneous dwarf spoons. In pre-podded homes, a pack of coffee filters is loosely pinned to the wall.

ZOLDER OF FORTUNE . . .

The Dutch are no strangers to the Western trait of hoarding unwanted keepsakes and other krap in the attic (*zolder*). Dutch attic experts estimate that, on average, each household shoves around €1,250.00 worth of stuff up there. In the past, the problem was how to dispose of some/all of it to make room for more. Flea market and car boot sales were ineffective since the funds collected after a whole day's bartering in the blistering rain would only net a few cents for a complete *zolder*ful of junk. Salvation came in the form of Internet auction sites, which have become the premier mechanism for selling unwanted clog-stuff at better-than-**Koningsdag** prices.

Once the **zolder** has been unclogged, it can continue to earn its keep by being converted into additional living space or rented out to a foreigners . . . or a short **Nederlander,** if one can be found.

HOUƧE PETƧ . . .

Favourite pets (**huisdieren**) include:

- cats (to catch mice)
- dogs (the smaller the abode, the larger the dog)
- fish (observation of which supposedly curbs violence)
- rabbits (for the children to cuddle)
- guinea pigs (for the rabbits to cuddle)
- rats (to carry about town on owner's shoulder)
- exotic birds (to feel sorry for, locked in their cages)
- ferrets (to impress guests or relieve depression)
- female goats (to provide milk and cheese in country homes)

Fortunately, the government has published a list of **mag-niet** *maison*-mammals, based on a study conducted by Wageningen University. The list does not banish ungulates such as water buffalo, but does blacklist bison, camels, raccoons, porcupines and Rocky Mountain prairie dogs.

In urban areas, the dog reigns supreme. Despite attempts to ban or otherwise dissuade residents from adopting such cute and cuddly breeds as the Rottweiler and the Pit Bull Terrier, big bad dogs remain ever popular. The main problem is the bigger the dog, the bigger the meals, the bigger the pile of excrement. Owners take their canine pets to special toilet places, best described as "neighbouring streets." Any visitor to the Netherlands will soon become aware of this. Local authorities, domestic industry and the framers of the District Dog Shit Policy (**Gemeentelijk Hondenpoepbeleid**) are continually attempting to solve the problem. Among the methods employed around the country are:

- the "free biscuit" (vending machines that dispense a clean-up bag and dog treat for €0.10)

- no-poop signs (e.g. graphic of crapping dog and **hond in goot!** "dog in gutter!"), carved at intervals on paved walkways

- the "poop scoop"

- pooch playgrounds

- high fines for repeat offenders (€1,000 in some areas)

- dog crap awareness campaigns and associated literature

- dog bans in inner city areas

- portable vacuum cleaners

- a free smartphone app that allows people to report the location (by GPS coordinates) of dog deposits in inner city areas

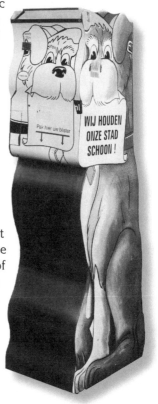

There is also an ongoing feasibility study whereby dog DNA is extracted from the streets to identify the culprit. This requires the country to develop a doggy database, but does not solve the problem of establishing a chain of custody of the evidence.

This wealth of innovative solutions, part-solutions and non-solutions to the problem doesn't appear to have made one turd of difference. For example: in 2004, Rotterdam's 20-member dog**shit** workgroup, after debating and imposing reams of rules and laws and codes and fines, declared the problem "unsolvable," a status that remains to this day.

HOUƧEBOATƧ . . .

There are over 10,000 houseboats (**woonboten**) in Holland, of which around 2,200 are bobbing up and down in Amsterdam. For reasons that will soon become obvious, Dutch authorities are attempting to reduce the number of ditch-dwellers by not renewing mooring permits.

Houseboats became prevalent due to the extreme housing shortage at the end of World War II. They are ideal living places for those who find the average Dutch house or *flat* too spacious. A houseboat is usually a shabby, converted canal barge which provides one or two cheap accommodation units. In general, canal boats have no rusty hook hanging from a gable; the *trap* is replaced by an unstable, narrow gangplank; the furnishings remain typical but fewer due to weight and structural limitations; the toilet cupboard is even smaller; and in places raw sewage still drains directly into the canal in which the boat sits. Ventilation is generally poor, heating is by means of an oil-fired stove and cooking is done on a butane, propane or natural gas hob. All this makes the habitat a potential floating-bomb, and a houseboat home on a busy waterway adds a whole new meaning to the word "hangover" (*kater*).

Despite these minor inconveniences, it still remains fashionable to live on a houseboat. Perhaps this stems from nautical traditions. For many, it provides temporary escape from the surrounding brick and concrete. In any case, houseboat living is "ethnic." Even though most houseboats have been permanently retired from their conventional roles and never go anywhere, the owners tend to work incessantly to keep the non-propulsion system in pristine condition.

In Utrecht, one of the red-light districts consists of a row of regularly rocking houseboats.

RENT VENT . . .

Most long-stay visitors want to rent their accommodation. This is an early sign that everything in the Netherlands does not always smell as sweet as tulips. The rental market is most definitely an owner's market and is divided into two sectors:

- Somewhat reasonably priced, rent-controlled properties (mainly owned or operated by housing corporations). These homes are strictly regulated by the government and local authorities. Rents are calculated on a points system (*woningwaarderingsstelsel*). But you won't even get a sniff of a chance to apply unless you fit the right lack of social qualifications. These properties are essentially only available to Nederlanders, low-income immigrants and refugees.

- Unreasonably priced, non-regulated free sector, where anything and everything goes—particularly your €uros.

Free sector renting is a minefield of problems. Landlords and/or agents will typically fleece a renter repeatedly before moving in, during moving in, after moving in . . . and before, during and after moving out. Here are some tips:

1. Try to avoid paying more than one month in advance rent and one month security deposit. The chances of even a model tenant getting it back are slim at best.

2. On moving in, check and review (with landlord) the condition and cleanliness of every square metre of wall, floor, ceiling, curtainage (include a ring count), carpetage (measure any stains, wears and tears), light bulbs (presence and function), mousetraps (incl. applied bait) and THE toilet roll—if installed (count sheets). Take photos of everything.

3. Throughout the rental period, pay utility bills (energy, phone, water) directly. Never allow the landlord to settle the bills and "recover the costs" from you.

4. Prevent spot inspections by installing supplementary locks or bolts on your front door. To avoid surcharges, do not tell your landlord.

5. Practice preventive maintenance. Never forget that "loose" fittings will be classed as "missing" or "broken" fittings when the day of *rekening* (aka End Inspection Report) arrives.

6. On moving out, repeat step 2.

As an example, here is how a €uropean software consultant described the flat-fleecing endgame played by one rental agency in 2009:

Last month the rental agency sent me their "End Inspection Report," and today their cost calculation arrived. It includes €21.98 (plus 19 percent BTW) for "Call out charges service man" and €43.95 (plus 19 percent BTW) for "Labour charges service man" giving that apartment what must surely be the world's most expensive curtain hook (since a loose curtain hook was the only breakage or damage identified in the End Inspection Report).

Strangely, it also includes €27.99 (plus 19 percent BTW) for "Replacement inventory from stock". Given that the

Start Inspection Report noted the only missing inventory as "2x mattress cover, 1x tea-towel, 1x towel" and the End Inspection Report records "2x fitted sheets, 1x tea-towel," then theoretically the inventory has actually increased by 1x towel.

Of course, they have not yet paid any of the outstanding refund. This, their letter says, "will be transferred to the bank account under deduction of eventually outstanding invoices."

*Please help me with one item: What the hell is **verontreinigings-heffing en ingezetenenomslag**? They have just decided to charge me €13.71 per month for this.*

Brian Bramson

COUNTRY LIFE . . .

Once you leave the city, you'll encounter some lovely, rustic old farms (**boerderijen**) as well as neighbourhoods of (mainly) free-standing modern homes. Although these independent homes are roomier than urban flats, one still often experiences the occasional twinge of claustrophobia in them. The toilet/bathroom tends to be characteristically small to downright dinky, but with friendlier flushers and more modern fixtures. Bedrooms are typically a few centimetres larger in length, width and height. Kitchens open onto the living room, giving a greater illusion of space. The meat-hook is ever present while the stairs remain steep. And don't worry—Bicycles, plants and pets are still omnipresent.

For those who want (and can afford) a unique, country home experience, there are the understandably rare bunker homes. Yes, that is correct. Those military emplacements, built mainly as a deterrent for enemy glider landings during the 1940s German occupation, are now available as living accommodation for the more forgiving who perhaps want a quiet life, free from city crime and vandalism. A 4-person apartment fetches €285,000 (2003 prices, landmine-free, excludes artillery). For those wanting a true "Atlantic Wall" experience, smaller installations that feature no toilet, electricity or hot water can be procured for €35,000 (2013 prices).

If the concept of bunker buildings appeals but country living does not, there is an urban equivalent that uses commercial shipping containers (see Chapter 19 – Gezondheid). Although they are built primarily for members of society who apparently have no place in society, it should not be too difficult to qualify for one, especially if you

Rusty Haller

have failed the **Bureau Nader Onderzoek Rijvaardigheid** driving test a few times.

FLOATING FLATS . . .

Having pondered for centuries the problem of how to find more land to build more houses on, Dutch ditch designers have recently reversed course: Waves of waterborne houses (*drijvende woningen*) and roads are planned and appearing in ponded areas around the country in an attempt to perfect the idea of the floating, flood-resistant city. Fleets of greenhouses are also being launched.

So what makes this more than just another mass of miserable houseboats? According to Dr. Chris Zevenbergen, the environmental director of the construction firm (and seemingly its chief salesman) and government advisor on flood defence, the new houses:

". . . are built of timber and concrete. The hollow concrete pontoons that serve as foundations will be able to rise, guided up a pair of 15-foot concrete piles, when the flood waters come. The clapboard superstructure, meanwhile, is light and boat-like. Flexible pipes and ducts are designed to ensure that water, gas and electricity supplies, and sewage disposal function even when the houses rise a whole storey. Boats can be moored

alongside. Inside, the houses are bright, breezy, split-level, unselfconsciously modern and understandably popular. Views from the bedroom and living-room balconies are a delight."

And so are the prices, at up to €600,000 per Dutch-sized unit. Amsterdam architect Anne Holtrop (whose ideas for 21st Century homes include houses without walls, and others floating on platforms made of disposable coffee cups and hamburger boxes) has taken the concept of "going green" to new depths:

"A building on the water is even more present than it is on land . . . The houses are fully covered with plants. First, they will make the houses look like green hills floating on the water. Second, the plants will make a number of relationships with the environment: mineral-rich water will be pumped out of the lake for the plants; the plants produce oxygen, compensating for the CO_2 produced when the houses are manufactured; and the plants will create a biotope for birds and insects."

With build rates ramping up to 200,000 water homes by 2030, the Dutch may have to reflood their reclaimed land to fit them all in. *"Everybody asks why didn't we do this kind of thing before,"* noted Gijsbert van der Woerdt, another of the concept's super salesmen. But all this does not necessarily mean that there ever WILL be 200,000 fast-food flats. For starters, bewildering and essential factors such as ***"waterberging"*** must play their part in mucking things up.

MONEY

he Dutch are the thriftiest people in all of Europe and do not part easily with their money (**geld**), even if they are rolling in it. It is usually not possible to spot wealthy Netherlanders since they hide it so well. Although this chapter is titled "Money," it is not the currency itself that has prompted the inclusion of this material but the manner in which it is revered and disguised.

THE TAO OF TIGHTNESS . . .

When confronted with the charge of fanatical frugality, the average Dutch person cites CALVINISM! as the root cause, then continues to practice safe saving. No attempt is made to shed the yoke of the archaic moralistic code. This is perhaps the only example of the Dutch accepting a principle such as predestination without question or protest. And why not—it's good for the purse.

The Dutch version of Calvinism has long been to:

- Guard every cent you own, and fight for every cent you can make.
- Deny, hide or apologize for your wealth to anyone that inquires of it.
- Plead poverty at all times.

This is a far cry from the original doctrine: *" . . . to learn to submit themselves to God, they must first be stripped of their wealth."*

If you want to blend in and "go local," try these examples if you are ever unfortunate enough to be in a position worthy of their use:

1. If you must buy expensive clothes, don't discuss the quality. Instead, mention the good bargain you got, thus making the garments seem less expensive than they were.

2. To someone who remarks on the obvious luxury of your home, reply, *"Yes, it is a big house, but in fact a bit too large and luxurious for us. Had we realized how costly it would be, we would certainly have bought something more modest."*

3. When hosting a party, ask your guests to make a contribution for the coffee, as if you can't really afford the gala affair.

4. On a luxury cruise, openly display your membership to The Loud and Proud Crowd by placing yourself above rules of etiquette and common decency.

5. On returning from the luxury cruise, criticize insignificant details, giving the impression that you've been on a cheap package tour.

Today, the two main remnants of CALVINISM! are:

- **LOVE OF THRIFT.** The Dutch see their thriftiness as a positive and even exciting trait:

  > *"I LOVE being tight! It's a thrill to get the most amount of value out of my money. Really quite an interesting hobby: how to spend as little as possible to gain as much as possible. The less you spend, the more you gain. I'm getting richer by the minute!"*
  >
  > Gerben van den Bergh

- **HATE OF WASTE.** Waste is something that REALLY bothers Dutch folk. If they find something to be necessary or useful, they do not mind parting with their pennies. But if something is perceived to be wasteful or extravagant, both the wallet and the mind shut tight.

BARGAIN HUNTING . . .

The Dutch enjoy spending time going to various shops all over town in order to take advantage of special offers and sales (**shophoppen**). They will gladly spend an extra two hours shopping in order to save two €urocents on a can of beans. Some will even spend more on public transport than they save at the sale.

When shopping for clothes, they will search the racks and shelves, frantically looking for a slightly damaged or soiled article. This gives them licence to demand a price reduction. If they find one, they will purchase it whether it fits or not. It can always be used as a birthday present or kept in storage for several years in case of weight gain or loss, or until their children grow into it.

In most of Europe, winter sales start in early January. In Holland, the sales begin towards the end of January. This eliminates the temptation for Dutch people to postpone Christmas until early January, thereby saving some of their precious pennies. January sales can be a violent experience in many countries. Risk the Dutch version at your peril.

All year round, sales and special offers abound, categorized as **uitverkoop** (sale); **aanbieding** or **actie** (special offer); **reclame** (advertised price, not to be confused with reclaimed land); **twee betalen, drie halen** (buy two, get three); and the irresistible **op is op** (sold out). None of these categories generate as much excitement as **alles moet weg** (everything must go). Beware of the fake "closing down sale" banners—these can adorn shop fronts for years.

A maze of complex and confusing rules governs price reductions (**reducties**). Foreigners would require the equivalent of a master's degree on the subject to begin to understand how to manipulate the system. The Dutch appear to be born with this ability.

STREET MARKETS . . .

Every Dutch town or city has at least one street market (**markt**). Whether open daily or just once a week, regular attendance is compulsory for self-respecting cloggies, as this is where they find some of the best bargains. Members of all walks of life surface at the street market, and tourists should be advised that this is the place to go to:

- have your wallet stolen (if you haven't already managed to do so on public transport)

- see everyday Dutchmen wearing their famous wooden feet (**klompen**)

- buy cheap imitation antiques, drugs, stolen goods and other miscellaneous merchandise

- experience the stench of rotting fish, vegetables and littered streets (not to mention the sweet aroma of stale urine)

- find yourself compacted among an endless throng of local tribespersons progressing at a snail's pace

For local inhabitants, the street market is an exception to their rule of penurious shopping. They'll pay over the odds (within reason) for the privilege of shopping at their favourite stalls and market(s). The pilgrimage is not complete until they orate about the visit to their friends, neighbours and family. This is the one venue where they refrain from bitching and whining about prices.

Laurie Boucke

A decade-long "closing down sale"

SECOND-HAND TRANSACTIONS . . .

If you advertise the sale of second-hand items, you must expect to waste time over numerous long telephone calls or e-mails probing for precise information on every imaginable detail about the *te koop* (for sale) item(s). Even if the item has been sold, Dutchies will want to know all the details in order to find out if they have missed a good bargain.

Getting the price you quoted is a difficult feat, for in the words of historian Simon Schama reflecting on commerce in 17th-century Holland, *"In matters of bond, for example, they could be as slippery as the eels on which they supped."* To assist you in dealing with Dutch barter martyrs, the following guidelines are offered:

COMPROMISE them before they compromise you. Upon entering your home, the prospective buyer will take an instant mental inventory in order to select a conversation piece to steer the topic in his favour. The ensuing discussion is used to prepare you for the I-can't-afford-that-price speech.

ATTITUDE. Adopt the firm attitude that the advertised price is the only acceptable price. Ignore arguments that the item can be purchased at a lower price at the local market. If that were the case, the prospective buyer would not have wasted his precious money and time on the phone call and journey.

CHANGE SYNDROME. Every good *Nederlander* will arrive with money strategically distributed about his person. If the advertised price was €45, a successful transaction will unfold along these lines:

- One pocket or compartment will contain €30, one will contain €10 and one will contain a single note of €100. Each banknote is neatly folded in half, twice. (This filing system is for the upcoming transaction only.) Your buyer's primary cash-stash is vaulted in a small girlie-purse that sits flat against the thigh.

- Upon eventual agreement of the price (€40), the buyer will produce €30 and rummage around to discover the €100 note, assuming that you will not have change for the large note.

- This is the crucial moment. Do you risk losing the sale if you maintain the agreed price, or call his bluff?

- You call his bluff. After a further reluctant rummage, he will produce the reserve €10 note. You are happy to receive the negotiated price. The buyer is content knowing that he gave you a good run for his money.

BANKƒ . . .

There are only three major banks in the Netherlands and, superficially, they appear to be professionally run. They manage this by minimizing or completely avoiding personal contact with their customers wherever and whenever possible. Thus the chances of finding a local branch that is equipped to deposit and withdraw cash sums can be quite remote. The first problem that confronts a would-be new customer is actually opening an account—so be sure to understand which bits of paper are required by whichever individual at whatever branch of whichever bank you are going to use (and expect a looong wait for anything to happen).

Where branches do exist (and accounts can be opened), the banks go to impressive lengths to protect your money when they are holding it (i.e. while they think it is THEIR money), sometimes to the extent that you can't get hold of it yourself:

- When moving cash into and out of a branch, an armoured security van will (where possible) park within centimetres of the door, to minimize the chances of a Mafia-style hold-up. During the transfer, customers within the building are effectively held hostage in order to prevent them from being held hostage.

- Cash is held in metal containers which self-explode if stolen. In the ensuing fire, your money will disappear to protect it from disappearing.

- Some premises are equipped with submerged vaults to protect customer investments from bank robbers who can't swim. (Theoretically, all Dutch banks are . . . well, work it out for yourself.)

- Personal experience indicates that debit transactions are balanced on a daily basis, while credits are acknowledged up to seven days after the fact.

Given the public's lack of appreciation for orderly queuing, busier branches tend to issue numbered tickets to encourage their customers to be patient and to give their elbows a well-deserved rest. As a bonus, this system eliminates the possibility of labelling the bank sexist, racist or withdrawalist.

Many banks impose a limit on how much of your hard-earned cash you can spend in one day. Link this with the fact that bank staff can adopt as unhelpful an attitude as possible, and you have a frustrating problem. Here is how Paul Claassen, a Dutch business owner, tried his best to solve it:

> *"I would like to withdraw €3,500.00 from my account."*
> *"Use the ATM machine."*
> *"It won't give it to me because I've reached my limit for today."*
> *"Then you have to wait until tomorrow."*
> *"No, I can't because (blah, blah)."*
> *"I cannot help you."*
> *"Why not?"*
> *"We do not have money other than what is inside the ATM."*
> *"But you are my bank and my balance says I have the money!"*
> *"You cannot get it here."*
> *"Why not?"*
> *"We are not a bank . . . just a local branch."*
> *"But it says ABN-AMRO on the door."*
> *"You need to go to the main branch in Eindhoven."*
> *"But that is in the centre of Eindhoven, I cannot park there."*
> *"You could go to Veldhoven."*
> *"Yes, but I would have the same parking problem."*
> *"Sorry but I cannot help you."*

Cashiers are most helpful in one respect: They happily share confidential banking information, such as your bank balance, with all within earshot. Once again, Dutch openness prevails.

ATMs (*flappentappen*) are about the only place where people voluntarily stand back and form an orderly queue. In fact, here they behave in a manner reminiscent of "punters" in line for a porno slot machine.

It is a false strategy to circumvent the ATM/cashier pitfall by "webbing it." Internet banking (once you've passed the initial test of completing the online registration form—and supplying all the backup documentation) is equally maddening, thanks mainly to a calculator-like instrument called an "e.dentifier." In order to perform a single transaction online, you, your smart bank card, the e.dentifier, and the bank's secure website must exchange a series of encoded, decoded and randomly generated code sequences to each other within tight time frames before you are permitted to e-move your money. This TV gameshow-like scenario is further hampered by occasional pop-up glitch*jes* that read **CARD ERROR** and **BATTERY WARNING**. Once you have navigated the entire electronic obstacle course, be prepared for the final insult—**CONTACT BANK**—before you repeat the whole performance for the next transaction.

IN/URANCE . . .

Netherlanders are amongst the highest insured peoples in the world. The average citizen spends over €2,600 annually on premiums. Why such a high amount by such frugal folks and in a land where the citizenry is famous for helping the underdog? Ironically, the fear and reality is that nobody will help if an insurance-preventable catastrophe happens. The basic attitude tends to be, "*You should have been insured. Sort yourself out,*" even from family and friends.

Insurance fraud is no stranger in Holland. As in other countries, many attempt to make money by filing false claims. In a well-publicized incident, a dentist from Doetinchem chopped off his dominant index finger with a cigar circumciser, then tried to collect €4.6 million in insurance by claiming his digit had been decapitated in a road accident. In the end, the eight insurance companies involved entered into a secret deal with the good dentist. They paid his medical expenses in exchange for his agreement to not file any insurance claims.

A /PORTING CHANCE? . . .

The Dutch love to be associated with sporting activities, provided the cost is not too high.

On a skiing outing, they will insist (from the very first lesson) on zigzagging their way down the slopes. After all, they have paid for the journey to the top and must therefore extract maximum value from the journey down.

The laws of magnetism dictate that the Dutch will be attracted to mountain climbing. Having no such natural features, they improvise by climbing man-made vertical barriers, such as an underpass retaining wall near the Amstel Station, Amsterdam. This activity, of course, is free of charge as the walls were erected for other purposes. If the weather is too bad to use an improvised outdoor mountain, they pay to visit a custom-built climbing wall (*klimmuur*) facility. Either way, cloggies can enjoy an authentic sub-sea-level training experience; after all, everyone knows that post-Victorian architecture and cement/plaster walls strongly resemble the snow-encrusted peaks of the Alps and the Himalayas.

When they fish, they religiously use two rods: Their fishing permit allows a maximum of two rods. Any fewer would be abusing their purse by not getting their money's worth.

Rusty Haller

Football (*voetbal*) is the national sport. TV programmes are cancelled without warning to show matches. If their team wins the cup, the whole town gets drunk. If they lose, the whole town gets drunk. During international tournaments they also bedeck themselves (and anything else they can get their hands on) in orange tones, and the unbearable festive antics intensify dramatically.

Ice skating (*schaatsen*) is another extremely popular sport, in large part due to the fact that anyone can skate for free on most canals, ditches, ponds and puddles. One of the most anticipated, exciting, financially rewarding yet unpredictable skating events is the eleven-city marathon (*Elfstedentocht*) which takes place in Friesland whenever nature and global warming provide enough ice along the 220-km (125-

mile) route. The last marathon took place in 1997 with over 16,000 skilled and unskilled competitors. The winner was a sprout farmer.

By 2008, with climate-change awareness reaching feverishly fashionable heights, the *Elfstedentocht* had acquired nostalgia status. In true Dutch style, an enterprising pair from Appelscha, Friesland, decided to expand the country's souvenir industry with a new product: e*lfstedenijs*—real ice harvested from the real 1997 *Elfstedentocht*. Fortunately they had foreseen the future, cut out a 50-litre chunk of frozen mosquito breeding ground, and dumped it in a freezer for a decade. For the sake of environment and economy, they decided it was time to stop wasting electricity on the freezer and make some serious *elfstedengeld* by chopping the hunk into 40 blocks, available for online purchase. Their dreams melted when the entire Cloud passed over this wonderful investment opportunity. They eventually sold all 40 *elfstedenijsjes* to a cloggy advertising agency for €2,500.

Potentially of more value than the 1997 ice blockjes is the amputated toe from a 1963 contestant (and frostbite victim), currently on display in the skating museum in Hindeloopen.

Rusty Haller

THE
NATIONAL
PASSION

he Dutch love to devote time to a "good cause." They express their devotion in the form of demonstrations, riots, debate, discussions and the inevitable collections. The common denominator is PROTEST.

When these principled pacifists are inconvenienced or their egos are ruffled, they instinctively resort to aggression and/or violence of tongue and word. They get their way—more so than any other nation. But it's never enough for them. They always find more to COMPLAIN and PROTEST about. This perpetual cycle of confrontation and inherent change has been instrumental in reducing excesses of the wealthy and powerful. Consequently, class distinction is minimal. The philosophy would appear to be:

- We hate anybody telling us what to do.

- Speak out! (At times the government and law enforcement agencies are paralysed by the thought: *"People would not stand for it."*)

- Defy defiance.

A favourite method of self-expression is the use of "profound" slogans and/or maxims. These are often presented in the form of pathetically unsubtle jingles. Such sayings are displayed in various ways: graffiti, buttons, stickers, T-shirts, logos, websites and banners.

Banners are typically made from old bed sheets (environmentally correct) and leftover house paint (cheap, if not free) and are erected or hung from the rooftop or windows of a protester's home or headquarters on the day of the official protest. Thereafter the device is left in place to rot, as a symbol of freedom and remembrance to all disinterested parties. Other banners are carried down the streets during supporting events.

A demo bed sheet   *Colin White*

The Dutch attention span is in some respects short-lived. In such a radically progressive and rapidly changing nation, it is no wonder that every few years each new wave of youth rejects the ideas of the previous. In this sense, labelling a cause or movement as old-fashioned discredits it and serves as an insult to any lingering, faithful followers.

DISCUSSION & DEBATE . . .

In the earliest and calmest phases, the national passion is disseminated through discussion and debate. Whenever and wherever more than one Hollander is present, they will engage in what they consider to be deep and meaningful discussion. They cannot stop themselves—even in close personal relationships. Many couples thrive on bickering and dialectics: *"Agreeing is boring. Life is dull without arguing. Why be alive if you can't discuss and disagree?"* Indeed, it is often a matter of argument for argument's sake. As one Dutchie put it:

> *"I admit that I suffer from this common Dutch ailment. I tend to get lost in the structure of the argument, rather than the content. And it can result in me going on and on and on until I feel the point has sufficiently been addressed in the correct way (or what I call correct). I am in therapy to learn to let this go."*

Cloggies like to interject a good dose of body language into their discussions, as illustrated by the following "Jan & Piet" joke:

> *"Jan had been expounding his views to his colleague Piet on a winter day. After a while, Jan said, 'You do the talking for a while, Piet. My hands are cold.'"*

After an argument, the Dutch do not generally harbour grudges. Heated debate is seen as a good and healthy sport, although the quarrellers will most certainly need to engage in a group sign-off rant (based on their "feelings," "intentions" and "reactions") before they move on to the next tournament. In this context, quarreling gains you respect as an equal.

In the office, meetings drag on endlessly since so much attention is given to the right to fully express one's personal opinion. A discussion is not complete unless everyone present has had his or her full say. The impression that something was actually settled in a meeting will be proven wrong when workers later remark, *"We didn't agree to anything yet. We only discussed it."*

This famously frustrating phrase prompts many to exclaim, *"Let's stop TALKING about it and DO something!"* and is summed up by the classic maxim:

It is better to debate a question without settling it than to settle a question without debating it.

This drawn-out method of comprehensive consultation (*overleg*), non-stop negotiation, compromise and consensus, when applied to economics and industrial relations, is called the "polder model" (*poldermodel*). Cloggies claim their formula is worthy of worldwide emulation . . . until the economy flops or the national mood festers. Suddenly, the polder model sinks under a tidal wave of demands with little or no negotiation, compromise and/or consensus, and the locals immediately launch into full-tilt tonguing over its demise. All sides frequently get locked into talks about talks, and discussions and debates about the lack of discussion and debate.

The third Wednesday in May is Dutch *gehaktdag* ("minced-words day," officially *Verantwoordingsdag* ("Accountability Day"), the government's yearly one-day discussion and debate on the results of their policies. The main focus of the 2009 (10th anniversary) session was the effectiveness of *gehaktdag.* Debate conclusion: Nobody is happy with it, but it will continue because it is *"a young tradition."*

COMPLAIN, PROTEST, OBJECT, APPEAL . . .

When discussion and debate do not settle an issue, Netherlanders escalate to the next phase where they voice their disapproval through the accepted and sacred channels of COMPLAINT, PROTEST, OBJECTION and APPEAL.

When the Dutch disagree with something, the first step is to COMPLAIN. COMPLAIN to anyone who will listen. Grumbling and COMPLAINING are part of the Dutch way of life.

Having found sympathetic ears, the next step in the process is to PROTEST. With the support of the ears and their associated mouths, the PROTEST can be made known to the offending party. This is usually accomplished through the medium of the written word.

Only when the PROTEST is met with overwhelming apathy does the disagreement gain momentum. The sympathetic ears and mouths now become an offended action (*actie*) group, and the disagreement automatically enters the OBJECTION phase. This phase is an overzealous form of the PROTEST and can include pleas, threats, demands and anything else that would likely win the day. The more determined objectors arrange for details of their dispute to be included in broadcasts, social media and specialist community publications.

The final conflict is manifested as the APPEAL. To win it requires all the support and cunning a Dutch(wo)man can muster. The APPEAL is a battle of wits and manoeuvring in both written and verbal form. If it gets too confusing (and it frequently does), ask a friend or lawyer to help you write a **blafbrief** ("barking letter") defending your APPEAL. When a Dutch neighbour was once asked for advice about a dispute, she advised, *"Je moet nu een grote mond opzetten,"—"Now you have to open your mouth wide."*

This four-element procedure is followed at all levels—official and unofficial, domestic and bureaucratic. It is valid in the case of an inconsiderate neighbour. Similarly, most official letters dealing with governmental finances end with a clause stating that you have the right to OBJECT (**bezwaar indienen**) to the government's decision, and flyers to this effect are provided free of charge in various languages. Even the annual income tax form states, *"After some time you will receive a reply to your letter of objection. If you do not agree with this reply, you can appeal."* You usually have 1–2 months to APPEAL. Depending on the circumstances, your letter can be sent to the office in question, or to the mayor or monarch.

Gerald Fried

Knowing how to whine (**zeuren**) is key to living a happy life in the Netherlands. One immigrant spouse described how her Dutch husband gives her lessons in complaining:

> *"My husband said that if I am going to feel at ease in the Netherlands, I would have to learn to complain in public! He is worried that I will get trampled if I don't know how to complain so he keeps saying, 'If you were to complain about that, what would you say?' Then he gives a nice review of how I did."*

CAUSES . . .

The causes, protests and incessant gum-bashing about "opinion" are all done in the name of freedom and the Dutch concept of democracy. As soon as a suffix such as *–vrij* (free) is added to a noun depicting a supposed evil force, the word is sanctified and warrants flagrant public display. In order to cater for people who can't (be bothered to) read, much use is made of suitable symbology encased in a "no-no" circle and diagonal bar.

Although the Dutch will scrimp and save every last cent, morsel of food or scrap of clothing whenever possible, they do like to give, but only to what they consider to be a worthwhile cause. This is usually through an organized foundation (**stichting)** with tax-free status.

The logic behind the **actie** movement attitude is described in promotional material from an Utrecht **actie** group: *"Actions, in which and through which, people are offered the opportunity to take action themselves."*

Any legal resident of Holland may hold a demonstration. It is a democratic right. Whether it is supported by 5 or 50,000, it is allowed to take place. Demonstrations must be well organized and coordinated with the local authorities. Every town or city has its own rules for this activity. Specifically, you must inform the local police of the intended date, time and especially the goal of the event, after which you will be advised of any necessary modifications to:

- date and time, which will be changed if any previously approved demonstrations or civic events conflict with your plans

- route, which will be changed or streets closed to traffic, depending on the anticipated support for the cause

When all is agreed, you will receive your demonstration permit, and the necessary preparations can be made for the day. During the demonstration, you will naturally notice increased police presence. Do not be dismayed. They are individuals first and policemen second. Some will even gladly display your campaign button on their uniform. If so requested, police car(s) will follow your demonstration along its defined route to ensure your cause is heard and not disrupted.

Non-approved demonstrations are not permitted, but are often allowed if the organizers promise to be orderly and not disturb traffic—and depending on the appearance of the protesters and the general acceptance of the goal. Police support during these proceedings is limited.

It must be emphasized that many of the causes have the good of the nation, the environment, minorities, the oppressed or all of (wo)mankind in mind. Whatever the subject matter, causes are an ongoing example of democracy in progress. What appears to be a Dutch addiction to this process strikes visitors to the country as rather curious. Perhaps these passionate demonstrations and debates account in part for the relatively low level of extreme violence in an increasingly violent era.

THE DUTCH WAY . . .

Today's "Dutch Way" is a reaction to an earlier "pillarization" (*verzuiling*) or social partitioning of Dutch society by religious, political and class affiliations. Each group had its own institutions and organizations, and people dared not stray outside their own group (*apartheid* anyone?) to engage in pillar-talk. However, realizing the futility of trying to change the ideas of others (no comment), the different elements learned to get along, thereby giving birth to "Dutch tolerance." (Ironically, contemporary cloggies frequently dive into discussion and debate over this point: Some blatantly believe that "getting along" is true tolerance while others describe it as a form of mere indifference.)

Pillarization began to collapse as part of the social revolution of the 1960s, resulting in the process called levelling (*nivellering*). This is based on the philosophy that everyone should be as flat as Holland and firmly demands: NEVER DEMAND! NO ONE IS BETTER THAN ANYONE ELSE. A popular Dutch expression for this is ***Hoge bomen vangen veel wind*** or:

Tall trees catch a lot of wind.

This philosophy allows the levelling lowlanders (*nivellerende Nederlanders*) to coldly deny any special status, praise or favours to people who would naturally enjoy these things in other cultures. As a result, staffers of some international organizations are fed up with being constantly leveled and are threatening to move abroad where privilege and rank are recognized and appreciated.

A sure sign of the "wastes of belevelling" is the lack of human statues in the Netherlands. There is a marked preference for ugly, abstract and inanimate sculptures rather than monuments to high achievers and heroes. A convincing explanation: *"These do not exist much in Holland, and even if they do, we'll be damned if we ever publicly recognise them as such."*

There are now two concepts of "The Dutch Way"—the actual attitude/spirit of tolerance (*tolerantie*) and legal permissiveness (*gedoogbeleid*). With increased sensitivies, tolerance is becoming more selective and limited. To some it appears that the main reason for tolerance today is that cloggies disagree on just about everything. The solution is to just look the other way. Many laws and regulations are liberally interpreted, thus they are either weakly enforced or not enforced at all.

A prime example of this is the case of *krakers* (squatters), who fanatically oppose building speculation and demand that uninhabited space be translated into subsidized housing (for them). In the 1980s, after years of invading vacant flats, offices, shops and warehouses, the *kraker*-cause evolved into passive rioting in Amsterdam—usually involving bricks, bottles, tear gas and tanks. The authorities conceded by agreeing to renovate and sublet a few occupied buildings, at the cost of more than €500,000. When the *krakers* agreed to "down bricks," a housing official described the compromise in the following words:

"We have the squatters under control now—an expensive way to deal with a little social unrest, but it's THE DUTCH WAY."

Twenty years on, the matter temporarily morphed into **anti-kraak** policies which allowed squatters to pay a low rent and occupy a building until the owner was ready to develop his property. But things soon returned to normal, with **kraak**heads and riot police taking each other on the next tolerance two-step. By late 2007, the Amsterdam police abandoned **kraker** tolerance by declaring, *"We will no longer let the squatters prepare by announcing evictions in advance."*

In 2010, the Dutch parliament proclaimed a ban on squatting. True to form, legislators left mayors, cops and municipal prosecutors to determine how to "implement" the ban. The future is predictably murky as the human rights card has now been played. Time to call in the EU.

VROUWENED UPON . . .

The feminists' "struggle" is probably the best example of a domestic skirmish which exploded into a national passion and held the country hostage for a number of years until women's rights were firmly and unequivocally established as a part of the national psyche. This has mutated into a fully fledged "save-the-women-of-the-world" campaign.

The *vrouwenbeweging* (women's movement) began as a wacky-women, man-hating, counter-culture thing that demonstrated itself so well that the government subsidized it by funding "gender awareness research" and creating a new cabinet position: Minister for *Vrouwen*ism. Feeling legitimized, the ladies of displeasure continued to give everyone else a hard time. They became so fanatical about their superior genetic characteristics that they elevated femininity to the highest pinnacle possible. They were WOMEN—and people/humans secondly. On the path to victory and with reinforcements of private funding, *vrouwen* gave birth to their own political party, *cafés*, books, websites, magazines, newspapers, archives, libraries, emancipation centres, theatres, travel agencies, unions, therapy clinics and, of course, Bicycle repair shops.

Vrouwen MANifestos were typically along the lines of, *"We are not against anything. We demand the right to live according to the custom of this country and not to be seen as half of a couple, but as an individual person and be treated as such."* Understandably, no one dared remind them that in the Western world, the custom is that MAN goes out to work and WOMAN manages the home and the family. Presently, "baby getting" is postponed (the average age of first-time mothers is around 30-35 years) or conceptionally withdrawn. In cases of divorce, strict laws are in place regarding child support payments, and women can purchase alimony insurance (**alimentatieverzekering**).

Ironically, many Dutch women emulate and incorporate the very masculine characteristics they seemed to despise so very intensely. These "butch-bitch" characteristics have been **vrouwen**-ed upon by concerned males for centuries:

> *"In their families they are all equals and you have no way to know the master and mistress but by taking them in bed together!"*
>
> Owen Feltham, England, 1652

> *"Dutch women are largely unfaithful. A co-worker told me, 'I am going to Spain next year with girlfriends so I can get some fresh meat. My husband is staying home with the kids so I can have some fun'."*
>
> Aurelia Hale, Holland, 2000

> *"Most of the women in Holland have no taste, are most unfeminine, and walk like farmers!"*
>
> Hans Algra, South Africa, 1992

> *"When surrounded by Dutch women, even a foreign man would become unromantic. I got my woman from abroad. I rest my case."*
>
> Anonymous, Holland, 2001

By the turn of the 21st century, **vrouwen** had lost much of their intensity (and subsidies). The new philosophy was, *"I'm fighting to liberate others, but I'm already liberated."* Membership in women's organizations plummeted, with most remaining members preferring to donate rather than participate.

The government set goals and quotas for women's employment opportunities, salaries and other advancements. At this point, many feminists lost the protest passion when realizing they'd rather work less hours (or not at all): *"I don't want equal opportunity employment if it means I've got to go out and work."*

The cloggy male had largely surrendered the family purse, and with equal employment a stalemate, the lowland lasses had to find a new set of complaints to add to the remaining issues of birth control, abortion, divorce, lesbianism, and their pathetic performance in the *Global Gender Gap Index* and the *Dutch Female Board Index*.

They found it overseas, perhaps while rounding up their straying males. The current tenet of *vrouwenemancipatie* is to liberate the remainder of female humanity from . . . well, you should know the thrust by now. The revised strategy is as predictable as a Roman battle plan, with its main body concentrated on government funding for new *stichtingen* to help "multicultural women." Consequently, the Dutch printing industry is enjoying a flowing period of prosperity due to the demand for booklets, pamphlets, leaflets and flyers in Arabic, Dari, Somali, Turkish—and of course Dutch, English and French—covering subjects from the right to go topless (i.e. not wear headscarves) to genital mutilation.

So far, MAMA CASH, a leading *vrouwen* funding foundation, has formed strategic alliances (mainly through dishing out dough) with such well-known influential international outfits as the Independent Association for Disabled Women of the Kyrgyz Republic and Daladda U Heelanayasha Danaha Haweenka (Somalian for "We Are Women Activists," better known to the world as WAWA).

This, of course, leaves the country in a state of anthropological chaos over the philosophy of leaving ethnic cultures uncorrupted by the customs and morality of "caucasia." Between the opposing factions sits a cowering government, fanning the flames of the fired-up contestants and refuelling them all with extra €uros as-and-when needed.

To stress that the matter of babes'-rights-to-no-babies ain't dead yet, the Women on Waves (WoW) Foundation (established in 1999) offers contraception and abortion advice to ex-maidens in countries where abortions are illegal, and performs "non-surgical" abortions via the abortion pill in international waters whenever and wherever possible. Commanded by WoW's grand admiral Rebecca Gomperts (who served her troublemaker apprenticeship with Greenpeace), their cargo ship carries a 25-foot freight container (to serve as a waiting room, examination room and non-surgical operating theatre) on its deck, and its crew of wenches wear bulletproof vests (just in case). The floating fetus free-er "foundered" off the coast of Dublin when 200 fallen Irishwomen requested relief (WoW expected less than five). To compound the problem, the Dutch government reminded the seafaring abortionists that they didn't have the necessary *stempel*-laden licence to perform. *"You have to ask what's next? Can we have a ship from the Netherlands selling drugs 12 miles offshore or carrying out euthanasia?"* complained Mildred Fox, Irish anti-*vrouwen vrouw* (or pro-baby babe) and former MP. With characteristic Dutch determination, the ship continued on its odyssey, but now distributing leaflets and counselling the world on procreation rights. After giving way to the stout Irish, the fleet of one moved on to Portugal (where they were almost blown out of the water by the navy) and then Poland (where they were pelted with unborn chickens). In 2009, WoW laboured over new licencing laws, cancelled its remaining tour dates and returned to Rotterdam, where the floating clinic became part of a feminist art exhibition. Meanwhile, the cause continues online through Women on Web or—you guessed it—WoW.

Regarding the disintegration of traditional male-female roles, Holland's only hope may be along the lines of the following:

> *"We men have become sensitive and sensible enough to know that women don't always appreciate flirters. So we're apt to leave it up to the ladies to make the first move.*
> *Last year a supermarket in the Jordaan had two colours of shopping baskets. If you were single and looking, you took a yellow basket instead of a blue one. You'd ignore the folks with blue baskets and home-in on the people with yellow baskets."*
>
> Anton Hein

Oh *vrouwen*, what on earth HAVE you done to us?

THE /ACRED UNION . . .

The idea of a European partnership was born shortly after World War II as a result of former old-world powers collectively crying about their lost glories. Over the next half century, they managed to turn a trading pact into the worst bureaucratic nightmare imaginable. And the Dutch national passion has been working its magic throughout the entire process.

When popular support for a European Economic Community was minimal, the Dutch urged it through protest, demanding equality and fairness for all. They made headway in 1992 when the Treaty of Maastricht converted the European Community to the European Union. After a brief honeymoon, they were at it again, this time protesting against it by seeking freedom from European oppression. The main whinges are related to:

- Fiscal fleecing in the form of unfair levying of fines, fees and taxes.
  For example, the EU threatened the Netherlands with a €1 billion fine for exceeding the allowable budget deficit, whereas France and Germany got away with it with a lecture. See also Chapter 9 for the Union

strike on Dutch dung. More recently, the EU fined the Netherlands €57 million for selling too much milk two years running.

- Overregulation and suppression of Dutchness.
A good example was the attempt to outlaw wooden shoes from everywhere but the tourist shops. *"It would be like Paris without the Eiffel Tower!"* exclaimed the impassioned owner of a company that manufactures **klompen**.

- Inability to "level" the EU.
One particular bone of contention is that the cost of membership per capita is considerably higher for the Netherlands than other member countries, yet Holland is awarded fewer votes than most.

- Ability of the EU to "level" them.
In 2009, the EU financed Entropa, a 250m² (2,760 sq ft) art sculpture representing various member countries. Holland was depicted as a submerged land, where half a dozen minarets protrude from the North Sea waves. There followed predictable cries of "**uit**rage!" from the offended Dutch. The fatwa fell flat when:

(1) Netherlanders noticed that other countries fared worse, Italy being represented by a bunch of masturbating footballers, and Germany depicted as a collection of *autobahns* forming a warped swastika.

(2) Maria van der Hoeven, Minister for Economic Affairs, admitted that she was not insulted . . . then confessed that she thought the minarets were oil rigs.

So just what has the billions of €uros in taxes brought to Netherlands? Protected status for **Jenever** gin and a bunch of cloggy cheeses.

FOOD FOR THOUGHT

SOME TRADITIONAL DISHES . . .

The international respect bestowed upon Dutch cuisine is reflected in the abundance of Dutch restaurants found in London, Paris, Berlin, New York and Baghdad.

Culinary orgasmic delights such as **stamppot** (mashed potato with cooked vegetable/meat/fruit fragments stirred in—as the concoction is pounded almost into a pulp, nobody is quite sure what the featured ingredient is) somehow do not entice the gentry as do *coq au vin à la bourguignonne* or *scaloppeine di vitello al Marsala*. And Edam **kaas** (cheese) is no match for *Caprice des Dieux* or Swiss *Gruyère*.

Appelgebak (Dutch apple pie) differentiates itself from other countries' traditional versions by the ritual around which it is consumed. Preferably accompanied by close friends in a **gezellig** *café*, the **appelgebak** (with or without **slagroom**—whipped cream) and cups of fresh, hot coffee, are slowly consumed, each mouthful garnished by deep and meaningful social intercourse.

Boerenkool met worst (kale with smoked sausage and smashed—not mashed—potatoes) is an interesting dish. Dutch smoked sausage usually has a unique but distinctly over-powering taste. When shovelled into the mouth with the vegetables, the sausage flavour is weakened and the recipient is confused whether the strange lumps are pig gristle or raw potato shards.

Bruine bonen met stroop (brown beans with syrup) is as exotic a concoction as it sounds.

Erwtensoep, aka ***snert met kluif***, is Holland's ceremonial centrepiece, succulent starter, majestic main course . . . whatever. It consists of a delicious, thick pea soup infested with lumps of ham or pig's knuckle and vegetable(s). It is served with spoon and bib and is available in kit-form at specialist shops and in canned- and powdered-form at supermarkets. It's as close as you can get to a national dish or national bowl.

Hutspot (mashed potato with onions, carrots and a suggestion of meat, swimming in a rich gravy) is a hearty dish, about as exciting as such a stew can be. It is most popular in the winter months.

Oliebollen (deformed doughnuts, sometimes with embedded raisins) are mainly a December fare and are a good tasty snack to munch on while waiting in the wind and cold for a bus or tram. They are normally dusted with powdered sugar (so avoid consumption if wearing dark clothing).

Uitsmijter (ham/cheese and two or three semi-fried eggs on untoasted toast) is mainly adopted as a lunchtime treat when even the Dutch cannot face the standard fare (see below).

There are, in general, little or no regional differences in the way traditional dishes are prepared, although some areas sport local delicacies such as **balkenbrij** (North Brabant): Flour, pigs' blood and lard, cooked and served with fried bacon.

MIDDAY MORSELS . . .

The standard lunchtime *pièce de resistance* is a tantalizing choice between open- or closed-sandwiches. Cloggy bread, which is rather dry and bland to the point of seeming stale, is lightly smeared with unsalted butter or unsalted margarine and topped with translucent slithers of processed ham or processed cheese. The unsalted lubricant is probably an attempt to counteract the effect of the highly salted topping. (Edam cheese is salted during manufacture in order to give it a bit of taste.)

For some strange reason, their salt sandwiches are delivered to the mouth by knife and fork (same goes for pizza), which often elicits looks of disbelief from foreigners. In the words of one particularly frustrated visitor, *"So help me, I swear if I have to watch another cloggy eat a slice of bread and butter with a knife and fork, I'm going to scream— not to mention licking jam off the knife and getting the last drop of soup by drinking from the bowl!"* Midday sandwiches are usually washed down with milk to avoid dehydration. Other non-solid favourites include *vla* (custard) and a revolting concoction called **karnemelk**.

The final course is typically one apple, pear or orange, peeled with the same knife that was used to dissect the main course. For an experience of poetry in motion, observe the way the Dutch peel their fruit:

- With apples and pears, a helical peel length is attempted: Whether it is achieved or not is largely irrelevant, unless you are superstitious. It is the style of execution that matters. The (blunt) knife blade careens around the fruit from stalk to stub in a continuous, poetic, lethal motion—a combination of Marcel Marceau and Jack the Ripper.

- For the superstitious, tradition dictates that if you hold the peel above your head, then drop it, the shape of the peel that falls to the deck spells the initial(s) of the peeler's next lover. Apparently ours are GIU and SCUG.

- With oranges, the top (and possibly the bottom) is first circumcised. A surgical incision is then made at what is left of the stalk-end, and the knife is drawn down to the ex-stub. Successive movements are made at roughly 30-degree intervals to divide the skin into regular segments. This done, the consumer manages, somehow, to split all segments in turn, and the inner sanctum of the deflowered fruit is laid naked for ingestion.

Consumption is secondary to the display of conquest, as the frockless fruit lies helpless in the hands of the rapist, like a British politician at a European monetary convention.

So from where does this exclusively Dutch characteristic stem? The most rational and likely explanation is the Dutch potato passion, the favourite recipe being whole, boiled potatoes, known as "boiled potatoes." There is only one way to peel a cooked potato while

Colin White

Peeling pleasures – apples

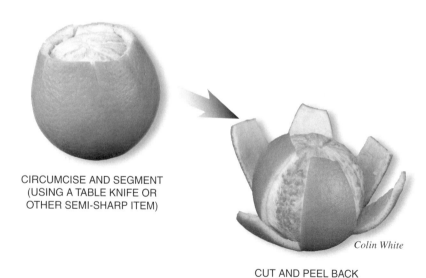

CIRCUMCISE AND SEGMENT
(USING A TABLE KNIFE OR
OTHER SEMI-SHARP ITEM)

Colin White

CUT AND PEEL BACK
SKIN SEGMENTS

Peeling pleasures – oranges

keeping it intact, and that is to use the spiraling-down technique, in one continuous stroke from the north- to the south-pole of the potato. This style of skinning spuds subsequently spread to the peeling of round fruits.

RE/TAURANT/ . . .

Locals will advise you to only patronize eateries that display a *horeca* sign. The term *horeca* refers to the Dutch catering industry (**ho**tel, **re**staurant, **ca**fé); all establishments that prepare/serve food—and display the sacred emblem—have solemnly sworn to observe *horeca*'s standards and codes under pain of (food)poisoning.

Foreign restaurants are popular social gathering points in towns and cities. Italian, Greek, Chinese and Indonesian eating emporiums are commonplace. Turkish, Indian, Mexican and Argentinian establishments are breeding fast. Unfortunately, the dishes served are often corrupted by substitutes for certain unobtainable original ingredients, as is the case in all European countries.

Dutch traditional restaurants also exist. They serve some or all of the dishes previously mentioned and soup-up the attraction by including other European classics such as *Wienerschnitzel*, *Jägerschnitzel*, steak (*biefstuk*)—child's portion—and *Tartar* (minced, raw steak (*tartaartje*). There are also speciality Dutch restaurants, the most popular being the pancake establishments (*pannenkoekhuis* and *poffertjeshuis*). You can't go wrong with these.

More important than the food in a Dutch eatery (*eethuis*) is the ambiance that permeates the place. Basically, the cosier the climate, the more popular the establishment. If the *milieu* is to their liking, the Dutch do not mind forking out a little more than usual. The incredible atmosphere of many of the restaurants is reflected in the overall *décor*, due to a *mélange* of all those wonderful and typical features touched upon in this work, such as flowers, plants, coffee, apple pie, cleanliness, mood music and price range. Lighting, furniture, architecture and style of dishware are also important. Political, health, religious or "good cause" affiliations are often used to lure customers; in these eating houses, posters and propaganda flavour the scene. All these elements, however tasteful, seldom detract from the rude behaviour and indifferent attitudes of the staff.

Whatever the locale, there is a definite etiquette that is followed when the meal arrives:

1. Before commencing your meal, wish your companion(s) *bon appétit* by uttering one of the following: **eet smakelijk**, **smakelijk eten** or **eet ze**.

2. Adopt the correct "utensology" according to the dish served:

   ALL MEALS: Frequently mix, toss and play with the food while displaying a trance-like expression on your face. Between bouts of this food-fiddling meditation, blab incessantly with your dinner partner(s). When you are done with the main course, first completely clean the plate by loudly scraping it with your utensils, then clean the utensils using a prolonged licking action. Knives may be slid down the gullet using a sword-swallowing technique to remove the last stubborn vestiges of edible matter.

   SALADS AND SPAGHETTI: Chop into small pieces and shovel into mouth. Allow a few half-chewed scraps to fall back onto the plate.

   DUTCH PEA SOUP: The special male-only ceremony for *erwtensoep* requires that after every three or four slurps, you must drop the spoon in the cup, wipe your mouth, rub your thighs vigorously while complementing the soup on its taste, then continue slurping.

3. Observe the "paying protocol." The paying protocol prescribes that if you are invited out for a meal, you pay for yourself ("go Dutch"). If someone else pays for your meal, reciprocate ASAP.

Another cultural anomaly, especially disturbing to Americans in particular, is the *serviette* (or table napkin) situation. The problem is more than adequately described in the following Internet posting:

*"Is there a national napkin shortage? Our local **pannenkoek café** seems to do a thriving business with families. Although they offer a special **kinderpannenkoek**, most of the kids seem to order **poffertjes**. However, when you order **poffertjes**, you do not get a napkin. So typically there I am with a table full of*

*small children, **poffertje** bits and powdered sugar and syrup*
flying everywhere, and no napkins.
*If you order a big **pannenkoek**, you get one small paper napkin.*
I ALWAYS have to call the waitress and ask for napkins . . .
and then I get ONE SMALL NAPKIN. This is typical in all the
***pannenkoek** houses I have been to, and I do love the Dutch*
pancakes, but is there a severe shortage of paper napkins or
something? Do Dutch kids never spew powdered sugar on their
siblings or drip syrup into their lap?"

Leslie Atkins

A word of warning for those who delight in visiting sushi-style or Chinese "all-you-can-eat" establishments: do NOT interpret this term as meaning "all-you-can-scoop-onto-a-plate." You can be fined up to €3 for not gulleting all your goodies.

LORD OF THE FRIES . . .

Snack bars introduced themselves in Holland long before the concept of "fast food" infested Western culture. Banks of heated coin-operated hatches (**automaten**) set in walls announce the presence of gastronomic goodies such as over- or under-cooked chicken (**kip**) wings, hamburgers and potato-and-mush croquettes (**kroketten**). At home, **kroketten** can be spread onto bread. The most popular varieties of mush fillings are:

satékroket	*rundvleeskroket*
kalfsvleeskroket	*minikroket*
meesterkroket	*kipkroket*
Kwekkeboomkroket	*kaaskroket*

NOTE: Don't worry if you can't savour all varieties. Most of them feature the same degree of blandness, and it takes around twenty glasses of beer to fully appreciate them.

Also popular are fried pancakes filled with a scalding creamy-coloured goo that vaguely tastes of cheese (**kaassoufflé**) and fascinating, tasty noodle slabs (**bamibal**). This type of convenient meal ("eating from the wall") provides just the thing for a healthy jogger to feast on after a strenuous workout. Curiously, it is also customary to park a Bicycle against the lower window hatches in order to allow the contents to "mature" properly (apparently, tourists tend to extract the contents before the item has properly crusted or burned).

Colin White

Modern Dutch cuisine in all its glory

The only thing you cannot extract from the wall hatches are freshly cooked salty French fries (***patat, friet, frietjes*** or ***frites***), usually served drowning in mayonnaise. Deluxe derivatives add diced raw onion and strong lubricants to the mayonnaise: ***patatje speciaal*** adds curry-ketchup sauce, and ***patatje oorlog*** adds peanut sauce.

Around one third of the potatoes (***aardappelen*** or ***piepers***) sold in Holland are used to make ***frites***. A poor potato harvest one year saw snack bar culinary experts protesting bitterly about the taste and texture of their chips. *"You can taste the water in them,"* they complained. Potato merchants retorted that it was not the earth-apples that were the problem, it was the Dutch consumers who were hypercritical: *"We are spoiled potato eaters who instantly detect a small variation in taste,"* said the commercial director of ***Farm Frites*** (a leading supplier). And so it came to pass that while the Netherlands boasted about being the world's leading exporter of potatoes, its domestic wholesalers were looking to Egypt and France to supply stocks for its snack bar industry.

Wherever there is fast food there is McDonald's. In Europe, the chain has achieved a higher status as an eatery than in its native USA and usually incorporates a local dish in its menu. Holland was treated to the "McKroket"—a standard, stale, croquette wedged inside an equally stale bread roll.

Nearly as popular are the normally filthy *shoarma* snack bars which identify themselves by the presence of a grilling device (containing a vertical rotary spit, heavily loaded with thin, wide slices of possibly rotting animal flesh which is rumored to be lamb) strategically located at the front of the ex-shop. These establishments assemble the Middle Eastern version of hamburgers, consisting of bisected pita bread loaded with hackings from the spit, weeping green-salad components and a hot sauce, guaranteed to mask any natural flavour. Delicious.

TIPP(LE)ING . . .

Most restaurants throughout Europe automatically include a 15-percent tip in the bill. Standard Dutch practice is to leave an additional coin or two on the table to express gratitude to the staff and thereby avoid appearing Dutch. That extra 10-cent tip is considered a tremendous token of appreciation by Dutch restaurant clientele. We doubt this sentiment is shared by the restaurant staff.

For those who prefer their sustenance in liquid form and a little stronger than milk, Dutch bars are also places of intense social discourse and atmosphere. Some are open 24 hours a day, some daytime only, some evenings/nights.

If you drink alone, there is no chance of boredom as most bars provide a monumental display of curiosities and collections on their walls. If the bar has a history, you'll find it on the walls; if the owner has a history, you'll find it on the walls; if its name suggests a theme, you'll find it on the walls; and so on. If you find a bell hanging from a rope, or a rope hanging from a bell, don't ring it, despite possible encouragement from the locals. By doing so, you're agreeing to buy all present a drink of their choice. Be cautious when using the phrase, *"Let's have a drink"* (**borrel** or **borreltje**), as it can easily be interpreted as, *"The drinks are on me."*

The prince of **borreltjes** is *jenever*—Dutch gin. It has been getting people legless since the middle ages, when some enterprising cloggy decided to mask the disgusting taste of his home-brewed malt wine by adding juniper berries. Consequently, the EU agricultural lords have granted *jenever* the status of "protected geographic indication," i.e. it can only be produced in the Netherlands . . . oh, and Belgium and parts of Germany and France. There are two basic types: old (**oude**) and young (**jonge**), the difference having absolutely nothing to do with age and everything to do with distillation processes.

Dutch beer (*bier*, *pils*) is sweet, tasty and strong. Ordering a beer can be confusing for foreigners who attempt to do so for the first time in Dutch. No matter how you refer to a "beer" in Dutch, the bartender will respond by using a different term. Here, the obsession with diminutives comes into play:

Mag ik een bier? (May I have a beer?)
Een biertje? (A beer? lit. "a little beer," doesn't refer to size)

Mag ik een pils? (May I have a beer?)
Een pilsje? (A beer? lit. "a little beer," doesn't refer to size)

For a small glass of beer, use the double diminutive:
Mag ik een kleintje pils? (May I have a small beer? lit. "May I have a small little beer?")

Een kleintje? (A small one? lit. "a small little one," refers to size)

Beer is generally served in small, flowerpot-shaped glasses. When poured or pumped into these containers, a considerable amount of froth or "head" develops, which is sliced flush with the rim. The resultant offering often shocks European visitors. Germans laugh at the sawn-off "head" and protest the lack of quantity (as usual) while Brits laugh at the lack of quantity and protest the overabundance of "head." French and Italians just drink it and think romantic thoughts of home, while Americans first eye it with pity then smile at the distinct "liver quiver" that comes with their first chug.

This ode to the Dutch brown *café* (*bruin café*) would not be complete without a tribute to its dealers. Ranging from nimble, spikey-haired, young mild-mouths to middle-aged, 100-watt, bloated baritones (of both genders), they possess an impressive memory for faces and places as they quench the thirst of 50 or more customers, collect empty vessels, and keep a written account of who-had-what and who-sits-where.

Their system relies on the ability to rechristen each patron with a nickname ("three drunk Brits" or "blue beard" for example) or geographic landmark ("broken stool") that their co-dealers can instantly recognise. More characteristically, they have an uncanny ability to invoke colour blindness and numeric dyslexia when the moment comes for a customer to settle the bill (*afrekenen*) at the end of a boozy evening.

The older urban bars tend to display banks of brown banknotes on its counter surrounds. Whether this is a tribute to the hoards of visitors it has "ripped-off" in the past or is in recognition of the international nature of its clientele does not take a degree in anthropology to conclude.

DUTCH ſUſHI . . .

Long before the Western world discovered the intimate luxury of sitting at a low, black, lacquered table to feast on Japanese raw fish, the Dutch were doing it in quite another manner and continue to do so in no lesser style. Standing in front of an open-air fish stall, ranks of cloggies hold raw, brine-slimed herring (*haring*) sprinkled with raw, diced onions in the air, and lower the ex-creatures into their gaping gates. Two swallows and a series of lip-smacks later, the onion debris is wiped from their mouths and clothing, and the feast is over.

The annual release of "new herring" at the end of May gives rise to a national celebration in the form of a stampede to the local fishmonger. *Hollandse Nieuwe* marks the official opening of millions of herring-hungry gullets and is preceded by fish-dealer reports on taste, fat content, etc. In the first few months of *haringseizoen*, 160 million stinky ex-aquatic vertebrates slide into the erect stomachs

Gerald Fried

Social scoffing: harvesting haring and Heineken

of drooling Dutchies. Demand is so great that the Netherlands often exceeds its EU quota.

One year, the season opening was delayed until 2 June—two days late! Herring were smuggled in from other European producers (typically Denmark), and a national hotline was set up so snitches could report this heinous and unfair activity. "High **Straat**" fishmongers can be fined up to €11,250 for selling *haring* before the official start of gulping season.

A similarly repulsive eating practice exists with eel (*paling*), the thin variety being smoked and the thick variety being fried or served in butter sauce. Here the vomit-buds are teased by the fact that the eel heads are left on for consumption at the more ethnic establishments. If this hasn't put you off yet, consider the following: Some of Holland's hatcheries breed eel infected with a strain of the herpes virus that originated in Japan. Netherlanders are assured that the infection poses no risk to humans.

If you are still contemplating savouring these icky ichthoids, **smakelijk eten**, and hurry up about it: the EU has threatened to impose a cessation to eel-chomping, thanks to *paling*'s promotion to the rank of THREATENED SPECIES.

DUTCH RUSK . . .

It's called **beschuit met muisjes**. Don't even try to pronounce it. It means something like "Dutch English muffin with baby mice," the **muisjes** being pink/white/blue aniseed sprinkles. It is highly inadvisable to attempt to prepare and/or consume this traditional snack without proper and thorough demonstration and instruction from a native.

Beschuiten are round, extremely dry, light and very fragile biscuits. You cannot cut a **beschuit** in half; it will merely disintegrate. The *mode d'emploi* of this delightful snack begins with butter which must be at or above room temperature for any kind of result. Spread the butter on the **beschuit**, trying not to break the brittle thing. The butter acts as glue for the **muisjes** which are sprinkled on top.

The next step, and biggest challenge, is to eat this delicacy without making too much mess. This takes quite some skill. Depending on the angle of entry into your mouth, the mice can roll into your lap and onto the floor if the ratio of mice to glue is not correct. Wherever they land, the piles resemble clumps of mouse *shit*. With or without mice, avoid eating a *beschuit* in bed: The crumbs you drop are worse than gritty sand between the sheets.

Beschuit met muisjes is traditionally served on the day a baby is born/comes home from the hospital, so do not be surprised if your grocer wishes you congratulations when you purchase the biscuits and anise sprinkles. Through a stroke of marketing brilliance, Dutch manufacturers have made *muisjes* available in pink and blue for obvious reasons. No further comment necessary, except perhaps to advise . . . don't ever confuse *muisjes* with *meisjes!*

DROPJEƒ . . .

The name of the Dutch national nibble is licorice, better known as *drop* or *dropjes*. It comes salty or sweet in different shapes and sizes, and since they are predominantly black, this helps in differentiating the various cultures. They are sold prepackaged or "fresh," the latter being a popular purchase at the local street market. Overdosing on *dropjes* is known to cause high blood pressure, but underdosing is reportedly good for the heart. Lower down, things take on a different shape: Seven grams or more per day for four days can lower testosterone levels in men by 44 percent. But relax, guys, if you drop dropping *drop* for a few days, things will straighten out.

Hollanders spend around €170 million on *dropjes* annually. They are consumed at the rate of almost 90,000 kg per day. Needless to say, the Dutch *drop* market is stable and healthy. (One producer uses 25 different recipes.) Among the selection to choose from are:

soft, chewy fish	coin-shaped (default style)
harder-to-chew half moon	English mix
filled baguette	sugar-coated varieties
single-salt button	traffic signs
double-salt parallelogram	witch's hat design
sweet-'n-salty farmhouse	cats (in various poses)
bite-sized Twizzler	Flintstones characters
Belgian boy pissing	coloured cubes
heart-shaped honey drop	spaghetti shoelaces
beehives	keys

Sex shops and hash bars (see Chapter 16 – Rocking and Rolling) may stock other shapes.

If as a visitor you decide to sample some **drop**, don't be embarrassed to spit it out after two or three sucks. Most normal people do.

Once you decide you definitely don't like the stuff, steer well clear of a favourite fairground fascination whereby contestants scoop up ladles of **drop** which they estimate to be a certain weight—usually half a "Dutch pound" (**pond**). If the scooped **drop**pings are exactly the target weight, the lucky contestant is awarded the batch free of charge. If the target weight is missed (even by a few milligrams), the contestant pays for the "goodies."

COVETED COOKIEſ . . .

When you are (finally) invited to a Dutch home for a cup of coffee, you will almost certainly be offered a **koekje** (biscuit, cookie) to go with your coffee. **Koekje** offering is a memorable event for foreigners. In more traditional homes, once the coffee has been served, a metal box is taken out of an impressive wooden cupboard. The mysterious metal box is opened, and you are invited to take a **koekje**—ONE SINGLE **koekje**—after which the box is slammed shut and put away again. If you decline the coffee, the **koekje** tin will be offered to all those who have accepted the **koffie**, and you will be bypassed.

Visits to a Dutch home have a regular pattern. First you are invited only for **koffie** and a **koekje**. If you are liked, you may eventually be invited to stay longer than coffee and be served alcoholic drinks and snacks. You've really arrived if you are invited for dinner.

DIRTY DIſHEſ . . .

If you do stay for dinner, you might be fortunate enough to observe Dutch dish washing (if you don't find yourself doing it) since the dining area often affords a view of this activity. Here is the basic procedure:

1. Force a plastic bowl the size of the sink into the sink.

2. Add environment-friendly washing-up liquid, scalding hot water and a sponge (optional).

3. Exchanging your sponge for a dish brush (**afwasborstel**) with handle, fish an item out of the brutally hot water with the stick-end of the brush.

4. Scrub the item clean with the brush-end of the brush. If the item is very deep, ignore the fact that the brush doesn't reach the bottom.

5. Once the item is clean, place it in the dish rack, making certain you do not rinse off the soap.

6. Let the dish brush sink to the bottom of the basin.

7. Make several attempts to fish the brush out of the hot water, and once you succeed, juggle the brush back and forth from left hand to right hand until it cools down enough to use it.

8. Search for another item to wash and repeat the process until the bowl appears to be empty. There will always be one or two teaspoons left at the bottom after the procedure is complete.

9. If necessary, restock the bowl with dirty dishes and repeat the sequence. If the water is dirty but hot, reuse it. If it is clean but only warm, replace it.

10. When all is done, use a towel to rub the soap deposit and any remaining food into the "clean" items.

11. Finally—and you're on your own with this one—concoct a method to lift the full, hot, pliant and snugly fitting bowl from the sink without spilling the water everywhere.

BOTTOM OF THE BOTTLE . . .

Cloggy kitchens are also a treasure chest of crude yet practical gadgetry. Best known, perhaps, are the uncleanable garlic press and the slotted spade-like cheese-slicer (**kaasschaaf**) that miraculously produces the stingy, stealth-like slithers of processed curd previously reported. (Try it on anything other than cloggy **kaas** and you risk being left with a pile of crumbled crud that resembles a scale model of the ex-walls of Jericho.)

But by far the most Dutch of Dutch kitchen drawer-ware is the *flessenlikker* or bottle-scraper. This wondrous, flexible wand is a pleasure to both behold and be held. With a few skillful flicks of the wrist, the experienced *flessenlikker*-driver can extract enough of those last few elusive smudgettes from a mayonnaise jar or ketchup bottle to (sometimes) save as much as a few cents over a twelve-month period. And those last few salvaged remnants taste so much better than the rest of the stuff!

This is one of the few items of kitchenware that Dutch people do not scrimp on. The standard HEMA/Blokker model is generally frowned upon by housewives as they (the *flessenlikkers*) have a cheap steel insert that tends to bow and rust after a few furious bottle scrapings. If you are presented with a meal that includes mayonnaise with brown streaks, it is a sure sign that your host has not spent his/her *flessenlikker-*€uros wisely.

This Dutch-declared device (invented by a Norwegian) has typically met with success only in Holland. It makes an excellent (read: cheap) gift or party piece abroad, as baffled foreigners try to figure out what it is:

> backscratcher • part of a lightweight Bicycle pump • mini-roulette scoop • flower embellishment • feminine hygiene/ gay-play device (*flikkerlikker*?) • instrument for removing Dutch doggy doo-doo from sufferer's shoe soles?

They'll never guess . . . and probably never want one . . . and ya can't blame 'em either!

A GROWING CONCERN

FLOWER POWER . . .

If you want to express thanks, gratitude or sympathy to a cloggy, give flowers (***bloemen***, sounds like "blue men" or "bloomin'"). If you would like to apologize or patch up a quarrel, resort to flowers. If you are invited to dinner at a Dutch home, be sure to arrive bearing flowers. Where some nationalities would send a greeting card or others would arrive with a gift or other token, the Dutch say it all with flowers. A cloggy on a Bicycle with a large bunch of flowers is as symbolic as a beret-bedecked Frenchman carrying a long, thin loaf of bread.

Bunches of ***bloemen*** should ideally be carried petal-down, in order for the excess water (from their previous abode) to leak through the wrapping and run down your leg. Display the "wrappered," soggy bundle in front of your hosts immediately upon arrival. They will transform before your eyes, as the essence of their being is reflected in an expression of ephemeral euphoria on their faces. A flower-grooming and rehabilitation ceremony will take place before you are invited to join them in their humble dwelling.

When you enter a Dutch home, be certain to take a machete with you to hack your way through the growth. The Dutch are proud of their obsession with plants and flowers to such a degree that the average living room resembles more a subtropical jungle than European living quarters.

Rusty Haller

Finding a place to sit

When you finally find a place to sit, your gaze will undoubtedly fall upon additional vases of freshly cut flowers, prominently and strategically enshrined in highly visible locations. Further growth is nurtured just outside the windows, in both the front and back gardens where available or, in flats, on the window ledges or balconies. Given the diminished dimensions of a Dutch dwelling, the lovely leaves limit *Lebensraum* to ludicrous lengthlessness.

The image of horticultural Holland is the tantalizing tulip. Yet these tulips are less visible than the purely green goddesses in the domestic environment. Tulips are bought by the bunch, box and bushel, mainly for the benefit of others, or as a showpiece. As with so many other things, the tulip has been made a symbol of Dutchness—of the Dutch, by the Dutch and for the non-Dutch. Chapter 20, The Flying Dutchman, explores this myth in greater detail.

POLLEN NATION . . .

Needless to say, the flower industry thrives and therefore is a major source of revenue for the country. In parts of the remaining countryside, flower fields resemble a colourful patchwork quilt and evoke the **Holland Bolland** (bulb land) image. Colder months and temperamental genera are no obstacle to the industry, thanks to greenhouses.

In towns and cities, flower shops, stalls and barrows are abundant, with prices to suit every pocket. **Nederland** is the largest exporter of cut flowers in the world. The flowers are sold daily to vendors in Aalsmeer at a collection of auction halls which handle about 80 percent of the world's floriculture. The method used is the democratic "Dutch auction" (called "Chinese auction" by the Dutch) whereby the sellers bring the price down until someone makes the first bid. Located almost on the threshold of one of the main runways at Schiphol airport, Aalsmeer contains roughly a million square metres of greenhouses and bulb fields. Tens of mllions of flowers and potted plants are auctioned daily. Tell THAT to the softies who believe that flowers are "the hieroglyphs of angels" and can only flourish in a peaceful, serene environment (and must be softly spoken to or serenaded).

If you just can't get enough tulips and windmills, you can always make a pilgrimage to **Keukenhof** and bask in 80 acres (32 hectares) of flower gardens and related goodies. The place is heavily advertised all year round, but don't be fooled: It is only open for two months each year (late March to late May). After annoying legions of tourists for half a century, someone finally hit upon the idea of a summer show. The **Zomerhof** takes place in August/September.

Every ten years, a huge horticultural exhibition called the **Floriade** is held in Holland. This is a doubly joyful occasion for Hollanders since they can bask in the excitement of two of their favourites: flowers and money. Or can they? The 1982 **Floriade** lost approximately €4 million, and despite this, it was considered an outstanding success. The reasoning (clogic) was that as the actual cost was €16½ million, they enjoyed a €16½ million show for only €4 million. The 1992 spectacle boasted 2 million bulbs and 3.3 million visitors, but the outcome was a negative profit of €10.5 million.

The 2002 event was held near Hoofddorp in the pouring rain. As the chosen ground was then in the middle of Dutch nowhere, and as there is nothing more depressing than standing in the cold wind and rain in the middle of nowhere staring at soggy plants, it should come as no surprise that the 2002 *Floriade* was an €8 million fiscal flop.

The site of the 2012 non-success was Venlo, a small city on the Dutch/German border, famous for another form of horticultural commerce (See Chapter 16 – Rocking and Rolling), but even the promise of a cross-cultural bud-bonanza couldn't rescue the event. Instead of following tradition and turning the area into another handful of hallowed hectares dedicated to fallen *Floriade(n),* Venlo GreenPark—yet another "business park"—is rising from the failed fields. Looking remarkably like a collection of multistory greenhouses, this development boasts *"sustainability, innovation, logistics, knowledge transfer and market orientation . . . aspects that are of vital importance for the welfare of our society, and that dictate the direction and the future of the green sector . . . developed according to the Venlo Floriade Principles."* Sign me up, Scotty!

A far more popular event (for the locals) is the *Bloemencorso*, an annual flower-float parade following a route through Aalsmeer, Amstelveen and Amsterdam, and which takes place in September (outside the normal European tourist season). It is a heart-warming moment to watch the local inhabitants delight in the colourful procession of flowered chariots as they pass by—enthusiasm due mainly to the magnificent arrangements, but also because they are free to behold.

With such large amounts of finances flying, flower filchers have inevitably entered the arena—big time. Organized crime has extracted much profit from the leaf-thief/petal-pusher circuits by stealing bunches of bouquets from flower cultivators and selling them anywhere and everywhere it can. On a more serious note, XTC, heroin and hemp have enjoyed a traffic route from Aalsmeer to the United Kingdom hidden in dead flower bulbs (for a while Dutch dog detectives ignored the shipments because of the overwhelming stench of rotting vegetation).

Horticultural hysteria is not the exclusive domain of petals. Anything green and growing is a certain money-spinner. Plants for home use and vegetables for export also command a large space in the fields and markets.

Acquiring a budding new family member is only the start. Plant paraphernalia (an ornate pot, special soil, humidity gauge, various types of plant foods, leaf shine and related items) is purchased/upgraded without a great deal of thought for the purse. Whenever necessary, the household horticultural library expands with do-it-yourself books such as *Caring for Your Favourite Hevea Brasiliensis* and *1001 First Names for Your New Euphorbia Pulcherrima.*

It has yet to occur to the Dutch that all this growing of flowers and house plants wastes good soil that could otherwise be used to grow crops. The crops could be sent to the starving masses in Africa, a popular subject for more protests in Holland. The world now waits with bated breath for the Dutch to protest this abuse of their assets.

Bertie Kaal

Flowers for the masses

TIMBER TALK . . .

In keeping with their love of plant life, the Dutch have elevated the tree to almost "national symbol" status. Cities and villages provide generous budgets for the care and maintenance of trees. Each public tree is logged, numbered and carefully monitored. Some municipalities produce *boom* brochures with detailed maps of tree locations, viewing routes and family history/heritage of the various species. Tree doctors study, examine, inoculate and perform surgery when necessary. Some even go to the extent of implanting microchips under the bark so that

Rusty Haller

A Dutch dendro-paramedic

a visiting **boomarts** can access a patient's medical history with his digital diagnostic device.

If a tree is fortunate, has the right roots, is well-behaved, lives long and leaves itself well, it can be granted "monument" status. (More than 10,000 trunks have achieved this rank.) Tree foundations and **actie** groups for trees do a blooming business. For instance:

- When a 130-year-old Leeuwarden sycamore tree was executed in order to make way for a theatre, a farewell ceremony was held at its last resting place. Flowers were laid in memory. (No doubt a memorial plaque for the tree will be erected in the theatre—this tribute being constructed from choice wood from another victim of deciduous decapitation.)

- A distracted milk farmer from Eibergen accidentally uprooted a sapling Japanese nut tree. Being a good, conscientious cloggy, he replanted the tree and advised the local authorities of the incident. Expecting to be charged for the broken stake and perhaps the €42 tree (if it did not survive), he was shocked to be presented with a bill for €1,766.91. The explanation he received was, *"Every felled tree must be replaced by one of the same size and quality."*

- The tree with arguably the best roots possible—born in 1850 and the #1 **boom** in Amsterdam until it was beatified in 2010—was the horse chestnut in the garden of the Anne Frank House/Museum. In 2007 it too was due to be shipped off to the shredder, due to a fungal infection. The entire country branched out to save it. After months of judicial jockeying involving the Borough of Amsterdam Centrum, the Dutch Tree Foundation (**Bomenstichting**), the Anne Frank Foundation, the Support Anne Frank Tree Foundation, the local district court, and the Mayor of Amsterdam, the deciduous darling was given a stay of execution. Corsetting costs ran at around €80,000 for the first year alone. Three years later it blew down.

This last example gave rise to another example of Dutch fiscal innovation. While the legal wrangling was taking place, Anne's tree's kind next-door neighbour thought it would be nice if other folk could also be comforted. So he supposedly leaned over the fence and plucked a seed from an ailing branch and offered it for sale via an eBay online auction. A short while later, the auction closed. The kind neighbour walked away with US$10,240 (€7,000) and the conquering philanthropist walked away with one conker of dubious parentage. Inspired by this, the Indianapolis Children's Museum somehow acquired eleven saplings in 2013, said to have grown from Anne's tree's seeds, for distribution to museums schools, parks and Holocaust remembrance centers across the USA—it's enough to make St. Peter jealous!

The only form of tree-abuse tolerated is that executed by another overprotected species—cloggy kids (see Chapter 18 – Children), who happily maim, disfigure and mutilate the vegetation whilst experiencing freedom and union with nature.

Having said this, we now encounter a choice double standard of clogism. On the one hand, they export forest-loads of wooden shoes around the world, as a symbol of their country. On the other hand, they are fed up with the stereotype of the wooden shoe/windmill. A typical example of this conflict manifested itself while we were originally researching this book. A Dutch illustrator pleaded to know:

> *"What kind of tune will the book whistle? Is it a book showing all Dutch people walking on wooden shoes, making porno pictures of their children for selling in the USA?"*

In this ecologically conscious, save-the-planet, celebrate-earth-day world, one wonders if the crime of **boom**icide in order to preserve windmill table lamps, footwear and footlockers is really valid (Holland is one of the largest importers of tropical hardwood). Foreign forests are apparently less sacred than the Dutch variety, as the Netherlands government has decreed that there should be no restrictions on the importation of wonderful wood from Latin lands.

ſHIT HAPPENſ . . .

One may think that incessant production of tulips, trees, tomatoes, turnips and taters would have rendered Dutch soil almost barren by now. Indeed not, for the regular application of cow and pig crap (*mest*) and other fertilizing agents has kept their hallowed ground rich—until recently, at least.

Fields became polluted with the residue from the 100-or-so tons of manure donated annually by the millions of cows and pigs (four-legged variety) inhabiting Holland. And then there was the chicken and sheep output to spread around. There was just too much *shit* there.

One reason for this had to do with Dutch dung rights. Each livestock farmer got a crap limit assigned to his farm. As soon as this rule came into play, so did some ways to beat the system. A swineherd would marry a pig farmer's (human) offspring to gain manure rights as a dowry. Alternatively, a betrothed could get the fiancé(e) to establish a new pig farm before they married in order to double their rights.

Ever eager to capitalize on the prospect of florins for free faeces, provincial authorities set up "manure banks" for deposit and withdrawal of the stinky stuff. To guarantee success, bank charges were levied on all transactions, and the whole nonsense was government-subsidized. The *shit* banks became a nationalized industry "to promote efficient use of the surplus." As a partial result, 90,000 homes in Moerdijk (near Rotterdam) rejoiced in receiving electricity generated from chicken crap . . . then cut their clucking when the process was declared to be "ungreen."

Then along came the EU with all its bureaucratic baggage, rules, regulations and fines, looking for its cut. When they saw the system set up by the Dutch government, they just couldn't let it pass. The message from Brussels was clear: *"Tidy up your **mest***!*"* The Dutch government has so far paid hundreds of millions of €uros to Brussels for exceeding their Euro*shit* allowance. Farmers strive to reduce the burden on the government by exporting the extra excrement and by engaging in clandestine dumping. Millions of tons of *shit* seemingly disappear into open fields every year—which completely defeats the object of the exercise. The Ministry of Agriculture has paid over €305 million to buy up *mest*-generation farms, in order to reduce the total livestock population.

Rusty Haller

To quote a well-oiled and rustic Dutch saying, *"There's nothing like the healthy stink of a farmer's field."*

UDDER THINGS . . .

Apart from their importance in providing fuel for the **mest** mess, cloggy cows also provide the main ingredient for Dutch dairy produce. Without cows, there would be no famous football-cheeses, no discus-cheeses, no authentic whipped cream for their authentic apple pies, no condensed milk for their coffee and no butter for their sober sandwiches, not to mention the effect on the thriving export market. The place would simply not function well without cows.

So what is being done to improve the production of raw materials in this sphere? Continually revolutionize the milking process, of course.

The Dutch firm Lely, a leader in milk-sucking technology, promotes "cow democracy" since cows are free to enter and leave their milking stall whenever they feel like a trip to the parlour. This supposedly reduces stress and increases production. It works like this:

1. On Daisy's arrival in the milking stall, the robot finds, cleans and titillates her teats with rotating scrubbers. This is called "maintaining maximum respect for cows."

2. Next, four suction tubes search for the teats and latch on to them. The cow doesn't seem to mind; indeed, she moves about trying to get in the right position (and avoid the threat of more scrubbing brushes).

3. Once the teats have been found, the suction tubes siphon off the milk. When the udder is empty, suction is released thereby freeing Daisy, who shakes herself dry and exits the stall, mooing "Ah, that's better!" or "Thank goodness that's over with," depending on the cow.

Lely calls this "the natural way of milking."

Now, if only some clever cloggy could adapt the system for use in urban areas to handle the output from dogs' rear ends!

"All hail the Dutch, long-suffering neutrons in the endless movement against oppression and exploitation. Let us hear it for the Dutch, bland and obliging victims of innumerable wars which have rendered their land as flat as their treats. Every one is an uncle, not a one can muster real courage.
All hail the Dutch, nonpeople in the people's war!"

Tony Hendra,
National Lampoon, 1976

10
ON DUTCH CUSTOMS

MANNERS MAKETH MAN . . .

Cloggies firmly believe their manners are impeccable, but to an aware foreigner they are as rare as a dike-mender's drill . . . or so it seems. If you feel you are trapped in Rudeland, you are not alone. The sharp tongue and lack of finesse are hard for many to stomach, but to the Dutch these are the hallmark of honesty and virtue since "you always know where you stand." The fact that we don't all want to know exactly where we are standing, sitting or lying is immaterial. This explanation by "Oud Mokummer" may be of some solace:

> *"My experience with the Dutch is not that they are terribly rude, but rather that they tend to see things as black or white, without any nuances. I feel many of them don't have a filter for their thoughts, as tact would dictate. They simply blurt them out unchecked, so really all you have to do is step back and let the remarks fly over your shoulder. They really aren't aware of the heft of their remarks."*

When abroad, lowlanders assume no one they meet will speak Dutch. They ridicule others by making sarcastic and derogatory comments about them in Dutch. Occasionally they find themselves attacking fellow cloggies. No embarrassment or bad feeling ensues as:

- Both parties realize that they are guilty of the same.
- On discovery of their common nationality, both parties will agree to transfer the ridicule to alien targets.

When being introduced to a Dutch person for the first time, a mutual monotone mumbling of names takes place, with a barely audible *aangenaam* (lit. pleasant) mixed in somewhere. Expressions such as, *"How do you do?"* and *"Pleased to meet you"* are not used. During the introduction, your gaze should be a vacant one. Avoid eye contact and wait for a right hand to be dangled at you. This signals the start of a ritual known as "hand-giving" (*hand geven*). Hand-giving consists of a few nervous, brief, damp and limp hand wobbles. Your facial expression should be one of boredom or indifference.

When greeting longer-term friends, a kiss on left-right-left cheek (three kisses in total) is appropriate. Handshakes and cheek nibbling can be abbreviated, prolonged or combined, and apply to male-female and female-female greetings (not male-male, yet). Never misinterpret these rituals. Two women engaged in a handshake/1.5-kiss greeting does not signify a reacquaintance between two lesbians who don't trust each other. It could well indicate that there are more important things to discuss.

The kissing insecurity gives rise to yet another national phobia: the fear of sweaty hands (*zweethanden*). Although a look of fear may at first be interpreted as mistrust of character, it is no cause for worry on the part of the sweat-recipient.

Correct adoption of parting gestures is as important as greetings. When leaving a friend's home at any time of day or night, stand outside the door and repeatedly scream *daaaag* at the top of your lungs. Then hop on your Bike and continue the serenade for a block or two. If your mode of transport is by car, drive off slowly, shouting *tuuuuut* as often as possible. Then speed up, making sure that the whole street knows that you have spent a lovely (in most cases, read: mediocre or boring) evening at your friend's home and that you are now leaving.

Another very common, affectionate way to say goodbye is to yell *doei* (pronounced "doo-ee") several times. This expression is apparently used by the lower class and is considered to be vulgar, stupid and a sign of lack of education, yet they all seem to do it.

To become an accepted member of Dutch society, we recommend you practice the following sign language, preferably in private:

- Place hand parallel to ear, three inches from ear. Oscillate hand in a forward/aft direction at medium speed. This means "delicious" (**lekker**).

- Make a double thumbs-up gesture with lateral pumping action from the elbows, whilst religiously chanting **OMSTERDOM**. This means, *"I like where I live."*

- Spread fingers, palms uppermost, and extend forearms. Tilt head to one side as you emit a sound not unlike a sick cow: **jaaaaa**. This means, *"I don't really believe you."*

See Chapter 4 – Driving, for special sign language when driving.

We would be remiss not to warn about the importance of the Dutch **agenda**. By "agenda," we are not suggesting some aspect of political skulduggery, but merely the Dutch word for a pocket diary. No non-welfare **Nederlander** would be without one. It is the focal point of social life. If you are in it, you're part of it. If not, forget it. Basically, you need to make an appointment to visit your Dutch friends. The gist of the **agenda** is that you cannot just drop in on a Dutch person. This is simply not done and is considered bad manners. Once you've been inscribed in someone's *Book of Invasions*, don't be late for the date. And don't be early, even if it means standing outside in the wind and rain for half an hour. Finally, should you be stupid enough to show up unannounced at mealtime, don't expect to be handed a plate.

BIO/COOP BEHAVIOUR . . .

If you want to SEE and HEAR a feature film in Holland, wait for the DVD. If you merely wish to preview the decline and fall of civilization (as we know it), Dutch cinema (**bioscoop**) is for you, but you must behave accordingly:

1. The number one rule is that you must set your mobile phone ringtone to LOUD, then giggle, chatter, belch and rattle your food wrappers as much as possible to ensure that no one can follow the film. If anyone's presence irritates you, throw your empty bottles, cups and other rubbish at them while making loud and nasty comments about them.

2. If the theatre is not yet full, be sure to select a seat directly in front of someone else and to sit up as straight as possible (preferably with a tall hat on) to block their view. Better still, fidget frequently.

3. Make every effort to arrive late so as to inconvenience as many members of the audience as possible by blocking their view and stepping on their feet as you find a seat. If you have missed part of the film, ask the people sitting near you (in a loud voice) to explain in detail what has happened so far.

The programme intermission provides a rest period for the audience:

1. Join the stampede to the foyer for obligatory coffee (to ease the throats of the better behaved), soft drinks or beer (to massage the throats of the worst behaved) and for restocking munitions of wrapped confectionery.

2. The middle ranks will remain in the theatre, rehearsing for the return game.

3. All persons over 6 feet (1.9 metres) tall must delay returning to their seats until the programme has recommenced.

4. Do not even consider prematurely finishing a conversation to view the film.

The latest antics involve genital-juggling, fighting, fornicating and generally behaving in a manner described by the Dutch as **bioscoophooliganism,** but best described by Americans (for once) as "being an asshole."

A BAD CA/E OF THE CLAP . . .

At the end of a show, the audience may actually burst into applause if the film is judged to have been exceptionally entertaining. After surviving celluloid sadism, what better way to finish the evening than to adjourn to a local tavern to drink away your embarrassment of having clapped at a blank screen. Alas, other cinema patrons will have beaten you to the bar and will be heavily engaged in interpreting, criticizing and dissecting whatever parts of the film they might have managed to see and hopefully hear. The criticism is far-reaching, as Dutch film director Paul Verhoeven (*Soldaat van Oranje, Starship Troopers, Hollow Man,* etc.) found to his cost: "[In Holland] *there was tremendous resistance from the critics and the Producers Guild who made life unbearable. I was driven out of the country by the Producers Guild.*" (Note that Verhoeven was "driven back into the country" by a Dutch "Lifetime Achievement award" and then went on to direct *Black Book*

(*Zwartboek*)—yet another cloggy film about Dutch families being destroyed by nasty Nazis who invaded the country to steal Bicycles.)

At the conclusion of a (classical) concert, a standing and thunderous ovation is given, irrespective of the quality of performance, in order to avoid *"understatement of the appreciation of concert performers,"* after which the concert is mercilessly analysed crotchet by crotchet. The Dutch are extremely critical of musical conductors. At least one prominent conductor has resigned after repeated bowing to the plausible applause.

In a class of its own is internationally renowned conductor/composer/violinist André Rieu and his "Johann Strauss Orchestra." With rock star demeanour, Rieu waltzes and cycles around carefully choreographed sets fiddling with his 1667 Strad, accompanied by up to 50 supporting musicians. Despite his world celebrity, nowhere is the applause more captivating than in his native Holland.

CAMPING . . .

Camping is a popular recreational pursuit. It is cheap and conforms to the Dutch obsession with being seen to be classless. Domestic campgrounds are havens of comfort, with hot showers, shops with microwave meals, built-in barbecues and more. Individual sites are marked, pre-planned by the owner, and there are obviously no rough spots on hillsides.

Almost every household owns a camping shelter of some description. It can be a 1–2 person ridge tent, a grand family tent with awning and rooms, a caravan or a trailer. Yet not all are used for overnight accommodation. For some curious reason, cloggies make a habit of erecting tents in public parks for a few hours during a sunny day. The practice is quaintly called "day camping."

It may take 2–3 hours to travel, pitch the tent(s) and arrange the accessories (collapsible chairs for seating, table for coffee paraphernalia, potted plants and/or flowers, etc.) for a mere 45 minutes of relaxing with nature, but they do it *en masse*. So much so, in fact, that a subculture of **berm**-tourists has developed. This strain of day-camper purposely seeks out space close to major highways in order to calmly complain about the excessive traffic and its consequences prior to becoming part of the problem on the way home.

Overnight public campsites are an excellent place for the young to sadistically impose their freedom on others. Around dawn, the little ones like to begin to sing Dutch children's songs; for a while, their parents will not interfere with this exercise of freedom and national pride. When the songs finally get on the parents' nerves, they gently tell their little darlings to hush. The children exercise perfect disobedience and carry on singing and shouting. Those cloggy kids who do not like to sing can find freedom of expression by talking in an obnoxiously loud voice.

Older children (up to 30 years of age) have their rights to freedom, too, and often express themselves by playing football through the campsite. Other great places for the kiddies to play football are restaurants, *cafés*, full car parks, golf courses and metro trains. Another favourite pastime is cussing and breaking wind. Making fun of others is, of course, a must, accompanied by lots of very loud giggling and cackling.

Rusty Haller

Dutch openness

Longer trips extend into other countries. The biggest difference here is that the inventory of survival gear is expanded to include sacks of potatoes, kilos of **koffie**, big bags of licorice and anything else they consider to be essential to existence abroad. Favourite European destinations are Scandinavia, France and Spain.

When they get to their getaway spot, a camp-wide collective inventory of Dutch requisites is taken. A rationing plan is then established so that stocks will last until new squadrons of Dutch holidaymakers arrive with reinforcements. In a well-conceived publicity stunt one summer, the Albert Heijn supermarket chain shipped truckloads of gastronomic goodies to Dutch campers in the south of France. The French retaliated by refusing to collect the resultant rubbish. This in turn was countered by lowland lorries hauling the waste back home.

ON MARRIAGE . . .

Weddings legally take place in the town hall (*stadhuis*) marriage room. Church ceremonies are supplementary and optional. Marriage prices differ, depending on the time of day and day of week. Same-sex couples are charged the same price as straight couples. The ceremony clearly defines the extent to which the partnership is to be taken:

Money under matrimony
is money shared.

For foreigners, the procedures go haywire, requiring the production of a stack of certified and recertified documents including an imaginary work called a "certificate of being single" and a birth certificate which may have to be verified by two or more local institutions, then formally translated into Dutch. Authorities may also probe your motivation for matrimony and/or require a death certificate from either divorced party.

Understandably, many couples opt to simply live together (*samenwonen*). For those preferring this level of (non) commitment, living-together registries provide an alternative means to register relationships. Couples enter into their living-together contract in front of a notary public. Living-apart-together is popular as it allows couples to have their own life most of the time, but also to be together and have an easy escape clause. Above all, certification is cheaper, and there are tax and welfare benefits.

The controversial Catholic issue of clergy and wedlock has been understandably fierce in Holland. The attitude is summed up in a BBC television interview with a Dutch theological student:

Q: *"How do you feel about the idea of a priest being able to marry?"*

A: *"No question at all. It's a question of the priest himself, and not of other people. When I want to be a priest and I want to be married; and the Pope, he wants a priest (who) is not married; I don't want to be a priest!"*

Get the idea? More on the consequences later.

THE COFFEE CULT . . .

Cloggies run on coffee. They can exist on over-boiled potatoes, but they run on coffee. On average, each Dutch person consumes 165 litres of the stuff every year (this doesn't include the cups of cold coffee that are fed to house plants as a healthy plant-food additive).

Fresh Dutch coffee is grown in politically correct countries charging the lowest price for the best quality, but always roasted and packed in Holland. Custom-built vending machines brew it and discard the unsold liquid at timed intervals. The armed forces take it on NATO manoeuvres in thermos flasks. Truck drivers and businessmen alike *en route* to other European countries gorge themselves with it before crossing the border and complain bitterly about foreign coffee, drinking as little as possible for the duration of their trip. At main railway stations and in intercity trains, vendors patrol the platforms and corridors with coffee carts. In all fairness, Dutch coffee far excels its dishwater-style cousins served in the UK and USA. It is strong and distinctive in flavour. Once you sup a cup, you will never forget it—in fact, research conducted by the University of Maastricht indicates that it has memory-enhancing powers.

In keeping with this endowment, for years the populace has been treated to annual coffee-rating tests, sponsored by various organizations, including the well-known magazine/publishing house of Elsevier. Each year, different blends are tasted by experts (apparently armed with digital thermometers, magnifying glasses and vomit bags) at locations around the country in order to establish the "cream of the drop" in the same way that France, Spain and Germany rate their wines. There follows an extract from the result of one coffee test conducted by the national daily paper *Algemeen Dagblad*.

ESTABLISHMENT	OBSERVATION	REMARKS
De Tukker, ALMELO	Smell of French fries prevents one from smelling coffee. Cheap mixture, not bilious. (68°C)	Every coffee shop gets what it deserves.
Artis Zoo, AMSTERDAM	A sour cup of coffee. Dirty cups. (70°C)	If the animals got the same care, that would be the end of the zoo!
Academisch Medisch Centrum, AMSTERDAM	Good honest espresso. New cup required when waitress dropped my change into the coffee. (70°C)	Quite an achievement!
Smits Road House, BELGIUM–NL Border	Cup of bile. Sore throat coffee. Inferior product. Stomach ache!	Welcome back to Holland!
Konditorei Gouverneur, BERGEN OP ZOOM	Great coffee served in beautiful china. Top class. Fine taste. (71°C)	People who love their business and take care of all aspects. First class!
Wegrestaurant v.d.Valk Oriental Palace, BREUKELEN	HORRIBLE! Undrinkable. Quality of mixture extremely poor. Dirty spoons, dirty brim on milk jug. Also cold. (57°C)	Rubbish, sir. Pure rubbish!
't Wapen van Delft, DELFT	Absolute loser. Coffee tastes like chlorine. Four dirty cups. (72°C)	Stale lubricating oil.
Centraal Station, DEN HAAG	Vulgar, bitter, rotten taste. Cheapest in existence. (70°C)	Cup of bile!
Hotel Restaurant Wienerhof, DEN HELDER	Even the most callous expert is disgusted. The mud wants to come down your nose. How dare they! Puddle in saucer soaked sugar bag. (66°C)	Just dirt.
Ferryboat "Counter," DEN HELDER–TEXEL	Black: practically undrinkable. With sugar: just syrup. With milk + sugar: lukewarm urine. (67°C)	Try tea.

ESTABLISHMENT	OBSERVATION	REMARKS
Restaurant Bellevue, DORDRECHT	Strange aftertaste. Moldy? Ditch water? (67°C)	Do not despair. There are other shops around.
Restaurant De Volder, EINDHOVEN	Tired waitress drops cups on table. Pure and honest. (74°C)	Satisfactory.
Freddy's Snackcorner, ENSCHEDE	Old coffee, absolutely unfit for consumption. (74°C)	Why is nobody protesting? How can this be . . .!
Cafe de Drie Gezusters, GRONINGEN	Sorry, no beating around the bush. A dirty, filthy cup of downright rotten coffee. A shock to your heart. (63°C)	Is there a doctor in the house?
Postiljon Motel, HEERENVEEN	Just bearable. Personnel evidently in bad mood as it's another workday. (72°C)	One cup in the morning wakes you up screaming.
Cafe Hart van Brabant, 's-HERTOGENBOSCH	Bad, uninteresting, dirty. Inferior mixture. (71°C)	Would the proprietor himself taste the coffee which he dares to serve to his customers?
Eethuisje De Gordiaane, LELYSTAD	Good blend, served with care but temp. differences. Sharp. (65–76°C)	Machine needs service. Good overall quality.
Engels, ROTTERDAM	Characterless coffee without aroma. Weak extract from poor mixture. Two dirty cups, spoons filthy, rings around milk jug. At first, change from waitress was HFl 75- (€34) short.	Why, oh why? It's about time somebody took care of this!
Restaurant Warenhuis Termeulen, ROTTERDAM	No aroma, stench instead. Simply dirty. Murdered coffee. (72°C)	My stomach revolts. In need of fresh air before I vomit.
Coffeeshop Drinky Met, UTRECHT	Disinfectant? Chemicals? Salt? Dirty aftertaste.	Horrible!

ESTABLISHMENT	OBSERVATION	REMARKS
	Undrinkable. (77°C)	
Bar Michiel de Ruyter, VALKENBURG	Well-groomed, clean, excellent blend. Perfect coffee, served hot. (81°C)	Champion espresso! Congratulations!

With this in mind, it makes you wonder why the stuff is so popular. But it is—it always has been—and unless one day it is proven to cause *fietsvrees* or genital warts, it always will be. Although the Dutch are renowned for taking packets of **Roodmerk/Aroma Rood** on extended overseas trips, there appears to be a problem in the exportation of brown-burned beans for extraneous brewing: It just doesn't taste as good! Numerous theories abound as to the reason(s) for this, the most popular being:

- The water has added chemicals that corrupt the taste (as if Holland's H_2O is perfectly pure).

- Foreign filters enfeeble the flavour.

But the obvious solutions to these claims do not seem to provide a cure. Typically, Netherlanders have gone to outrageous lengths to find a fix for this devastating dilemma, which reveals much about the Dutch psyche. In this regard, and for the benefit of any readers who may be tempted to join the quest, we can advise that:

- The absence of a **waardebon** on the package does not affect the taste of the contents.

- Using sweetener or powdered milk sachets "liberated" from a local restaurant does not improve anything.

- Brewing in a basement or other underground location makes not a millimetre-of-mercury's difference.

- Stirring with a spoon soaked for a week in Dutch dishwashing detergent will only ruin the spoon.

The accepted method of drinking Dutch coffee is an art in itself:

1. Check that all the necessary components are present: cup of piping hot coffee; dwarf-sized spoon or stirring stick; condensed or powdered milk; and sugar.

2. Support cup in one hand. If a saucer is provided, do not hold the cup, but grip the saucer as if it were a frisbee about to be thrown.

3. Add milk to cup to colour (optional).

4. Add sugar to cup to taste (optional).

5. Stir continuously until cool enough to drink. If you use sugar cubes, pound the lump until dissolved, then stir vigorously for the remainder of the cooling period. If you added milk and/or granulated sugar, alternate between clockwise and counterclockwise stirring. If you drink your coffee black, stir however you choose. The important thing is to stare hypnotically into the cup while you stir.

6. Remove stirring implement from cup. Tap wet end 2–4 times on the rim of the cup. This indicates to your colleagues that you have completed the stirring phase and are about to enter the drinking phase.

7. Return stirring implement to cup.

8. Hold cup with fingers and thumb diametrically opposed. (If a saucer is present, do not use the hand holding the frisbee.) If the cup has a handle, insert middle two fingers through the handle. Extend index finger upwards and across the cup to clamp the stirring thing against the far end of the cup. This is important as it prevents the thing from entering your nose in step 9.

9. Raise cup to mouth and slurp loudly while drinking. After first slurp, announce: *lekkere koffie, hoor!*

THE OTHER CULT . . .

The Dutch possess a proven passion for religion. Traditionally, the country is divided between the Catholic and Protestant faiths (reference books are contradictory about the exact ratio; apparently even the Dutch can't agree upon what they are). Whatever the divide, it is modified to roughly 100:1 for the customary sport of POPE-BASHING.

The origins of this appear to be the archaic policies of the Vatican in respect to contraception, abortion, divorce, clerical celibacy and acceptance of homosexuality, not to mention, of course, women's ordination (*vrouwen* priests)—in short, fucking and females.

The canals of Catholicism finally overflowed when Pope John Paul II—Public Enemy No. 1—visited Holland as part of an altar-stop tour. The warm welcome provided by the Netherlands consisted mainly of street riots, demonstrations, protest, pop songs (*Popie Jopie* was the top-selling song) and satirical comedy in schools and on national television. The regiment of slogan writers originated such absolute gems as POPE GO ROME; PAUS RAUS (get out, Pope!) and PAUS ROT OP! (piss off, Pope).

The following Sunday, the Dutch were back in their Catholic churches, praising the Lord. No large queues were evident at the confession boxes. There was no apparent shame or embarrassment. No one, royalty or commoner, condemned the rioting, and then Prime Minister Lubbers reflected, *"The Pope came here as a man higher than others. That is not the Dutch way."*

The infamy of the Dutch disapproval of Rome's religious rantings is so intense that a popular Vatican joke explains: *"One Dutchman is a believer, two make a church and three make a schism."*

In 2005, with a puff of smoke, John Paul II was gone. The Dutch never made their peace with him—even the royal family gave him a final snubbing by boycotting his funeral: *"The Vatican is a very small state. We are not required to attend the funeral of every head of church,"* was the official reasoning.

Two Popes later, things have been rather subdued with regard to Vatico-Dutch relations. Pope bashing appears to have gone out of vogue, but be prepared for another storm surge at any time.

THE BIRTHDAY PARTY . . .

Birthday parties begin around 8 pm and are held at the home of the birthday boy/girl (*jarige*). As soon as you arrive, shake hands with the *jarige* and say *gefeliciteerd* (congratulations). Be sure to bring flowers and a gift if you want to be invited again.

The event somewhat resembles an open house. After entering, you will be ushered into the living room which, for the occasion, will resemble a doctor's waiting room, with chairs arranged in a circle. On them will be seated an array of relatives interspersed with the odd friend and neighbour. The relatives will welcome you to what at first appears to be a group therapy session, with all the appeal thereof.

The welcoming ceremony consists of walking around the room and shaking hands with each other person. For some unknown reason, the relatives will extend their congratulations to you, the guest, then mutter their name unintelligibly. Normal etiquette allows for this so that should you have the opportunity to enter into forced conversation with the person later on, you can always reopen the chat by asking for the name again.

Just when you feel you cannot put on another false smile, the tension will be alleviated by the unveiling of coffee and cake. You should now join in with the echoed expressions of ecstasy, enthusiastically exclaiming *lekker!* to no one in particular about food and drink that you have not yet tasted. The atmosphere generally loosens up a little between cups, and people may rave about the lovely birthday gifts on display, about a course they are taking or about a recently acquired bargain. During this enlightening and captivating conversation, you will have ample opportunity to compile your next day's shopping list.

Coffee and cake consumed, round two invariably commences with beer or soft drinks, a few savouries and more conversation. This is your cue to evacuate your chair and socialize further afield. You can always retreat to the toilet or bring a premature end to a conversation that has become too overwhelming by spilling the remains of your coffee, beer or soft drink.

At some point, the conversation will be broken off for a round of *Happy Birthday* (in English) and/or the unfortunate Dutch equivalent which appears to be entitled *In de gloria*, *Lang zal hij leven* or *Verjaarslied.* (The absence of an official title for the song illustrates the national shame and embarrassment at such idiotic lyrics.) The singing is followed by a number of "hip hip hurrah's" as everyone appears to be having the time of their life.

When you feel the evening has reached its climax, or else any time between 10 and 11:30 pm, you may mark your departure by moving around the room once more to shake each person's hand again, mumbling goodbye and flashing your smile yet again. CAN'T WAIT FOR THE NEXT ONE!

Just when it seems the celebrations can't get any worse, you'll find yourself at the cheesiest of 'em all—the 50th birthday bash. At this time, the honoured person may be blessed with a multitude of embarrassing childhood photos plastered on trees and poles around the neighbourhood. A life-size doll, puppet or scarecrow, supposedly representing the wisdom of the biblical figure of Abraham or Sarah, appears in the garden, on the *jarige's* desk at work or in gifts, as do Abraham/Sarah cakes, chocolates and so on. As biblical students will appreciate, the Old Testament couple had no children until God intervened. In the case of this abomination, it would probably be more productive (and compassionate) to put their faith in Viagra.

Rusty Haller

URINE TROUBLE . . .

You're in trouble if you're caught short in public. Traditionally, one of the unspoken delights of living in Holland has been the freedom to urinate when nature and bladder demand—provided a fairly private place could be found. Not so in 21st-century Holland. The days of instant and unpaid piddling are over. The piss police (*plaspolitie*) are on patrol. Drivers will be relieved to know that an exception is made in traffic jams where a hard shoulder provides a suitable receptacle.

If a chap manages to find a public *pissoir*, the stench and filth are likely to asphyxiate the sphincters. Many public toilets are so unsanitary that it is a health risk to use them (this includes schools). Ironically, the Dutch term for pissing outdoors is "wild pissing" (**wildplassen**). **Wildpoepen** is also possible. In some places barbed wire and electric fences have been deployed in an attempt to discourage the practices.

Laurie Boucke

Wildplassers defying the plaspolitie

The most annoying custom, however, is the pee fee levied at the tollbooth entrance to lavatories in shops, restaurants, hotel coffee shops, museums, concert halls, train stations, warehouses, expositions and any other place where you feel the urge. You'd think the lady collecting the change in her begging bowl could at least clean the toilets from time to time, but no. That is not her purpose. That is not what you are paying for. Even more baffling is the fact that the amount of change she collects each day is less than her daily wage. One of 2011's most popular Dutch words (according to leading dictionary publisher van Dale) was **plaswinkel** — a shop with pay-toilet facilities.

FURTHER FESTIVE OCCASIONS . . .

King's Day

King's Day (**Koningsdag**) is the royal birthday bash. It is celebrated 27th April (birthday of King Willem-Alexander).

Many cities turn into a large flea market for the occasion. The Dutch save up their old junk and try desperately to sell it tax-free on this day. There are infinite street stalls, selling all types of food and beverage, spread throughout the town centre. In larger cities, the crowds are unbearable and at times unruly. An atmosphere of orange (the royal colour) prevails as many celebrators dress in orange-coloured clothing and wear silly hats. There are parades, live bands and other forms of public entertainment. All in all, it is definitely an occasion to be experienced.

If you have recently moved to one of the larger cities in Holland and want to do as the townspeople do, you will probably not take part in this event. Urban tradition requires that you shun the celebration by boycotting the city centre (in order to nurse the hangover that you will be suffering from the full dress rehearsal on **Koningsnacht,** the night before).

Rusty Haller

Carnival

During the winter months when the northern lowlanders are praying to the gods of the *Elfstedentocht*, the southern lowlanders are getting ready for carnival (c*arnaval*).

Each city or region of the south has its own blend of carnival. Among the traditions are presenting a cabaret in the prevailing dialect, giving speeches while standing in a barrel, changing a town or city's name for three days and other spectacles. But that is the cultural face of the festival. To the layman, carnival is a big beer festival with float parades, brass bands, gaudy costumes (some taking a whole year to create), street parties and more street parties. In the greater scheme of things, some carnival venues can be considered as "*Koningsdag* on steroids."

Rusty Haller

Remembrance/Liberation Day(s)

Remembrance Day (**herdenkingsdag** but also known as **dodenherdenking**) is on the 4th of May and honours ALL war victims . . . except Germans. Flags are flown at half-mast, wreaths are laid at appropriate places and the ruling monarch makes a public appearance. At a specified time, the whole country makes its annual attempt to observe two minutes of silence. As a visitor, your main awareness of Memorial Day may be that your tram comes to a grinding halt for a short period.

Liberation Day (**Bevrijdingsdag**) is on the 5th of May and celebrates the freeing of the country from its Teutonic oppressors in 1945. Due to prohibitive costs, this historically important event has been demoted from a national holiday to a paid holiday every five years. If, as a foreigner, you want to have the best time imaginable, pretend you are Canadian: The free food and drink will stock you up for months.

Two Christmases

On the third Saturday of November, the Dutch Santa Claus (**Sinterklaas**) travels from Spain to Amsterdam by ship. After clearing customs for parking fines, electronics, excess toys and sweets, he is greeted by the monarch before stocking up with soft drugs, **pepernoten** (mini biscuits) and chocolate letters. It is **leuk** (nice) for Dutch persons to receive a chocolate letter in the shape of one of their initials. To keep everyone happy, the manufacturers "claim" that every letter contains the same amount (weight) of chocolate.

Santa has a long white beard and a decidedly Catholic look about him, epitomized by his long red robe, tall red/gold mitre and golden crook. Traditionally, he is attended by his black manservant Peter (**Zwarte Piet**), who has been shining his shoes for around 160 years. Pete was invented by a Dutch teacher in 1852.

In contemporary times, up to a dozen caucasian-featured **Zwarte Pieten** provide security at **Sint**'s various gigs and protect the **pakjes** from being liberated by pickpockets and muggers. Parents con their children into believing that the Petes are not the victims of racism, but are black from the soot of the chimneys that are used to deliver the gifts, even though there are practically no open soot-lined stacks left in the country. As an aside, note that the term **zwartepiet** has some other uses in Dutch; it is linked to laying blame, passing the buck or the Jack of Spades in card games.

Traditionally, the Dutch celebrate Christmas (**Kerstmis**) on the 5th of December and again on Christmas Day/Boxing Day. There are two Christmases in order to split the material one (gifts) from the spiritual.

Gifts are exchanged on the evening of the 5th of December (**pakjesavond**) in celebration of the birthday of **Sint Nicolaas**. At night, children place their shoes by the fireplace. The shoes are filled with surprises from Santa during the night, which partly explains why Netherlanders have such big feet. Another tradition consists of "creating" and exchanging prank gifts. Each of these presents is accompanied by a silly or rude poem (the more

embarrassing the better) about the recipient's character and bad habits. The "giver" understandably strives to remain anonymous.

Perhaps in order to compensate for the tacky gift ritual, employers devised the **kerstpakket**—typically a box consisting of a variety of quality food items plus one or more quality non-edible gifts. Some companies give a gift certificate or extra paycheck. Suspense builds until the **pakketten** are finally distributed at work (a joyous occasion) on or shortly before the second Christmas.

New Year's Eve

New Year's Eve is called Old Year's Evening (**oudejaars-avond**). As this is the only time fireworks (**vuurwerk**) are allowed, it follows that, for many, the celebration lasts from 15 December to 15 January. Your first experience of New Year's Eve in Holland may give the distinct impression that the country has gone to war. It can be dangerous to walk about town after 10 pm, as cloggies take extreme delight in throwing these mini-bombs at passers-by. This form of entertainment continues throughout the night. For safety reasons, bars and restaurants close at 8 pm and open again around 11 pm or midnight when the carnage is at its peak. To pacify the pacifists, a recording of fireworks and other explosions called *Veilig Vuurwerk* was released on CD as an alternative to the real thing. In its first year, sales reached the platinum level, but have since fizzled out.

Nowadays fireworks are difficult to purchase in Holland, due largely to increased **regel**ing of the industry. Many cloggies therefore get them from the one place in Europe that always seems to have plenty of gunpowder . . . Germany. Please note that the Dutch authorities impose a hefty fine for possession of German fireworks that do not include instructions in Dutch. The carnage caused by illegal fireworks and the quantities seized usually increase with each new year: 2008 damages totalled more than €4 million and included 22 schools that burned to the ground. In 2012, Justice Minister Ivo Opstelten declared that setting off illegal fireworks after midnight was an "important tradition."

National Windmill Day

National Windmill Day is not observed nationally. Of all the areas that do sail away with it, most do so in May. Around 950 designated sites (which are normally semi-open to the public) are decorated with flags, flowers . . . and donation boxes.

National Bicycle Day

National Bicycle Day (*Landelijke Fietsdag*) has been observed for over three decades. It is the largest single-day cyclist event in Europe, drawing nearly a quarter million bell-dinging participants and is usually held on the second Saturday in May.

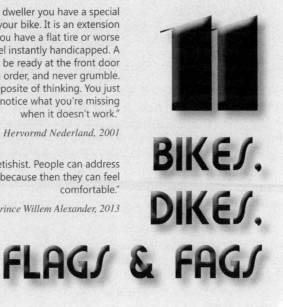

BIKEƧ, DIKEƧ, FLAGƧ & FAGƧ

his chapter focuses on some traditional and contemporary things for which the Dutch have received a measure of global recognition. The list is understandably short and is headed by the tourist money-spinners: windmills and tulips—both of which occur and recur in other chapters of this work. Here we include BIKES (in honour of Dutch perseverance with the infernal machines); DIKES (those all-important irrigation features, without which this book would be a collection of blank pages); royalty and patriotism (those ancient traditions that the Dutch simultaneously love and hate, typified by the practice of flying FLAGS at every slightest excuse); and homosexuals (unfashionably referred to as FAGS in English-speaking countries).

BIKEƧ . . .

There are almost 20 million of them in Holland (the highest density in the world), with an estimated 900,000 of them creaking away in Amsterdam alone. Whether this only counts roadworthy vehicles or includes the mangled, decimated lumps of rusty no-wheelers chained to bridges and lampposts throughout the city is unclear. What is clear, however, is that the Dutch are SO fond of them that at least 91 percent of households own at least one, and over 21,500 miles (35,000 km) of dedicated paths honour them. They come in various shapes, sizes and vintage—irrespective of which, they are all dearly loved and respected. There is a thriving black market industry in them, and facilities for spares and repairs are almost as plentiful as dog *shit* on the pavements.

They are called *fiets* (plural, *fietsen*), probably because that's what powers them. Their drivers are Kings/Queens of the Road (Queen Juliana would ride one to the local street market) whose wanton disregard for other road-users encourages them to careen from kerb to kerb, up to four abreast. This and the typical refusal to install/maintain a working bike light—25 percent of all cycling deaths are attributed to this—or protective headgear turns the night-riding *fietser* into a "kamikaze kloggie."

Public buildings, parking facilities and public service vehicles are all designed with the two-wheeled wonders in mind. Most major roads (except highways) include a personal Bike lane (*fietspad*) for them. Whenever and wherever possible, this lane is a separate thoroughfare, complete with its own road signs and traffic lights. The *fiets de résistance* of roadway real estate is the motorless motorway (*fietssnelweg*): super-smooth surfaced, immaculately maintained and often built in isolation to regular roads, *fietssnelwegen* provide Formula One-style cycling for fast-lane *fietsers*.

Bicycles are used in many roles: as personal limousine, goods vehicle, freight wagon and taxi, thanks mainly to a twisted tubular steel accessory—the carrier. The carrier carries crates, kids, cats and canines alike (special child seats can be installed at the front and rear of the frame, for larger families). In the absence of these household items, it provides a rear seat for one or more passengers (traditionally the girlfriend, boyfriend, wife, husband, friend, house plant—or any combination of these). Heavier cargo such as pianos and cupboards require the borrowing/rental/purchase of a *bakfiets*, a sturdy *fiets* modified to incorporate a large wooden box or platform at the front.

Predictably, the criminal element has not been blind to the possibilities of an attractive income from the resale of rustled rigs. The cream of Dutch technologists has been busily engaged in protecting the freedom of this threatened species for decades. The number of stolen specimens peaked at around 1 million per year before a phased introduction of uniformed *fiets* patrol teams, video cameras in special stalls, and surgically implanted microchips and barcodes in the cycle's

Rusty Haller

1. DYNAMO-DRIVEN HEADLIGHT (PREFERABLY DENTED AND BROKEN).
2. MOBILE TELEPHONE (USE WHILE IN MOTION, ALTHOUGH ILLEGAL).
3. HAND-KNITTED (OR P.L.O.-STYLE) SCARF.
4. TYPICAL CARGO.
5. STIRRUP PUMP (NOT TO BE LEFT ON BIKE).
6. PASSENGER SEATING/FREIGHT COMPARTMENTS -- MAX LOAD 250 LB (112 KG).
7. SIZE 10 EMERGENCY BRAKING SYSTEM (2-CHANNEL).
8. ANTI-THEFT DEVICE (OFTEN COSTS MORE THAN BIKE IS WORTH). MAY ALSO BE WORN AROUND NECK OR WRAPPED AROUND SADDLE SUPPORT.
9. BUNCH OF DUTCHNESS.

Nedlanderthal Man

anatomy dramatically reversed the trend. Once the firm domain of junkies, bicycle peddling is now largely performed by cloggy cycle cartels who transport truckloads of them to Belgium, Germany and Spain. For ten percent of the cycling population, the only way to avoid theft is through abstinence—they have stopped pumping their pedals.

The future of safe-cycling is assured on two fronts:

- Pedal Protection
  Generous governmental programmes extend to "bunkers" consisting of revolving lockers which can only be accessed electronically. Even the Dutch railway service has joined the game with the "Bike Shelter of the Future"—a *fiets*-lovers' paradise where old machines can be laid to rest inexpensively, and expensive racing

types can be stored in a private vault. Magnetic cards (including the hallowed *ov-chipkaart*) are used to access them via PIN codes for owner identification purposes. Robot cranes may be employed in a form of valet parking service.

- Pedaller Protection
  Primarily concerned about *fietsers* receiving bigger dents than cars in two-vs-four-wheel collisions, the Dutch Cyclists' Union (surprisingly called the *Fietsersbond*) has embarked on a campaign to force car manufacturers to fit air bags to the windshields of automobiles. If that doesn't reduce the annual death toll by a whopping 60 (as claimed), perhaps they could fit air bags to car wheels as well.

By far the biggest Bycycle theft cartel is operated by a branch of the local police known as the *Buitengewoon Opsporingsambtenaar*—the BOA. BOA's systematically kidnap misparked pedal*tjes*, stash them away in a Bike pound called an *Algemene Fiets Afhandel Centrale* (AFAC, commonly referred to as "ah fuck") and return them to owners for a ransom of €10 or more.

Lastly, some words of encouragement for prospective cyclists: Do not be scared to mount your machine and pedal off. Nobody knows that you are a novice at cycle-ology. Your secret weapon to build confidence is mounted on the handlebars—it's that rusty round audio alarm called a *fietsbel*. Here's how to use it:

1. Select your target of opportunity (aka pedestrian).

2. Stealthily approach the pedestrian (preferably from the rear) and maintain a collision course.

3. Two seconds from impact, sound the alarm device with one "ching-ching." Any more than a single "ching-ching" will reveal your true cycling status.

4. The tricky part: Immediately swerve to the left or to the right to avoid the impending collision. Note that it will take a few practice runs before you can accurately predict the evasive action that the target will take.

5. Fire a salvo of verbal insults into the air, then select your next target. Repeat procedure.

If you can't get the hang of this after 4–5 attempts, or if you're thirsting for revenge against other *fietsers*, consider a motorized version of the bike called a *bromfiets* or its ecological successor: the

Laurie Boucke

Laurie Boucke

End of a life-cycle

motorscooter. The rules of engagement are much the same, except now your vehicle is far noisier, faster and more dangerous, enabling you to terrorize everyone and everything on or off the road, including motorists.

The *bromfiets*' long reign of terror was based on its motorized-mosquito whine, in much the same way that the *Stuka* dive-bomber struck fear in the hearts of civilians during World War II. But it was not until the early 21st century that *KlogJugend* hit on the idea that more shock and annoyance could be instilled in kerbside *café* customers if they had a little less warning of an impending buzz-by. Hence the rise of the marginally quieter motorscooter as the weapon of choice amongst urban *asolijers*.

Dike∫ . . .

The Dutch have been building dikes, dams, ducts and ditches for about 1,000 years—and they still need more. They've been seriously messin' about with water for longer—and they've still got plenty left. They've tried to blow it away with windmills, pump it away with windmills and convert it to paper and flour with windmills—and have created a tourist industry in the process. The product of their labours is called the Dutch "landscape": a subaqueous plain, or (almost) dried-up seabed, which would completely disappear if the sea level rose by 60 feet (20 metres).

Perhaps due to their inability to tame the raging waters, they have become experts and innovators of waterways and bridges. They partitioned an area of the North Sea, formerly known as the Zuiderzee, into a freshwater lake and reclaimed large areas. A motorway runs across the 30-km partition (*Afsluitdijk*). The southern delta region (prone to periodic flooding) has been harnessed by a series of hydraulic dams, and the port of Rotterdam is protected by a pair of swinging doors (the *Maeslantkering*) that behave like a horizontal version of London's Tower Bridge. None of this could have been achieved without serious protest, debate, demonstrations and compromise.

In 1958, Parliament made positive moves to protect the country against flood disasters as a response to public disquiet following the devastating floods of 1953. In the late 1960s, protests were voiced about the project. The completion date of the last and most complicated part of the project was set for 1978. This was delayed due to protest and debate focusing on the barriers being "normally open" (to maintain the natural environment) or "normally closed" (to ensure the safety of the population at all times). In other words: plankton vs. people. Complete closure, for which contracts had already been awarded, was out of the question. The compromise called for the barrier to be kept open in normal circumstances but to be closed during heavy storms. All in all, the project was delayed some eight years and cost 30 percent more than estimated, with Queen Beatrix officially opening the storm surge barrier in October 1986. The *New York Times* acknowledged the feat with the following quote from Louis van Gestern:

> *"This will end the mythology of the dumb little Dutch boy with his stupid finger in the dike to save his country."* (See Chapter 21 – Another Brick in the Waal.)

Ever eager to profit from their talents, the Dutch have exported H_2O control technology to the extent of creating picturesque coastal landscapes in countries where a barren interface previously existed.

Back on the domestic front, the remaining water does have its uses. A primary mode of industrial transportation is the canal. Barges are more commonplace than articulated vehicles. In mid-wintertime, when the water becomes ice for a few weeks, nothing is wasted. Ice skates are donned by all from 2 to 102 years of age for a season of free travel—for leisure, business, sports and fitness.

FLAGS . . .

With true originality, the national flag is the French *tricolore* turned sideways, that is, blue under white under red. It is displayed at every excuse by the patriotic. Some will argue that the Dutch flag predates the French one by around 200 years, but the fact of the matter is that it took four centuries of debate and demonstration (until 1937) for the Dutch to officially agree on the complex design and colour scheme.

The post-World War II period saw the Dutch in the forefront of the drive for a unified Europe. During this phase, patriotism declined and fewer flags flew. With the goal of unity a supposed reality, Dutch fervour has refocused on the fear of losing their national identity. Flag manufacturers are reporting record sales. If homeland sales start to flag, they can always cut 'em in half, turn 'em around and sell 'em in Paris on Bastille Day.

If other flags are present, all should fly at the same height and be of the same size, quality and material. When fluttering with foreign flags, the whole flock is lined up in alphabetical order. Citizens and businesses can fly the flag at memorable events such as a wedding or if a Dutch kid ever passes an exam. On such occasions, it is not uncommon to accent the flag with a suitable thematic device.

Rusty Haller

National events with royal connections are denoted by the introduction of a long, fraying strip of toilet paper or ribbon, stained orange, and known affectionately as ***oranje wimpel.*** This streamer is intended to flap and fly freely above the horizontal *tricolore*, but given the Dutch climate, it tends to wrap both itself and its partner around the flagpole in one soggy, saturated wad.

The Netherlands is one of the few European countries which still retains a monarchy as a figurehead—adored and well loved, despite the obligatory scandals and obscene levels of personal wealth. The House of Orange-Nassau (also called the House of Orange or ***Oranjehuis***) has "governed" since 1815. The royal family (***Koninklijke Familie***) is among the most wealthy in the world, and this fact leads to the occasional bout of anti-royalty sentiment.

Queen Juliana (1909-2004) reigned supreme for many decades as hands-down favourite royal, largely due to her unpretentious manner.

She preferred her bike to a posh car and rather liked to be called *mevrouw* instead of *majesteit*. Unfortunately, her husband was left to his own devices to find things to do. Consequently, he enjoyed the fruits of favour "donated" by American defence firms. After the inevitable scandal and equally inevitable "investigation," the government dropped the matter, providing that Bernhard Leopold Friedrich Eberhard Julius Kurt Karl Gottfried Peter zu Lippe-Biesterfeld (aka Bernhard van Lockheed) resign from all "official duties" (not including repeated acts of infidelity). At the ripe age of 93, Bernhard joined the great Starfighter in the Sky after losing his battle with cancer.

Next to inherit the funny hat was Juliana's daughter Beatrix. German husband Claus von Amsburg had long been rumoured to have links with the Nazi party through associations with the *Hitlerjugend* and the *Wehrmacht*. At the regal betrothal (1966), some 1,000 cloggies violently demonstrated, shouting, *"Claus, raus!"* (Claus, get out!). After 17 years, the process turned completely around. The general public displayed much sympathy and compassion for THEIR Claus who had suffered from a mental breakdown, severe bouts of depression (necessitating frequent travels to Italy to play golf) and had been diagnosed with Parkinson's disease. By the time Claus *raus*'ed in 2002, he had added throat, lung, kidney and prostate problems to his popularity resumé. In return, the Dutch dropped their flags for him, although his German blood still denied him a good *wimpel*ing.

Queen Beatrix threw in the royal towel in 2013, after a reign of 33 years during which her popularity hit a high of 90 percent (for pedalling in public) and a low of 70 percent (at a time when the monarch's constitutional role was considered too political, powerful and "undemocratic").

Most citizens are (so far) supportive of their new King Willem-Alexander. Although he had been groomed for "crownship" along traditional lines, his assurances that he is "much more informal" than mum and will strip the Dutch crown of what is left of its political powers, are a good start for "Wim-Lex," formerly known as "Prince Pilsner." His earlier social missteps have been largely forgiven (if not forgotten) and his new image as a monarch of the masses now conveys a 21st century *Oranje superheld.* Willem-Alexander Claus George Ferdinand, King of The Netherlands can or has:

- Piloted jet planes
- Skated 200-km marathons in sub-zero temperatures
- Run the New York marathon

- Managed national water boards (*waterschappen*)
- Served on an Olympic Committee

King Wim's choice of spouse followed in the family tradition. When his romantic association with Argentina's Máxima-Zorreguieta was first announced, the country searched for a Claus-like conundrum—and found it. Miss Zorreguieta's father was tied to a brutal military dictatorship. After the predictable venting via heated debates and a large dose of exquisite royal PR, the country moved to a fully fledged national doting over Maxima (*née* Máxima).

The fact that the vast majority of the Dutch love to own a royal family may at first seem out of character for obvious reasons. As one royal supporter explains, *"As long as the royals are not too pretentious and talk sense, we don't mind supporting them. A president wouldn't be much cheaper—we have already calculated this!"* Supporting this view, a 2013 poll showed that cloggies have more faith in their monarchy than in their politicians.

The matter of patriotism would not be complete without discussing the world-famous heroism of the modern-day Dutch military forces. Until 1995, Dutch military service was compulsory and limited to just over a one-year period for young males. Now it is strictly a volunteer affair. To some its hardship equals that of a stay in a holiday camp. The ranks are permitted to retain essential jewelry in the form of ear-, nose-, lip- and nipple-rings, and other symbols of their mid-childhood, and enjoy full labour benefits (controlled working hours, public holidays and more). Even the officers have a union contract. Gays are welcome and received at all entry positions.

Back in the distant days of conscription, the alternative to military service was to become a conscientious objector, officially recognized and categorized. A *dienstweigeraar* (service "refuser") performed civilian-type work, or a *totaalweigeraar* (complete "refuser") lounged around in a military prison for about two years. Even after sentencing, a *weigeraar* could conscientiously object—and still have a chance of beating the system.

With the changeover to "professional" status, one would think that there would be no further need for "refuser" rules. In actual fact, a new breed of *weigeraar* has evolved. Upon reaching the age of 18, Dutchmen are registered with the Ministry of Defence and informed that their services will not be needed except in the case of war. The killer is that they cannot object to military service during times of peace, but they can during times of war. They now protest losing the right to be able to protest when there is nothing to protest about, and thus . . .

We demand the right to go to prison for not wanting to do something we are not required to do.

But even Holland's armed forces have to engage in a little bit of conflict now and again—albeit begrudgingly—and when they do, it is performed with that good old Netherlandic nature:

- When a MIG-29 Fulcrum was shot down by a Dutch F-16 over Serbia, an air force spokesman rationalized the event on the basis of relative cost rather than implied threat: *"An AMRAAM [Advanced Medium Range Air-to-Air Missile] is expensive. But if the missile breaks something that is more expensive, the concept works!"*

- Moving ahead to the Dutch military role in the US-led attempted occupation of Afghanistan, the conflict reverted to firing verbal salvos at whoever would listen. This time the problem was that the military union called General Federation of Military Personnel (*Algemene Federatie van Militair Personeel*) did not know how to represent its members properly: *"It is a secret operation—we don't know what the rules are!"* and *"We are concerned that the International Security Assistance Force cannot do its work because you cannot fight and make peace in one construction."*

- During the Libyan civil war of 2011, Dutch F-16s flew with other NATO forces, but were forbidden to drop any bombs. Their mission objective was to be "as useful as possible."

In 2013, in order to further prepare the armed forces for future overseas conflicts, Minister of Defence Jeanine Hennis-Plasschaert introduced special troop training in the art of befriending *buitenlanders* before other NATO forces blew them away. Rather than ship battalions to Botswana, companies to Cambodia, or regiments to Ruanda, she chose to put 40 squaddies on a train to Amsterdam, where they would better experience a "live environment." The orders required that the soldiers wear dress uniforms rather than battledress, so that the not-so-local locals would not think that they had been invaded. But that same year, while the rest of Europe was aghast with the revelations that the USA was pretty much digitally spying on the whole world, Holland learned that Volkel Air Base (near Uden, North Brabant) was still home to 22 Cold War era nuclear weapons. Ruud Lubbers, Dutch Prime Minister for much of the period, confirmed the continued presence saying, *"I would never have thought those silly things would still be there in 2013."*

Reporting back on the bladder problem seemingly experienced by Dutch males, it is interesting to note that their armed forces have also recognized this strategic deficiency and acted accordingly. The four-person portaloos used so effectively in domestic encounters such as King's Day are also deployed during overseas UN/NATO exercises in an attempt to prevent Dutch urine from defoliating forests and jungles—an admirable gesture that will finally put paid to the devastating consequences of "Agent Orange."

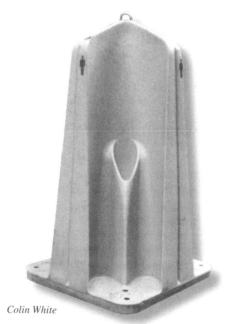

Colin White

The stealth portaloo

FAGS (AND FAGETTES) . . .

Gay boys and gay men (*flikkers*) came out of the closet in the 1960s. The discovery of the fact that there were other *flikkers* about, fired by their inherent (Dutch) rebelliousness and permissiveness, led to the formation of *actie* groups, followed by demonstrations, gay rights movements, gay centres, gay bars, hotlines and periodicals.

The inevitable reaction of **vrouwen** homosexual movements took place soon thereafter, with lesbians (**potten**) demanding equal rights and more-than-equal facilities. Holland was one of the first (if not the first) to provide generous welfare benefits to a lesbian couple who "had" a child through artificial insemination.

Despite their common homosexual *raison d'être*, gays and lesbians are separate entities. In general, women are marginally accepted in gay bars while men are more taboo in lesbian bars and *cafés*.

Amsterdam's liberal locals constructed the world's first monument to homosexuals in 1987—an obvious structure in the form of three large triangles, painted pink. Soon after, work started on a portable homomonument which was presented to the British government as a protest against proposed anti-homosexual legislation. The rest of the population strives to be extra "open" and accepting of homosexuals, bisexuals and portable monuments. Meanwhile, in 2001, Holland was the first country to make gay marriages legal for Dutch nationals or resident foreigners living with a Dutch partner.

Large events such as Gay Pride in August attract homos from around the world. For many, the feelings of freedom and euphoria are on par with that of soft-drug users openly enjoying joints in public places. Even the liberated Dutch gays enjoy being in the majority one weekend a year. (Surprisingly, some still experience a minority status at times.)

Obtaining gay rights and gay acceptance in Holland has required less of a struggle than in most countries. The gays fought their battle according to Dutch rules: long and detailed discussions; non-violence; demonstrations; playful behaviour rather than being aggressive, obnoxious and pushy; and appealing to Dutch tolerance. In addition, many Netherlanders consider it a plus rather than an effeminate minus for men to be cultured and artistic—traits often associated with the gay community.

Gay rights are part of a general pattern of rights for all groups that demand (and obtain) a place in Dutch society. The phenomenon known as **verzuiling** (pillarization, see Chapter 7 – The National Passion) was largely responsible for the original acceptance of gays in the Netherlands. For the majority of homosexuals, the struggle is more or less over and it's business as usual, even though the supposed tolerance for homosexuality is often superficial, or in the case of some orthodox religious groups and ethnic minorities—lacking completely.

"The Dutch nowadays have forgotten how to deal with violence (until the 1950s we were pretty violent in, for example, Indonesia), and we are in danger of having Muslims, Christians and atheists opposing each other, destroying everything we have been trying to build since the 1970s."

Rene Prins, 2004

12

IDENTITY CRISIS

his book has blossomed in part through its ability to define and describe the Dutch identity. For years, it was smooth and steady sailing until a maelstrom of unresolved social problems rocked the boat. These social problems largely revolve around immigration policies. Dutch identity has slowly eroded over decades of attempting to absorb and accept other cultures into its protective purse. Inviting members of former colonized countries, importing cheap labour and absorbing people from the EU have diluted the Dutch identity to the extent that their very own Queen Máxima failed to find it after supposedly searching for seven long years.

ID-OLOGY I (proof of identification)

Dutch can and do demand essential credentials from anyone over the age of 14 at the slightest excuse, so keep your ID with you at all times. Note that when the Dutch bark *legitimatie* at you, for once they are not being rude; they are not probing into your family history or parentage. The word is harmless, meaning "identification," and refers to paper or plastic documentation that must bear the requisite symbology and scribbling to be considered valid.

When examining certain forms of Dutch ID, you will immediately become aware of the Dutch obsession with paraffin (misspelled *parafen*). A Dutch *paraaf* (signing of initials) consists of one or more large, illegible scribbles, used mainly to ensure that no one but the originator can decipher the initials. The formal signature (**handtekening**, lit. hand-drawing) is equally as enigmatic as the initials, only there is more of it. Whether using the **paraaf** or hand-drawing, the process of bold and daring scribbling provides positive identification of the Dutch nationality. Of equal importance on some documents is the **stempel** (rubber stamp). While some documents require only a **paraaf**, others need the hand-drawing and yet others need the stamp. Sometimes a combination of **stempel+paraaf** and/or stamp+hand-drawing are necessary. With plastic documents, a hologram, barcode and/or magnetic strip replaces the **stempel**. Other vital ingredients of a legal Dutch document include the date and place (**datum en plaats**), despite the fact that the place can easily be falsified and is inconsequential.

If you find all this too perplexing or suffer from legitimitis, it gets worse. You are expected to know exactly which **legitimatie** is legit **legitimatie** for a given occasion, and who is entitled to see what. In this regard, it took the combined resources of the Ministries of Justice, Home Affairs, Finance, Social Affairs and Employment, Transport & Public Works and Welfare, Public Health and Culture to work out what everyone needs to lug around:

PASSPORT. No description necessary (if you haven't got one, how did you get there?). You can use it for most things (including retrieval of your mail at a post office, even though it does not show your current address).

VERBLIJFSDOCUMENT. The Dutch alien residency card issued to non-Dutch dwellers LEGALLY living in the Netherlands, requires strong proof of identity and purpose for its issuance. Yet this card is not considered a form of identification by many institutions, including the post office, even though the card bears your name, photo, hand-drawing, birth date, place of birth, nationality and alien registration number, verified by a minimum of two holograms and an official hand-drawing by an authorized member of the aliens police. Of course, if you are a citizen of an EU member state you do not need to . . . well, usually not . . . well, sometimes . . . to qualify for . . . unless you want . . . er, perhaps on Tuesdays.

DUTCH DRIVING LICENCE. Can be used in many situations (including football hooliganism), except for anything to do with taxes, employment, insurance, welfare or illegal alien investigations.

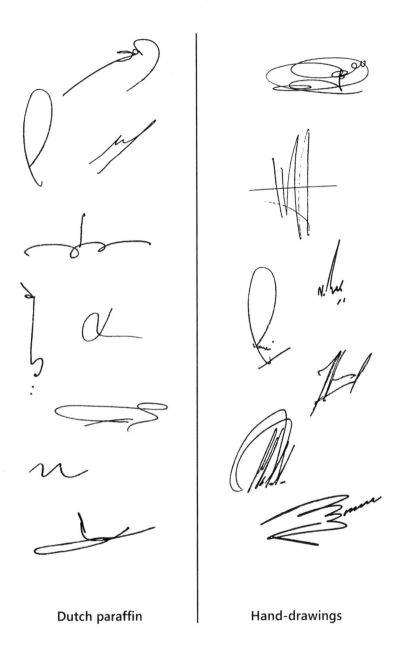

Dutch paraffin | Hand-drawings

NATIONAL ID CARD (NEDERLANDSE IDENTITEITSKAART or NIK).
Doubles as a passport for travel within the EU.

If you really want to feel that you are an integral part of Dutch society, a **burgerservicenummer** (BSN) is the ID of choice. Although it sounds like a fast-food crowd control ticket, it is the all-important social security/tax code/welfare-benefit registration number. Without it, you can't work and you can't claim money for not working—but rest assured they WILL find a way to tax you.

ID-OLOGY II (how to get it) . . .

If you want to stay longer than your tourist visa allows, you will inevitably need to deal with the Immigration and Naturalization Department (**Immigratie- en Naturalisatiedienst** or IND) to beg for a **machtiging tot voorlopig verblijf** (MVV). Experiences vary, and each is unique, but by far most are described as frustrating, confusing and expensive to say the least. The game is a modified version of "dog go fetch," and the rules—neatly packaged and presented as the Modern Migration Policy (**Modern Migratiebeleid**, or MoMi)—require the authorities to inconvenience wannabe residents by whatever means possible, making them run around town to gather various documents that are unobtainable. For example:

- An officer tells you that you must have health insurance in order to obtain a residency permit.

- You waste a few days on the insurance scent, only to learn that you cannot be insured without an MVV.

- You then return in a dejected and nervous state, fearing deportation or worse.

- The officer inhales a compassionate **ja** and then nonchalantly tells you, "*I'll give you a temporary residency permit. With this, you can get your health insurance, then you can come back and get your full permit. By the way, have you already obtained your . . .?*"

Occasionally, your fearsome IND-man will revert to being a standard Dutchie clown, as evidenced by the following account from an American resident-hopeful:

"After hearing many horror stories of the US Immigration Service, I was a bit nervous when I went to the Dutch authorities to request a residency permit. When I walked in,

there was an officer sitting behind the counter. Wanting to be polite, I asked him, 'Do you speak English?' He replied, in perfect English, 'No, not a word!' Okay, silly question. Still nervous and not really knowing where to begin, I said, 'I'm here for some information.' He immediately jumped up, placed his hands on the counter and leaned over it while looking past my shoulder. 'Well,' he said, 'It's a bright sunny day. Looks to be about 8 degrees outside. The pool is open–at least the pool across the street from my house. Is that the kind of information you are looking for?'

Thoroughly dazed by this encounter so far, I proceeded to ask for a residency permit. He then asked me if I had a [mumble, mumble] in my passport. I said, 'No. What is that?' as my heart began to sink. He replied, 'You were supposed to go to the embassy or consulate in your country and request it. You then need to come here and show me the sticker, and I give you this form to fill out, which I am going to give you because you are standing in front of me now.' I was stunned! If this was the way that the Dutch were going to handle bureaucracy, then I was going to like it here."

A. D'Auria

The earlier mentioned dog-go-fetch sport applies to many other situations, such as obtaining a business permit from the Chamber of Commerce (**Kamer van Koophandel**) and registering at the Registry Office (**bevolkingsregister**). Staff at the latter locale can demonstrate flair and originality in their challenges: If you are married, you will need to provide a copy of your marriage licence; if you are single, you may need to produce the non-existent "certificate of being single" (which in this instance is called a "certificate of non-marriage"). In some towns, the **bevolkingsregister** requires you to provide your Internet home page as well as your physical address. Do not be surprised if, after spending months gathering reams of forms, qualifications and certificates (from both your homeland and Holland), you are asked by a sadistic supervisor to return next week with translations, authentications/verifications and legalizations of all paperwork that is not Made in Holland.

Don't try to garner sympathy from the civilian population—they do not have to play this game, and they won't believe YOU have to either.

THE REGELS . . .

Learn this word: *regel* (pronounced ray-gull, with a guttural g). Expect to hear this word often. It literally means "rule" and little Holland is BIG on *regels*. As at least one exasperated visitor has observed, *"In my home country, we can do almost anything we want to as long as there is not a law or rule that says we can't do it. Here in the Netherlands, we can do anything we want to as long as there's a rule that says we CAN do it."*

For such a seemingly liberal country with so many freedoms, it is surprising to foreigners how repressive, deeply ingrained and far-reaching the *regels* are. They provide the locals with a finely balanced barrier between the laws of the land at one end and absolute anarchy at the other end. There are a multitude of *regel* levels (national, provincial, municipal, street and even individual buildings such as blocks of flats), each dictating acceptable behaviours in just about every social and economic setting possible. The multitude of regulations can cause confusion and frustration.

To add to this confusion, some *regels* are compulsory, some are optional, some are voluntary, some are conditional and some are improvised/invented on the spot if a Netherlander wants to get his way (so you don't necessarily have to obey them all). After Somali refugee, feminist-activist, writer, intellectualist and Dutch Member of Parliament Ayaan Hirsi Ali got dis-Membered for perjuring her immigration process, one of her Dutch protectors in the European Parliament justified the lowland lies with, *"Naturally, rules are there to be 'adapted'."* With the situation clarified, Hirsi Ali has been largely forgiven and is now practicing her craft in the USA.

Another foreigner living in the Netherlands offers some good advice. After being summoned for a fourth tuberculosis examination, she asked if she could officially refuse to take another and learned that only one such medical exam is *verplicht* (required). Her advice:

> *"Whenever you are stuck by a Dutch regulation, ask directly if it is obligatory or voluntary. This is because many regulations are not clear and apparently are kept this way to ensure more compliance from foreigners who don't understand how the* **regels** *work."*

When applied to the burgeoning urban tourist trade of sex and drugs, the *regel* concept permits the authorities to impose informal and flexible rules and regulations under which otherwise illegal activities can be tolerated. Furthermore, the *regels* can be rapidly repaired, replaced

Enjoy Amsterdam, but...

...not everything is allowed

- Do not use the street as a toilet

- Hard drugs such as XTC, heroin and cocaine are illegal

- Soft drugs are not to be used in public places. Go to a coffeeshop!

People who do not adhere to these rules run the risk of a fine. Call 0900 8844 for more information.

Regeling in Amsterdam

or removed to respond to problems without resorting to ponderous legislative procedure.

Even so, in some places, regulations have become so overbearing and stifling that measures are being taken to remove *regels*. Numerous websites (including local governments) now feature a *minder regels* page where pissed-off people and browned-off businesses can electronically lobby for selective de*regel*ization.

Punishment for breaking municipal *regels* is often in the form of monetary damages called *boetes* (fines). Pay your parking tickets if you ever plan to return to Holland! If you fail to pay a ticket and attempt to enter the country by air at a later date, you run a high risk of being detained by the police at the port of entry. They will require you to pay for the ticket, even if it's years old, plus a fine. The same applies if you inadvertently miss paying your last rubbish collection bill or if your residency permit expires while you are outside the country. When you re-enter, you will likely be invited to the "explanation chamber."

Dutch nationals are not exonerated from Schiphol fines. In fact, one of the highest airport fines to date was issued to a Dutchman who had "incorrectly" filled out his tax forms. At the outgoing passport control desk, he was presented with a tax bill for nearly €100,000 which he paid on the spot, then went on his merry way.

The most common means of extracting money are the **bekeuring** and **boete**. A **bekeuring** is a ticket with an on-the-spot fine. If you can't cough up the cash, it becomes a **boete** that must be paid within a defined period. Both hits are on the increase as more and more regulations pass in order to keep people in €uro-line and grow the government—all for a good cause, of course. As more new laws are passed and more fines levied, both government and public are ever alert and mindful of maintaining the critical and intricate balance between tolerance and punishment. As an example of the erosion of once-commonplace activities, it has long been considered fair game to stick your tongue out at, or otherwise ridicule cops. But now insulting "law enforcement personnel" has become a more serious matter. The case of a homeless man who called a cop a **mierenneuker** (ant-fucker) for confiscating a beer can reached the high court. The home- (and beer-) less victim was eventually exonerated, after which a Member of Parliament questioned, *"If you can call a police officer an ant-fucker, then it worries me what you can call a social benefits officer!"* The fine structure is particularly fierce when using visual insults—obscene finger or hand gestures, or t-shirt slogans, with or without verbal insults.

CRIME AND PUNISHMENT . . .

Public acceptance of bureaucratic madness is largely based on the perception that Dutch law enforcement has become ineffective and that escalation of serious crime in the country is largely due to the influx of foreigners. Typical attitudes are along the lines of, *"The cops here are more social workers than police officers,"* (foreigner's view) and a public opinion poll that revealed a growing unDutch leaning: *"The police should use truncheons and pepper spray to become the boss of the streets again"* (locals' view). But there remain two forms of vandalism that are acceptable to the majority of the Dutch citizenry:

- Blowing up parking meters and touchscreen **parkeerutomaten**, as this promotes free parking for one space up to a complete **straat**. (Authorities have countered this activity with the installation of seismographs and heat detectors.)

- Destruction/theft of speed detectors and cameras, as this eliminates fines. (Authorities have countered with the installation of more high-tech stuff: motion detectors, proximity sensors, heat and smoke detectors, vibration/tilt meters and bullet-proof glass. For extra coverage, some municipalities are installing cameras to monitor the cameras.)

Trial by jury does not exist. Perhaps the Dutch are better off without it, as a jury would spend weeks defining their role, debating a case and squabbling over their opinions, with the result that they would probably never reach a verdict. Instead, judges are left to their own ends to deliver verdicts and penalties.

While the public becomes increasingly alarmed at worsening crime statistics (one-quarter of Dutch people are crime victims, one in three no longer feels safe in Holland), the courts, prisons and social services continue to play "Mr. Nice Guy" to the bad guys. Some warrants for drug trafficking and other criminal activities are often never served. With prisons stocked to capacity and due to the Dutch tendency towards forgiveness, sentences are often extremely lenient. A judge in Sittard routinely reduces defendants' sentences if they have to wait "too long" for a court appearance—*"I can't stand waiting around for hours either,"* the judge confessed.

Prison terms are served on a space availability basis. Thus, a criminal (sorry, "victim of society") will be released upon conviction, pending an empty cell. If a criminal does go to jail, chances are his or her stay will be carried out in relative comfort, not unlike a hotel stay. The idea is to provide prisoners with as normal a lifestyle as possible. Consequently, in addition to the introduction of flat-screen HDTVs, "sex cells," smartphones and voting rights, some prisons have taken the concept of creative confinement to undreamed of levels. Psychic healers, tarot-card readers and astrologists are employed at some facilities. Paul van Bree—a prison service clairvoyant in Schiedam—puts prisoners in contact with dead relatives: *"That brings them peace. Big strong men burst into tears,"* he explained. At an overstocked prison in Doetinchem, prisoners are given €5.00 extra "pocket money" if they share a cell with another inmate. The *mede*cons make their own house rules. For example: *Niet schijten als ik aan het eten ben* (Don't shit while I'm eating). Another rule provides that prisoner A can smoke a *blowtje* (joint) in the cell if prisoner B snores at night.

Then there is the problem of prior commitment. Many criminals are just too busy to find time to languish in jail for a few months or years. Many hire a substitute to serve their time under the *euro's voor uren* doctrine. The ploy works because the authorities are lax in checking the true identity of people who report to prison when a suite finally becomes available.

It is part design and part necessity that the Dutch have instigated forms of "alternative punishment" and "educational projects" in order to rehabilitate their victims of society (e.g. a 67-year-old woman from Oisterwijk, Brabant, was sentenced to 180 hours of knitting for fraud). More heinous forms of punishment may include a 22-day excursion to a mountain camp on the Mediterranean coast, enjoying the local countryside and cuisine. Consequently, theft from automobiles is commonplace, as is pickpocketing and similar crimes. To have your car broken into and the expensive radio-CD-cassette player stolen is considered no big event.

The attitude of the police? One of inconvenience—your ex-property will be on sale in a bar the next evening where you can buy it back at less than half price, and you should be grateful for such a bargain!

As an example of how emotionally devastating this attitude can be, we offer the following from Nakita DiGuardi:

> *I had my first run-in with crime in Holland. I had my house robbed . . . Supposedly two Moroccan men used steel bars (which are still in my house) to break in our windows. They then came in, grabbed our computers and took off down the street.*

> *I'm pissed as hell and feel totally violated, but life happens. So now we have done the most unpleasant thing of ordering bars to be put on our lower level windows.*

> *Later, we actually found out some new information on our computers that were stolen.*

> 1. *The three Moroccans that broke into our house live literally right around the corner from our house.*
> 2. *The laptops were sold the next day at the coffieshop right across from our house.*
> 3. *The police refuse to follow up with any of this information. We found out this info from another neighbor who actually buys stolen goods at the coffieshop but didn't buy our computers. (Who knows if that is true? He won't go to the police of course.)*

My concern is this. The police keep telling us to just leave it alone because if we aren't careful they might retaliate. I know these three guys know what I look like, and they can see when we leave our home. I am honestly scared at this point. I asked the police if they could give me mace to carry for my safety. They told me that I am not allowed to carry anything on me for my protection."

Rusty Haller

Stolen moments

Confidence in the police is so low that the main reason many people report a crime is to obtain the police report required by their insurance company.

But according to the police, their nonchalance has good cause. They feel they are treated as a ***pispaal*** (pissing pole) by the general public. It's not their fault that much of the crime cannot be solved or justice be served, as they are seriously bogged down in bureaucracy. Huge files are created for each crime, using different colours and **stempels**. There are complicated formulas and forms to complete for the most elementary of crimes . . . *"four hours of bicycle patrol leads to three hours paperwork,"* sighed the newly resigned leader of the **Algemeen Christelijke Politiebond (ACP)**.

In some respects, one can sympathize with the law enforcement legions as their own judicial system promotes crime by rewarding it. Dutch law allows criminals to deduct the cost of their crime from any penalty that may be applied by the court. After being caught robbing a bank of €6,500 in Chaam, the perpetrator was forced to pay back €4,500 as he had supposedly spent €2,000 on the gun. A legal expert explained, *"It's about the costs a criminal would not have incurred if he had not committed the crime. He had to have a weapon in order to rob the bank!"*

NON-RACIST NATION? . . .

When it comes to racism, the Dutch suffer from a perplexing identity crisis: Are they or aren't they?

They like to boast that they are a non-racist nation. In the 1960s, they were extremely proud of the lack of prejudice and racial problems in Holland (although in the 1940s the first Indonesian immigrants were looked down upon as second-class people). But there was a reason for this situation: Non-Caucasians were a rarity in Holland in those days. The result was that darker-skinned people were idolized by the Dutch.

Things began to change when cheap labour was imported from countries such as Turkey and Morocco. When Suriname became independent in 1975, hoards of Surinamese flooded the country. The crime rate, drug abuse and number of people on welfare increased phenomenally. Immigration procedures tightened somewhat as public dissent began to manifest itself:

- The unspoken sentiment: *"We support your cause, we appreciate your dilemma, but don't want you here."*

- In the words of Amsterdam clergyman Dr. H. G. Boswijk: *"When Surinamers come to our churches, people observe a friendly distance. They say, YOU ARE WELCOME BUT LEAVE US ALONE. It's a kind of implicit apartheid."*

- From a former Mayor of Lelystad: *"Many immigrants come from countries where little or no culture exists. If they bring anything with them, it is their bad habits."*

With the arrival of political correctness and "multi-culti," the Dutch collective conscience reflected on their recent outbursts and felt the pull of the tide which soon washed up feelings of guilt over their colonial past. The country synchronized with the rest of white mankind in dutifully being seen to abhor apartheid. This naturally evolved into indignantly demanding "equal access" for all. As part of the ground-swell, the use of euphemisms to refer to "coloured" people took hold, such as:

allochtonen	("immigrants")
buitenlanders	("foreigners")
gastarbeiders	("guest workers")
immigranten	("immigrants")
medelanders	("fellow citizens")
minderheden	("minorities")
nieuwe Nederlanders	("new Dutch")
rijksgenoten	("members of the state")

Predictably, Dutch creativity took hold when the opportunity to invent new terms for people presented itself. Hence the list expanded to include the more specific **kut-Marokkanen** (Moroccan cunts) and **geitenneukers** (goat fuckers). Somehow the term **allochtonen** prevailed and by 2004, hardly one media-hour could elapse without the A-word being hacked to death. It got so bad that Rotterdam and some other municipalities, in a rare display of political correctness, outlawed the A-word in favour of terms such as *"Rotterdammers of Moroccan descent."*

The nation had already plunged into a sustained downer following two unrelated tragedies: Pim Fortuyn, a charismatic, anti-immigration gay politician, and Theo van Gogh, an outspoken and inflammatory (even by Dutch standards) mediocre moviemaker, were both murdered for mouthing off. Although these killings happened two-and-a-half years apart (conspiracy theorists insist the period was 911 days) and the circumstances were unrelated, rising anti-**alloch** feelings magnified to the point that immigration became the blame child for everything bad that had happened to the country over recent decades. Immigration laws were tightened, and the old **verzuiling** system reared its head again.

Many believe the Netherlands has sunk to its deepest level since World War II. The prevailing feeling focuses on mouth psychology and the concept of tolerance. On the one hand, the murders of Fortuyn and van Gogh are seen as an example of the intolerance of tolerance. On the other hand, many feel that *"The Netherlands has been too tolerant of intolerant people for too long."* (Geert Wilders, 2004). Whatever the outcome of immigration policies, van Gogh-ery has a firm future:

- **We laten ons niet monddood maken** (We won't shut our mouths)

- **We moeten vaker onze mond opentrekken** (We need to open our mouths more often)

With racism being officially blacked, it is surprising that many Dutch continue to resent their nearest neighbours—the Germans. Yes, we all know about the Nazi atrocities committed over half a century ago, but much of today's venom is spat by a generation that was then largely unborn. So what is the root cause of this rampant rejection; why do the Dutch doubt **Duitsers**? After all, they were mates during World War I (Anthony Fokker sold 'em pacifist machine guns and red, three-winged, anti-war air-superiority fighters), and they were mates during earlier significant conflicts. There have been few trading disputes (in fact, Germany is by far the Netherlands' most important trading partner); they both make good beer; they both delight in eating raw, minced beef (**tartaar**) and pig's feet; their respective aristocracies are undeniably meshed; and their languages and looks are . . . er, similar. The most common explanations for anti-German sentiment are:

Older generation(s): *"For sure it is about the war—not just the invasion and the treatment of our people and the Jews, but also about the Bicycles that they stole and used to make tanks and guns to kill people in their try for world domination."*

Younger generation(s): *"It is because we Dutch lost the 1974 World Cup when a German referee made a mistake. According to research done by the University of Amsterdam, we are more angry about a soccer match than about the invasion of our little country."*

Feeling decidedly *unwillkommen in den Niederlanden*, the German tourist presence in Noordwijk, Zandvoort and other vacation spots has dropped off dramatically. When German cars were vandalized and set ablaze in the town of Hoorn, the German Ambassador advised tourists to take the train rather than drive down into the lowlands, adding, *"It might be an idea to punish the perpetrators with community service, so they can brush up on their knowledge of history."*

If German drivers do manage to escape the fritz-blitz, they may want to choose their parking places v-e-r-y carefully:

"People will park so close to you that you can't get out again. You will be subject to constant abuse—verbal and quite possibly the other kind. You will get ticketed, clamped and towed; your wipers will get broken off; scratches and dents will develop on your car. Not much different, really, from the average experience of any motorist in Holland, except that it will happen to you about ten times as often and ten times as bad."

Tom Bijvoet

The aversion to "Germanity" manifests itself in many walks of life. People speaking German in public places are often met with ridicule and rude comments by annoyed Netherlanders who assume the **moffen** (krauts) don't understand Dutch. *"Friends of mine choose to speak English among themselves to avoid being immediately found out as Germans,"* explained one disillusioned *Deutsch*ess. Fewer and fewer Hollanders are interested in learning German, which is threatening the shutdown of many German departments in secondary schools, colleges and universities.

As a more extreme example, a Dutchman driving home from Germany left his teenage son as "collateral" at a petrol station in Essen when he ran out of fuel and funds. He was apparently so "fed up" with *Deutschland* that he drove back to Venlo and swore never to set foot in Germany again. Attempts at mediation were ineffective, and the man refused to finance the return of his child. The Red Cross had to repatriate the lonesome lad.

Of course, Holland would not be **Nederland** without a healthy counterculture that promotes Germany as a fun, clean, freedom-loving neighbour: a country that has replaced France as the top holiday destination (except for overnight stays and amount spent!).

13

"We believe you must give people a basic wage, and let them choose whether or not to work."

*Gerrit Jan Wolffensperger,
senior Amsterdam council
member*

WORK VS WELFARE

utch domestic culture has cunningly managed to interweave work and welfare with the concepts of individual rights and social justice in ways never fathomed by the rest of the world. In their perpetual process of innovation and rejection of older ways, the Dutch keep themselves proud and content whilst distributing billions to those perceived to be less fortunate than themselves.

UITKERING . . .

If you truly want to integrate with Dutch society, you must have at least one type of **uitkering** (national assistance; closest English pronunciation is "out-caring").

Applying for welfare and reaping the benefits is not a social disgrace—it is a right. At times, as much as one-quarter of the population is on welfare. Those governmental bureaucrats whose role in life is to approve your **uitkering** will give you all the assistance you require, to the point of helping you rewrite your application to receive maximum payment. If you don't qualify by answering *ja* (yes), then answer *nee* or *neen* (no), the social worker will likely advise.

Once you are legal in the country, there is only one requirement to obtain your **uitkering**: You must be prepared to spend a long time in dismal, unventilated waiting rooms on numerous frustrating occasions.

Advantages of having an *uitkering* are as follows:

- It kills any incentive you may have had to work. This is excellent training for the Dutch youth.

- It gives the Dutch government an excuse to have one of the highest tax rates in the world.

- It attracts thousands of foreigners, especially Turks and Moroccans (so the Dutch can claim they are not racist).

- It encourages those who get the urge to work to do so illegally to supplement their income. This is known as "black" (*zwart*) work by those who engage in it and "white" (*wit*) fraud by welfare institutions. Be careful which term you use when speaking with strangers.

- It encourages many to live abroad on welfare benefits at the expense of those who pay taxes. Senior citizens can be absent from the country for up to half a year before their benefits are affected.

- It offers a wealth of local government benefits, from free admission to the community swimming pool, to discount purchases at welfare-club shops. As an example, "minimum-wage supermarkets" (*minima-supermarkten*) sell date-expired meats, vegetables and dairy produce to welfare recipients.

An even better deal is to be declared disabled (preferably "permanently"). Until recently, about 10 percent of disability dole recipients were fraudulently awarded this honour. A further 10 percent joined the club through depression and 25 percent of women aged 25–35 were inaugurated after giving birth (understandable). The rewards included 70–100 percent of salary for the first year and thereafter around 65 percent. The degree of disabled dosh delivery is based on a sliding scale, starting at "less than 35 percent disabled" and rising to "80-100 percent disabled" by the *WIA*. In theory, those who fraudulently claim to be disabled will be caught during medical "rechecks." Their punishment? They are downgraded to regular welfare benefits.

Some cities, organizations and websites publish a free monthly newspaper or newsletter for welfare recipients. The publications provide them with all the latest benefits they are entitled to receive, demonstration dates/locations and ways to manipulate the system. Enticements for getting folks off welfare include:

- Free magazine, newspaper/newsletter subscription and e-mail updates (for "better societal orientation").

Rusty Haller

A minimum-wage supermarket

- One year of free adult education.

- Scooping up dog **shit** (hourly rate is less than welfare entitlement). This supposedly grants the scooper or scoopess greater self-esteem. This is a very secure job, but promotion prospects are **shit**.

- Free money to form a "permanent relationship" with someone who has a job.

- Free computer, training and Internet accounts.

Although Holland has one of the richest and most generous welfare systems in the world, the natives still voice their disapproval. They want more. And they want it free (**gratis**). Many women, youths and foreigners rally behind mottos such as **Bijstand Mis$tand** (Welfare = $-Abuse). Others use the same mottos to indicate their opposition to welfare because it makes people dependent and therefore is a "capitalist slave-making system." The point here is that the Dutch themselves cannot agree on the meaning of mottos around which they rally. This includes officials who strive to end **uitkeringsfraude** while at the same time fear the consequences should they succeed.

Local authorities organize occasional mini-clampdowns (such as reducing welfare payments to recipients with three or more cars) in order to be seen to be taking a proactive position. But sometimes the clampdowns backfire. In 2004, the Secretary of State shut down the "toothbrush police" by decreeing that pensioners (**AOW'ers**) with two toothbrushes in their bathrooms can no longer be automatically classified as couples "living apart together," a situation that lowers an **AOW-uitkering**.

Abuses withstanding, the system DOES provide help for the genuinely underprivileged, the chronically ill, the elderly and children in a far better and more humanitarian manner than the various so-called social security programmes which operate in other Western countries.

NO FIXED ABODE . . .

Whether or not by choice, there are tens of thousands of people who call the streets, parks, alleyways and ditches of Holland "home." Much of the country is in denial about this, as the *vox populi* has long been: *"There are NO homeless people in Holland."*

Before someone can be one of the non-existent homeless, he/she must first decide whether to be houseless-homeless (**thuisloos**) or roofless-homeless (**dakloos**), or both, as the degree of inherent freebie-goodies varies considerably. It has been suggested by some observers that the distinction is present merely to create more job opportunities for welfare bureaucrats.

In Utrecht, due to a lack of space in homeless shelters, free hotel vouchers were sometimes offered to the abode- or roof-denied. *"Life is expensive on the street. You can't just grab a sandwich from your fridge,"* explained one enlightened, compassionate **gemeente** geezer. Inspired by **gemeente** geezer's gravitas, Utrecht has now gone one step further by organizing annual "pamper the homeless day" events where the unfortunate are showered with free clothing, food, drink, and live music, before being thrown back into the streets or hotel rooms. The city's record on helping the homeless has impressed Amsterdam's **Daklozenvakbond** (homeless union), whose own efforts include poviding postal addresses and benefits updates for its own houseless and roofless members.

ſUBſIDIEſ . . .

Generous subsidies of all types are available. Although the Ministry of Housing, Regional Development and the Environment has published a series of booklets in Dutch, Turkish and Arabic on the subject, the system for qualification is so complex that **subsidiologie** is a required course for Management Economy and Law students at some colleges.

The most common is the housing subsidy (**huursubsidie**) which is doled out to over one million people. Also widespread are educational grants and subsidies. These include the arts. Often the financial encouragements are in the form of a purchase of the subject matter by the government, in order to help the aspiring artists. Some of the works are displayed in a multitude of public buildings for all common taxpayers to savour. The rest (the greater majority) are stashed away in storage while their owners offer daily prayers that the works will achieve masterpiece status in later decades. A psychiatrist was once subsidized to pose on a pedestal in a museum, proclaiming himself to be a work of art. (Hopefully he also was hung in a multitude of buildings.)

Life is based in large part around the amount and types of subsidies one receives. Recipients carefully weigh the financial consequences of starting part-time or full-time work. A job seriously affects their welfare and subsidies.

THE WORKING WAY . . .

Despite the attraction of generous unemployment benefits, some choose to actually work for a living. The process of getting a job is relatively simple, requiring only:

1. Production of the requisite documentation (see Chapter 12 – Identity Crisis).

2. A "reasonable" knowledge of the language. Newcomers who do not speak Dutch are now "required" (read: requested) to learn basic Dutch.

3. Selling yourself by convincing the interviewer(s) that you can—and, more importantly, will—perform the defined duties.

A prospective employer can require applicants to furnish a "Certificate of Good Behaviour" (**Verklaring Omtrent het Gedrag** or VOG). A criminal background check is run and if nothing of "importance" is found, the certificate is issued. If the applicant fails the investigation, the complain/protest/object/appeal process can be trudged through, by which time the job will have been filled by someone else. This can be an effective means of increasing and/or extending **uitkering** benefits.

Selling yourself may at first seem the most daunting phase of job acquisition, but the reality is that **Dijk**land often overflows with unfilled labour requirements. Unskilled/manual vacancies exist mainly because most eligible Dutchies (like some other Europeans) believe themselves to be above menial tasks, thereby encouraging the growing influx of foreign workers. Professional positions abound largely due to the obsession for hiring [latest technology] "experts." Whichever level applies, the interviewer(s) are under strong pressure to fill the gap with the least unsuitable applicant. In many instances, the concept of "bullshit baffles brains" is triumphant.

Once hired, the task becomes one of impressing the employer for a period of three months, after which it is difficult to dismiss you, as will be seen later. During the probationary period, you will without doubt experience some frustration regarding the lack of effort extended by your colleagues. In turn, they will be relatively cold to you while they pursue the philosophy, *"First you prove yourself, then we see what we do with you."* However, once you complete your three-month trial, your working life takes on a completely different character. You are now a fully fledged **medewerker** (co-worker). In short, you now belong and will thus be required to follow the **medework**-mantra: *"There is no point in working hard on projects that are sooner or later going to be scrapped."*

Rusty Haller

With this new-found status, you can now concentrate more on the "social aspects of work." Work now interrupts coffee breaks. A heated, two-hour debate over the validity of your boss's instruction receives higher priority than the five-minute task of executing it. A colleague's birthday takes top priority—the important event allows various workers to arrange a collection, purchase celebration requisites and organise the compulsory office "surprise" party. You, as birthday boy/girl (*jarige*), are not left out as it is your duty to provide edible delights. The party, of course, takes place during company hours.

Timekeeping is no longer a matter of conscience. Remember that the Dutch form of the expression "The early bird catches the worm" is:

The early bird is for the cat.

While all this travail is under way, the employer does his bit to keep the ship afloat. When faced with unwanted staff depletion, the company may well embark on a series of office extras, pitched as "incentives to stay" (for employees) or "productivity enhancements" (for investors). Examples include office haircuts, baby-sitting services and arrangements for in-home needs (e.g. plumbers, electricians, handymen or dry-cleaning).

One cardinal rule is: Never discuss your remuneration with other employees. The idea of salary differentials in Holland implies that vile, obnoxious and inhumane concept: INEQUALITY.

Employees need not worry about their (lack of) customer service skills. Customer service is a good way for staff to level the best of buyers. In short, the degree of customer service appears to depend on the personality, mood and perceived degree of busyness/business at hand. As an example, upon arrival, hotel guests at a 4-star Golden Tulip Hotel found a bottle of wine and two glasses on a table in their room. On contacting the hotel receptionist, the following transpired:

Q   *Is the wine complimentary? It's not on the minibar list.*
A   *Well, then, I suppose it must be free if it's not on the minibar list.*

Q   *We don't have any way to open it. Is there a bottle opener*
    in the room?
A   *I don't know but I have one here. You'll have to come down*
    to use it.

/UPERVI/ORY /UBJUGATION . . .

Opinions and views about Dutch supervisors vary. Foreigners tend to feel their boss is friendly, understanding and approachable. But this is not the attitude of Dutch employees. The FNV or **Federatie Nederlandse Vakbeweging** (Dutch Labour Union) claims that nearly 40 percent of employees are "afraid" of their bosses. They also whine about poor communication, long workdays(!) and, predictably, low pay. Others say their boss is too authoritarian. An even more disturbing recent development, heretofore heresy in Holland, is the occasional attempt to sabotage traditional channels of discussion and debate about company policies and other domestic issues, as typified by this particular gripe from one middle-aged veteran Dutch employee:

> *"The new boss, who is all jolly and charming in the hallways,*
> *lets people leave the job without even saying 'Sorry to hear*
> *that.' He takes the largest room of the whole building all for*
> *himself and puts others in tiny ones. He dares to write memos*
> *stating, 'It has been decided,' without consulting us first! Maybe*
> *this is perfectly normal in the USA or some east-European*
> *dictatorship, but not in the Netherlands where organizations*
> *are flat, workers can think for themselves and bosses cannot*
> *slam their fist on the table but are supposed to involve all levels*
> *before taking decisions."*

One thing is for sure: when a department, division, or even the entire company is at its most efficient, it will be reorganized by changing job titles and personnel duties to the extent that no one knows what the hell anyone is supposed to do. Reorganization is usually planned by omniscient managers, with no consideration given to individual workers' strengths, talents or coffee-making skills.

DI/MI//AL:
FAILURE OR /UCCE//? . . .

An employer must give you a "reasonable" (but unspecified) amount of verbal warnings as to your misconduct. Next, three written warnings must be issued (on separate occasions). These are only officially recognized if you (the accused) acknowledge acceptance in writing. Without your acceptance, the matter goes to arbitration.

With your signature, the case is presented to the local authorities for assessment and possible authorized dismissal. The word "possible" is used here meaningfully. Should the authorities decide your dismissal is valid, your new-found unemployed status is likely to qualify you for welfare. Welfare through unemployment is typically 70 percent of your last salary, paid by the same local authority. Given the Dutch affinity to the purse, it follows that the local authority will be hesitant to approve a dismissal.

At work, employees have little or no fear of being fired. They can basically do what they want. If they don't like a particular task, they refuse to do it. Some days or weeks later when their supervisor asks them how the project is progressing, the employee(s) typically reply with a shrug and inhale the word *ja!?!*

If for one reason or another you find you are experiencing stress on the job, one of the most popular and successful tactics is to stage a nervous breakdown and go on paid sick leave for several months. By the time you return, your employer will either make you work harder than ever to catch up, thereby putting you under stress again, or will ask you to resign. The solution will likely be a negotiated settlement wherein your disappearance is rewarded by a large payment made in such a manner that your welfare claims are not compromised.

When you have absolutely no choice but to actually DO something at work, you could join the 10 percent of Dutch employees who suffer from "burnout" (characterized by feeling emotionally drained, empty, tired, exhausted or "used up"—pretty much the standard Monday morning feeling). Burnout rewards are similar to stress rewards. You really can have a nice time working in Holland.

TIME OFF . . .

Every person recognized by the social security system, employed or otherwise, bank president or street sweeper, is entitled to a minimum holiday entitlement each year (on top of the seven national holidays and ten family-leave days). Although the total entitlement seems to hover around 30 days, it is impossible to tie down specifics. We asked some experienced Dutch employers for an explanation, and the clearest/most concise response was from Paul Claassen:

*"The number of vacation days depends on what branch you work in, but generally speaking it is 21 days per year. But, and here it comes, it also depends on the CAO. For instance: within the metal-working industry there are 2 different sides: '**Groot metaal**' versus '**Klein metaal**.' '**Klein metaal**' includes companies like re-grinders and small businesses up to say 50 employees. Everything above counts as '**Groot metaal**.' Each branch has its own result in the negotiations with the unions and thus the number of vacation days differs.*

*Then there is something like '**ADV dagen**' which is a way to reduce the number of hours worked without having to change all the contracts. This can mean that a person working 40 hours per week within a '**Groot metaal**' company gets some extra days off because the maximum allowed number of working hours is 38 per week. Do the math: 2 hours per week means on average 13 extra days per year. Then there are branches with only 36 hours per week: on a 40-hour contract that means 26 days per year. Banking has a work week of 35 hours so another 6 days extra. But remember these are not vacation days: part of them are planned in by the employer. Yes, they have a day off but they can't decide on when (in most central agreements the split is 50-50).*

Then there is something else: the older you get the more days you have. Per 10 years is about one day, but this also depends on the branch you work in . . ."

This may seem overly generous until you consider that a large part of the holiday pay (*vakantiegeld*) is deducted from the individual's wages throughout the year and paid back during the holiday period together with the employer's contribution, after taxation. Thus the thrifty Dutch award about four weeks' holiday and pay for roughly half—a classic example of "going Dutch." Again, it is the *uitkering*-ites who win, as they receive a *vakantie* bonus with their welfare payments for four weeks of the year.

Sick leave is yet another way to maximize an employee's welfare benefits. When you report an illness, representatives are sent to your home about once a week to "confirm" that you are at home and are genuinely ill. The visits are only allowed to take place during specified hours (typically Monday to Friday, mornings until 10 and afternoons from 12 to 2:30) of the first three weeks of your illness. This procedure rightly allows the critically ill sufficient latitude to shop for the necessities of life, such as flowers and coffee, without the fear of losing any welfare entitlement.

COMMERCIAL CUNNING . . .

Dutch businessmen come across as charming, enticing, jovial and extremely cordial to new foreign business contacts. The higher the stakes, the more a Dutch negotiator seduces his unwitting clients into a masterfully executed act of contractual copulation. He builds your confidence, makes you feel special and gives the clear impression you are getting a fair deal, all the while creating an atmosphere of *gezelligheid*, comfort and caring. In truth, he couldn't care less. The only YES he really understands is the ¥€$ you'll bring to him and his company. The Netherlandic negotiator is the commercial equivalent of the Venus flytrap: His true nature is camouflaged—then he strikes and consumes his prey before the victim realizes he is financial fodder. Be especially wary of utterances along these lines:

The price is important but so is the cost.
There are costs on top of the quoted price.
I am sure we can do business along these lines, providing it is something we can work with.
In former times, this has worked quite well.
This is something we have managed to do with others.
If we awarded this to you, would you feel responsible?
I am authorized to make a full commitment/offer.
I don't see how this could fail.
It does not fit well.
It is so good to do business with someone who understands.
Of course. I cannot see it any other way!

Don't ever bother looking for financial sympathy in the form of a price break. Whatever your problem is, your host will upstage you with a bigger and more expensive sob story: *"Your costs have gone up by 30 percent since last year? Well, ours have doubled in the last few weeks!"*

It's helpful to know in advance that you are not likely to get properly wined-and-dined by anyone in Holland—unless you happen to be the guest of the "big cheese." Lunch is a real shocker. If one of the managers takes you out to lunch, expect it to last about half an hour (as he looks anxiously at his watch) probably at some unheard-of, dingy, fast-food place that claims to have won the "best-tasting *uitsmijter* in the world" contest. He will lavishly lash out and pay for your fried-egg sandwich but may opt to bring a brown-bag lunch for himself. This is not an embarrassing situation in Holland (well, not for them at least).

Deal delays are inevitable. The main causes are:

- The ***bespreking*** (although you have arrived for a meeting, another one will have kidnapped your contact beforehand). EXPECTED DELAY = 10–30 minutes.

- The ***cursus*** (employees escape to courses on a regular basis). EXPECTED DELAY = 1–2 days.

- The ***snipperdag*** (a day off, planned moments before your arrival). EXPECTED DELAY = 1–2 days.

- The ***vakantie*** (there will be plenty of these). EXPECTED DELAY = 1–2 weeks.

The worst time to accomplish anything with the Dutch is between April and August, plus most of the month of December, because . . .

Work revolves around holidays.

∫TRIKING BACK . . .

The name of this game is "Haggle & Scheme." Expect deception, and learn to deal with it. Here are some guidelines to give you a fighting chance:

1. If a cloggy has made a written offer, DO NOT respond immediately. If anything makes Dutch businessmen nervous, it's not hearing about money straightaway. If you wait a few days to reply to their offer, it weakens them, thus improving your position. (Remember that this can work both ways.) On the phone or during meetings, employ the "pregnant pause" to achieve the same result.

2. After the obligatory introductory session, avoid business dealings in person. Use the written word—letter, fax or e-mail wherever possible. Dutch businessmen have an aversion to paper trails, for obvious reasons.

3. In written communications to you, be very suspicious of strange wording. The worst you can do is to reason, *"Well, he's Dutch so his English/French/Italian isn't perfect. But I think I know what he is getting at."* Always seek clarification, just as your opponent would.

4. Avoid sending long or pushy e-mails, faxes, etc. If you ask a lot of detailed questions or keep requesting speedy replies, your communications may well go unanswered. Dutch people tend to ignore you if they think you haven't planned things properly or when they decide you're using up too much of their valuable time.

5. NEVER fall into the "specific response" trap. In this ploy, your contact will answer specifically and literally to the exact question being asked. Example: When trying to reach a buyer or contract manager by telephone, you may ask, *"Is Mr. van der Sloot there?"* If the specific response trap is in play, the answer will be, *Ja!* followed by a line disconnect tone—call over. This trap has the effect of destabilizing you and forces you to focus on your precise choice of words, to the detriment of the overall negotiation strategy.

On that rare occasion where your tormentor has unintentionally made a mistake by overcharging you, remember the following:

1. The more nonchalant or dismissive he appears to be about the situation, the more embarrassed he is about it.

2. He will usually make light of the situation. Don't react, just ignore any silly comments.

3. Any apology will have a qualifier attached—"confusion" and "mix-up" being the more popular. Respond with Dutch directness: *"Oh that? There wasn't any mix-up. You just didn't pay!"*

Good luck.

A TAXING SOLUTION . . .

The freebies and fun stuff revealed in this chapter may seem like utopia to the newcomer, and in many ways it is. But it all has to be paid for, which is why it takes around seven months of gross income to pay one year of Dutch taxes.

The dialectic between overtaxation (*"**Ja**, we must be sure everyone is taken care of"*) and entitlements does not seem to rattle most workers. Perhaps one reason for this is the never-ending changes in tax laws to effect social justice. By the time workers realize something is unfair, the offending law has either been abolished or has morphed into something that appears to be more acceptable. As an example, a 2001 tax regulation granted a "social benefit" (tax refund) to a non-working spouse or other "domestic partner" rather than the wage earner/taxpayer. How nice.

Having gotten away with giving people's refunds to others, the ***belastingdienst*** attempted to instigate a scheme whereby they would send completed income tax forms to taxpayers who then just have to sign and return the form (and payment). Just how this would provide social justice is anyone's guess, but, as always, complaints and objections were a part of the equation and the plan melted into the IJsselmeer. Hare-brained schemes such as this, together with the incapability of the ***belastingdienst*** to organize its own IT division, has given rise to yet another citizens' ***actie***: "FIST AGAINST THE FISCUS.

PUNTENEL
& BEL HELL

hey blurt it out whenever and wherever possible—*puntenel* this and *puntenel* that—a refrain that reverberates in the brain. You won't find it in any dictionary for the simple reason that *puntenel* (or more correctly, *puntenèl*) is the pronunciation of .nl which is the identifier of Dutch websites.

Hollanders have a history of stubbornly resisting, then passionately embracing, emerging technologies. This includes not only computer technology but also the use of the mobile phone *(mobiele telefoon* or *mobieltje*). Thus you will encounter both *puntenellers* and *bellers* in all parts of the land.

Rusty Haller

HACKER HAVEN . . .

Holland harbours some of the world's most adept hackers, forever foraging for computer networks and Internet services to scuttle. A successful intrusion affords them their five megabytes of fame and perhaps even a place on the Dutch hackers' roll of honour. Top hits so far include:

- Thirty-four US military computer systems during the 1990-91 Gulf War. The bandwidth bandits offered tactical information to Iraq, but the customer declined as the source was "not credible."

- Infecting around 1.5 million computers worldwide (300,000 in the Netherlands alone) to steal Internet banking data and plunder PayPal accounts in 2005. The keyboard crooks hailed from Loon op Zand, Tilburg and Rijswijk.

- Hacking the website of the huge online eatery Just-Eat, resulting in over €30,000 worth of orders for pizza, sushi and *shoarmas* being served up for €0.01-€0.05 per order (2009).

- Launching an "unprecedented" distributed denial of service cyberattack targeting anti-spam/web hosting partners in the USA, the Netherlands and the UK in 2013. The perpetrator, Cyberbunker (who originally operated from a disused nuclear-hardened cold-war shelter near Kloetinge in the province of Zeeland) sent up to 300 billion bits of data per second via its computer networks.

Holland hosts an internationally recognized hackers' convention about every four years. The hippy-style geek-gathering attracts thousands of experts, enthusiasts and eccentrics for a few days of keyboard fondling (*"It's like a blind date with 3000 people,"* reported past attendee, Klaartje Bruyn) and diverse lectures ranging from digital passports, biometrics and cryptography to government lobbying and mayhem.

- Version 2005 (named "What the Hack"), held in the village of Liempde, was attended by Dutch police in numbers, in order to educate themselves on new technologies and techniques. Security was largely self-enforced—an unmanned baggage scanner was provided for people to screen themselves, and *gratis* disposable rubber gloves were provided so that attendees could perform a DIY body cavity search. Civilian visitors wore green armbands and plain-clothed police officers wore pink ones. Curiously, one of the favourite attractions was a computer-free area where Internet access was banned.

Rusty Haller

What the Heck?

- Version 2009 (named "Hacking at Random"), held in the small town of Vierhouten, was attended by 2,300 geeks and assorted androids and was pretty much an excuse to try to catch pneumonia by sitting in a soggy cow field and celebrating 20 years (=5 events) of hackerfests by attending such spellbinding lectures as "All Your Packets Are Belong To Us" (sic) and "Hacking with Plants."

- Version 2013 (named OHM2013 = Observe. Hack. Make.), promised "An open atmosphere where you can learn the basics of blacksmithing, contemplate in the zen tent or hack on hardware and software . . . the target audience includes free-thinkers, philosophers, activists, geeks, scientists, artists, creative minds and a whole bunch of people interested in lots of interesting stuff," according to the official, secure, website.

TELEPHONE TORTURE . . .

In Holland, you must state your name every time you answer your phone. If you fail to do so, the other party will either lapse into silence or demand to know who you are (*Met wie spreek ik?*) before uttering another word. Cloggies are seemingly incapable of holding any type of telephone conversation without knowing your name:

> *Can I speak to Mr. van Doorn?*
> *What is your name?*
> *John Smith.*
> *(Bluntly)* ***Ja!*** *The switchboard is closed. Call back later.*
> *Can I leave my name or a message?*
> *No!*

Some Dutch suffer from an affliction known as telephonophobia (*telefoonvrees*). The symptoms include anxiety and extreme nervousness when dealing with both incoming and outgoing calls. The Dutch are at a loss to explain the origin of their phone fear, but admit it is not unknown for the weak-hearted to go into cardiac arrest at the sound of a ringing phone. An answering machine only makes things worse, including the grotesque word for the associated hang-up:

telefoonbeantwoordapparaatvrees

Perhaps one cause of telephonophobia is that their subconscious minds are scarred with past experiences of bureaucratic *bellen*. They all know what to expect when dealing with calls to or from a business, public office, etc. If you are lucky enough to reach a human being but do not know the toadstool (*toestel* or extension number) or department (*afdeling*), it will be necessary to explain in great detail precisely why you are calling, and why you are calling this particular place. Just as you reach the interesting part of your lengthy explanation, the ear on the other end of the line, not knowing what on earth you are talking about, will either:

- cut you off, or
- connect you to a toadstool, seemingly selected at random. When someone answers, you must begin your explanation all over again . . . and again . . . and again.

Phone frustration continues to increase as callers access more and more useless menu selections or are put on hold indefinitely. The *Er zijn nog tien wachtenden voor u* message (There are ten people ahead of you), which is at least a little helpful in that you get a vague idea of how long you have to wait for a human response, is gradually being replaced by *Al onze medewerkers zijn in gesprek, een ogenblik geduld alstublieft* (All our staff are busy at the moment, please be patient), followed by loud unfashionable music which is interrupted every 30 seconds by the same message. *Telefoonvrees'ers* seem to prefer the original countdown-message system, but with some reservation:

> *"The countdown when on hold is good because you can prepare yourself and attempt to calm down your heartbeat of 180. At the same time it's bad because the countdown itself is absolutely nerve-racking, especially when you get to* **Er is nog ÉÉN wachtende voor u.** *OMG!"*

> Lonneke Kersten

When you finally reach an operator, the can't/won't *(kan/mag niet)* factor kicks in. Be prepared for the following lame laments:

> *We can't do that.*
> *I can't find him, call back later.*
> *That is not possible.*
> *I can't help you.*
> *That is not our policy.*
> *That isn't how it works.*
> *There's a waiting list/waiting period.*
> *He/she's on a lunch break.*
> *He/she's on another break.*
> *I'm very busy.* **Sorry!**

Then there are the perennial favourites that are guaranteed to drive anyone *op*'ping mad:

> *He/she's* **op cursus.**
> *He/she's* **op vakantie.**
> *He/she's* **op** *another* **vakantie.**
> *He/she's* **op bespreking.**
> *He/she's* **op een afspraak.**
> *He/she's* **op zakenreis.**
> *He/she's* **op zakenbezoek.**

When you ring the police, expect to have a long wait until someone replies. Offer the burglar or murderer in your home a cup of coffee to stall him while you wait for the police to answer your call.

With much of the country *vrees*'ing, *mag-* & *mag-niet*'ing and *op*'ping on a regular basis, it comes as some surprise to learn that this open and friendly place boasts the highest number of telephone taps per capita in the EU. In 2008, the Justice Ministry authorized 26,425 "lawful interceptions" (compared with 1,881 in the United Kingdom). To add to the paranoia, these statistics do not include taps by Dutch security services. This insecure security costs the country €4,000 per intercepted number (includes croc clips, connection fee, human monitor, written transcript, and a *kopje koffie* while listening in).

If you are reading this book while languishing in a Dutch police station or prison-hotel, remember that Dutch law allows law enforcement to record ALL conversations made by crime suspects. This includes discussions with your lawyers.

THE HOLY ROAMIN' EMPIRE . . .

As with computers, the Dutch resisted the advent of mobile phones (*mobieltjes* or *gsm'etjes*). Originally, they were strongly associated with criminal activities (in the same manner as paging devices), then reigned as expensive toys for youngsters who had never known the terrible ravages of *telefoonvrees*.

Next came the trendsetters and posers—*"Hey, don't I look cool with this little gadget in my pocket?"* Within two years, all levels of Dutch society succumbed—although there still remains a diminishing element who insist that they will never, ever have a use for a *mobieltje* (until their employer or *Sinterklaas* offers them one for free).

By 2005, mobile phones managed to equal the entire Dutch population. Then came smartphones with their access to the World Wide Cloud. By 2012, 53 percent of Dutch consumers were pedalling around with a characteristic smartbulge in their pockets, branding the wearers as "Internuts" who cannot move another chain's length without accessing their e-mail, downloading the latest tulip-futures prices or tweeting. In short, much of the Netherlands has gone from *telefoonvrees* to mobile madness (*gsm gekte*), including the global obsession with "texting" or *sms*'ing. The display of the name or number of most incoming calls has led to a reduction in *foon* fear and the new-found freedom of being able to answer calls from friends or family with *hoi* or some throat-clearing equivalent.

COPIN' WITH KOPEN

he Dutch love to window shop and to browse while dreaming of the ultimate bargain. Perhaps in fear of relenting to sales pressure, many also suffer from the bizarre affliction known as ***drempelvrees*** (threshold phobia—fear of entering shops, restaurants, offices and other places). Having managed to cross the ***drempel***, they revert to type.

CODE OF CONDUCT . . .

No matter where you make your purchases, expect to encounter seemingly rude and pushy people on both sides of the counter. The overall smallness and crowded conditions that prevail in retail premises frequently give rise to constant griping and grappling for personal space. There is a general "code of conduct" that you are expected to observe. Memorize the following:

1. For smokers, before entering a shop, find a waste bin containing dry, combustible material in which to throw your burning cigarette.

2. When entering stores, let the door slam in the face of the person behind you. If you hear a loud thump or bang caused by a person in a cast, pram or wheelchair, nonchalantly turn around and mumble, *"Surrey whore"*

(see Chapter 17 – The Dutch Language). If you're in a particularly benevolent mood, you can further announce that you didn't notice the person's cast or wheelchair. The concept of holding a shop door open for someone is so alien, if you make the mistake of doing so, they will likely think you are mentally deficient, about to rob them, or both.

3. If someone gets in your way, place your hands on his/her shoulders and impatiently push the person aside. If you are feeling especially convivial, show off your French by uttering, *"Pardon."*

4. If your purchases amount to less than €5 and a queue of more than three people has formed behind you, take at least five minutes to search for your plastic payment device. Alternatively, delay the transaction, using whatever means possible until the queue has extended to eight people.

5. Hunt for bargains and complain about the prices of ALL produce and merchandise.

6. Expect to argue long and hard to attain any form of justice or satisfaction. Remember: The customer is always wrong. This is especially true when returning defective merchandise or spoiled food. When it comes to overcharging and short-changing, a salesperson or waiter will not feel guilty or embarrassed when caught red-handed. Minor relief is sometimes possible if you don't mind shouting or throwing a tantrum.

IN ∫UPERMARKET∫ . . .

There is nothing "super" about a Dutch urban supermarket. In cities they are small units that cram a wide range of goods on narrow shelves separated by equally narrow aisles. Lack of space also means that inventory levels are kept to an under-minimum, so don't be surprised if the shelves are half empty by 5 pm. In rural and recently developed areas, supermarkets tend to be larger, offering some relief to customers. Irrespective of location, observe the following for a fair shot at a successful shopping spree:

1. Take a few coins or similar sized annular items as deposit for use of shopping carts. Until €uroisation, the peel-off ring-tab from a beer or soft drink can was

considered by much of the population to be legal tender for this purpose.

2. If a cloggy offers you an empty cart in exchange for the deposit amount, beware! Either the mechanism for refunding your money is broken, or the wheels malfunction (and you will bump around the premises, extremely inconvenienced and embarrassed).

3. Frequently block aisles with your shopping cart and, if possible, a few kids. If someone dares to stand in front of you or move too slowly for you, ram your cart into their heels or shins while nonchalantly studying the wares.

4. Recruit kids to covertly load other customers' shopping carts with expensive items.

5. Inspect egg cartons for quantity and condition of contents. Often at least one egg will be broken or missing. Check on the local definition of "Dutch dozen" (*dozijn*). In some shops, one *dozijn* can be ten, in others it means twelve.

6. Prod and poke delicate items. When about to leave, complain to the shop assistant about the poor quality of the produce.

7. Place little faith in bar-code scanners and the like at the checkout. Review your receipt for errors before leaving the supermarket. If you don't, you may well come away unaware that the price reductions which attracted you in the first place were never applied.

8. At the checkout, the cashier makes a series of greetings:
   Dag, which means "good-day."
   Bonuskaart, which means "discount card."
   Zegels, which means "savings stamps." (This is NOT a guttural *Sieg Heil*, as many Germans have learned to their cost.)
   Air Miles, which means "air miles." (Don't expect *luchtkilometers, vluchtafstand* or any other true Dutch equivalent.)

   Answer *dag* to the *dag* and grunt for the rest. The savvy-visitor strategy here is to get as many discounts as possible. A grunt may be construed as a "yes," and you might just be awarded a discount.

Rusty Haller

9. After your responses are processed, you will hear an animated "**en een bon!**" followed by a scrap of paper being thrust into your hand (if you are lucky, the paper scrap will reflect your purchases). Only at this point can you pack your purchases into the bag(s) that you brought with you (oh, we didn't mention that?). Take care not to package the next customer's items that are now streaming down the conveyer and mixing with yours.

10. When leaving the supermarket, never abandon an empty shopping cart. In pouring rain, gale, hail, sleet or snow, you must return it to collect your sizable investment. Failure to do so will immediately brand you as a dumb foreign tourist with no idea of the real world.
If you feel that you simply MUST abandon it, get out of the way as quickly as possible. You may be crushed in the rush to redeem it.

To avoid all of the above annoyances, look for a neighbourhood Muslim **minimarkt**. These are often owned and run by Moroccans, Turks or other **allochtonen** and offer cheap prices, fresh produce and "exotic products." Assuming you can speak **alloch**, you will find the proprietor/salespersons polite and respectful to their customers (if you can't speak their lingo, you still come away with the same impression). As a bonus, adopting your local minimarkt allows you to pose to your friends over delights you'll never find at Albert Heijn: *"My Moroccan butcher saves the most tender, tasty mutton for me!"*

AVONDVERKOOP . . .

In the bad old days, when regular Dutch shops had to close at 5 pm on weekday and Saturday evenings, and could not reopen until Monday afternoon, a renegade breed of retail establishment devised the concept of **avondverkoop** (night selling) to service those who needed to buy stuff outside the normal business hours.

Avondwinkels (night shops) sell staple necessities such as beer, wine, condoms, bread, snacks, plant food and toilet brushes. Prices are higher and the range of goods smaller, but the shops satisfy their customer base well.

People gripe about the inflated prices but shop there just the same. When regular store hours were extended up to 10 pm in 1996, many people saw this as the just demise of the pricey night shops. But the public had failed to take something into consideration, namely in night shops, you don't have to put up with crowds, pushy people, shopping carts and screaming kids.

RECOUPING RICHE/ . . .

Topping-Up

The Dutch have fallen for the Western fashion of carting around little plastic water bottles when venturing outdoors. Given the inflated prices charged for "designer water," this may at first seem highly uncharacteristic of the thrifty nation. What hides beneath the surface is the revelation that around 75 percent of the hydrochuggers engage in **flesjes hervullen**—the clandestine art of refilling the bottle*tjes* with tap water. The Spadel Group, purveyors of the top-selling Spa brand, positively pout at the practice: *"With every sip, a little spittle gets into the bottle and forms a breeding ground for bacteria."* Apparently, this does not happen if one refills the tiny bottle from a three-litre bottle of **Spa rood**, **blauw** or **groen**.

After 12-or-so refills, or when the screw-top thread has worn away, or when a growth of bacteria starts to form on the inside of the bottle, it is time to employ the final rite: **statiegeld** reclamation.

ʃtatiegeld

Statiegeld is the word applied to deposits on beverage containers. A beer bottle has a certain **statiegeld** value; a full crate has the quantity value plus some extra for the plastic container.

For discarding different types of glassware and plastic bottles with no value, there are colour-coded recycling bins on street corners. You may have to wait your turn to use these bins since it requires some studying before throwing bottles away. The owners want to make sure first that they don't subject themselves to financial ruin by inadvertently throwing away a bottle for which they paid **statiegeld**!

No self-respecting standard could be christened "decidedly Dutch" without a corresponding EU threat of extinction. In the case of **statiegeld**, the attack comes in the form of the "standard, single-use, disposable container"—a supposedly environment-friendly plastic bottle that the EU wants to flood its empire with. The attack on the common recyclable bottle has attracted Dutch collaborators in the form of beverage companies (who decry transportation and recycling costs), retailers (who protest about storage and bureaucracy costs) and, worse still, people who think that reusable containers are "old-fashioned." The Dutch resistance, headed by environmental organizations such as the **Recycling Netwerk**, launches salvos of complaints about secret government meetings and deals with big industry, and uses slogans such as **red het statiegeld** (save our **statiegeld**) in their fight to preserve this temporary taxation. Meanwhile, as the war escalates, the streetwise Dutchie still reserves his Bike's carrier for his weekly refill of capped and crated liquid gold . . . and always will, no matter who wins.

RED HET STATIEGELD

Borgsom

Borgsom is similar, but is applied to video camera rentals, safe keys, Bicycle rentals and other things of value. Anything that will make it, they'll take it—and sometimes they'll fight you tooth and nail not to reimburse it.

If you are not sure if you are paying **borgsom** on a transaction, a good indicator is when the vendor asks you for some **legitimatie**—although it is unclear why a vendor needs proof of your identity in order to borrow a €uro or two from you.

We strongly doubt that **borgsom** will be threatened with commercial extinction in the foreseeable future.

Spaaracties

Spaaracties include savings stamps (**spaarzegels/koopzegels**), club cards (**klantenkaarten/bonuskaarten**), discount coupons (**kortingsbonnen**) and redeemable coupons (**waardebonnen**) that are issued as an enticement by supermarkets and manufacturers/producers. They are ever popular in Holland, as they give the impression and satisfaction of something-for-nothing.

In the early 1960s, the Albert Heijn supermarket chain upped the ante by offering appliances through their **spaarzegel** programme, which resulted in almost 200,000 cloggies acquiring their very first refrigerator. Today some 70 percent of the country covertly collects the Douwe Egberts **waardebon** coupons from packs of coffee.

SHOPPING FOR CLOTHES . . .

1. When visiting fashion shops, take ear defenders with you to avoid permanent ear damage from the compulsory "in" music blaring incessantly therein. On a lucky day (for your ears anyway), you may witness the environmental police (**milieupolitie**) issuing the shop with a hefty fine for "noise pollution."

2. If you notice someone searching through a full rack of clothes, stand nearby and push the clothing apart so that you close the gap the person has made.

3. Take your children and encourage them to play hide-and-seek amongst garment rails.

AT ƧTREET & FLEA MARKETƧ . . .

1. If you see an item you wish to buy, show minimal interest in it. Tell the vendor you saw the same thing for less than half the price at another stall, in order to launch into a healthy bartering session.

2. If a crowd has gathered around a particular stall, push into the crowd, dig your elbows into those in front of you and breathe heavily in their ears to give them the hint to move out of your way. Conversely, if you are in the front row of a crowd studying the display of a stall and others try to elbow their way in, hold the fort. Do not leave until the crowd has dissipated.

3. When the market is extremely busy, walk against the flow of traffic, stopping frequently for no particular purpose.

Rusty Haller

16

> "Wealthy Dutchmen would
> rather talk about their sex
> lives than their money, and
> their sex lives are far
> less interesting."
>
> *J. van Hezewijk,*
> *The Top Elite of the Netherlands*

ROCKING
AND ROLLING

he three major cities of Holland are cities for the young-at-heart and the nucleus of open vice, crime and corruption. Every few years, Amsterdam is anointed the gay capital of Europe and the drug capital of the Western world.

In some rural areas, diluted forms of vice, crime and corruption are prevalent. In others, strict Calvinism and other moral standards have stemmed the tide of indecency to the extent that cigarette vending machines are emptied at midnight on Saturdays to prevent trading on a Sunday.

SEX AS AN ACTIVITY . . .

It has been said that the Dutch approach the subject of sex with the warmth and passion of an ice cube. Sex is an act society encourages of individuals aged 14 and up. (Or is it age 12—from time to time, pressure is applied to lower the age of consent from 16 to 12 years.) Many mothers monitor their young teenage daughters for signs of their first menstruation. This is the time to present the flowering female with her first birth control lecture/kit. The male situation is quite different. At the first signs of pubescence, it is not unusual for a Dutch lad to be hounded by his father to experiment with sex, sometimes with no concern for the consequences.

These magnificent displays of understanding and tenderness sow the seeds of sex attitude in the developing children. In school, emphasis is placed on the mechanics of pregnancy and sexually transmitted diseases, leaving the frustrated and curious youngsters to solve the remaining mysteries by roaming around Internet chat rooms asking, **Hoe moet ik pijpen?** (*How do I blow?*) and **Wie moet er boven?** (*Who goes on top?*).

By the time they reach adulthood, performing the sex act regularly is considered part of the daily routine. In the words of a housewife, "**Ja,** *having sex is something you do in the morning and at night, like brushing your teeth . . .*"

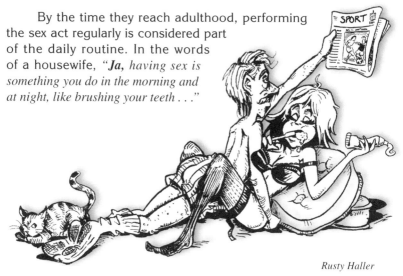

Rusty Haller

After 20 years of ramming free soft porn shows down Dutch throats, TV stations decided to pull out of that particular market largely due to limp viewership. As Expatica columnist Kevin Lowe observed, *"The Dutch have become so blase about pornography that they can't even be bothered to tune in when it's free on television."*

Sex can be mentioned coldly but candidly with dinner guests: *"The children had fun at the beach yesterday. We had good sex last night. I must go to the dentist soon."*

The Dutch word **vrijen** refers to both petting and penetration. (You will recall that the word **vrij** also means "free.") The topic of **vrijen** is freely discussed just about anywhere and with anyone, without embarrassment, shyness or hesitation.

Spontaneous stripping and nakedness on the part of cloggies should not necessarily be interpreted as a sexual gesture. They peel off at the slightest excuse and in front of whomever happens to be within visual range. An unwitting visitor meeting a relative for the first time, upon presenting an item of clothing as a gift, may be shocked when the new acquaintance eagerly undresses in front of everyone present in order to try on the clothing. Likewise, visitors to the country are expected to nonchalantly flash their flesh when and where the natives would. When visiting a doctor, there are no dressing gowns, and patients are expected to undress and remain stark naked in front of the doctor, staff and medical students for the duration of many procedures. Holland is the only EU country that has not freaked out over the use of "naked" body scanners at airports.

The subject of abortion (a *vrouwen* birthright) is treated with similar nonchalance:

> *"Did your period start yet?"*
> *"No, I had an abortion. On the way home, my Bicycle had a puncture . . ."*

/EX A/ AN INDU/TRY . . .

Prostitution in the major cities grew and flourished from the lusting natures of seafarers arriving from long journeys. The Dutch, ever alert to the prospect of easy florins, soon established dedicated districts (**gedoogzones**) for the plying of the trade. These areas are principally found in the Randstad. They are not sleazy. In fact, they are major tourist attractions and are generally located amongst other businesses and/or flats.

Prostitutes accept cash, major credit cards, cheques, foreign currency—anything that represents MONEY. These purveyors of pleasure exude pride in their profession, making no attempt to disguise their business when on duty. They are required by law to have regular medical check-ups and enjoy a healthy relationship with the tax officials who will generally grant deductions for a wide range of occupational necessities.

The Red Thread (**De Rode Draad**) was a foundation for prostitutes. In representing ladies and gentlemen of pleasure, **De Rode Draad** frequently protested governmental attempts to tighten up on things such as lighting, toilets, wash facilities and working arrangements. Originally their struggle was to work towards full acceptance and legalization of their **sekswerkers**, with social benefits (such as sick pay, special tax rates, pension benefits, pregnancy leave and compensation for time off during menstruation). **De Rode Draad** opened its curtains in 1985 and finally closed them in 2012.

Rusty Haller

Hmmm, do I get air miles, too?

Legalization in 2000 provided the industry with a new sales outlet: the ***uitzendbureau***. Women seeking employment through a job centre should not be surprised to be offered a position in the sex trade as an alternative to secretarial work and other more traditional jobs. (It is, after all, a form of temping.) When the owner of a sex club in Kerkrade needed 10 ladies of pleasure, he advertised the vacancies through the local employment agency, gushing about the excellent work package:

> *"They will receive a regular pay of 1,600 euro a month, can go on vacation, can receive sick pay and have a mortgage. For the job, they don't need experience. They will have a medical examination four times a year, they have the right to refuse clients and can choose how to **vrij**."*

To further stress the point that penis payment is profoundly permissible, a high court ruled that a severely handicapped man was entitled to a monthly grant towards the cost of a female "sex aid worker." The sum involved was ruled no great burden on the local government of Noordoostpolder. The man's claim to entitlement was based on a psychological report that he had need of sex once a month.

Some months later, the chair*vrouw* of the Netherlands

Association of Psychiatric Nursing (Nederlandse Vereniging voor Psychiatrische Verpleegkunde or NVPV) campaigned for the rights of patients at a psychiatric hospital near Maastricht: *"Some patients want sex and are going to brothels and being badly treated. Others are doing it with other patients in toilets, which is not nice."* City authorities responded by engaging a local "madam" to arrange the necessary discount therapy, so that patients would be in "safe hands." *"I told one patient, 'You can have as many orgasms as you like in half an hour.' The man didn't believe his ears and shot upstairs to the girls."* FORM A LINE HERE, PLEASE, GENTLEMEN!

For those who prefer synthetic sex, the availability of all things pornographic is overwhelming. Sex shops are in such abundance that one can rarely pass through more than two streets in larger city interiors without spotting a shop window openly displaying devices, films, clothing and literature of a diverse sexual nature. Cheap peep shows, interactive digital video cabins with Dolby Pro Logic audio and live sex shows reveal everything from "banana shooting" (whatever that is) to human/animal acts.

DRUGS 1 - STILL SMOKIN' . . .

The heavily reported Dutch over-tolerant attitude towards drug abuse is as famous as their tulips and wooden shoes, but it should be noted that the most active areas are in the Randstad, with relatively little activity in villages and the countryside. Progressive Dutch attitude excludes soft drugs such as cannabis/hashish and marijuana from the "problem drugs" category.

What seems shocking to tourists is run-of-the-(wind)mill for the urban Dutch. In Amsterdam, it is normal to see marijuana plants growing in homes and occasionally even in public places; the locals think nothing of people smoking a joint in public. However, tourists should note that even in the Randstad, the principle of the **gedoogzone** (tolerance zone) applies, which means paradise is not pervasive, and there are places where weeders are not welcome.

The cannabis *café* or "coffeeshop" abounds (Amsterdam alone supports around 220 coffeeshops which are visited by 1.5 million "tourists" every year). Since these shops are not allowed to advertise, they instead gloriously announce their main attraction by a marijuana leaf painted on the front window and/or outside sign. They offer a menu of several types of grass and hash. Coffee, soft drinks and souvenirs are also on sale. Ironically, many of these specialist shops are not

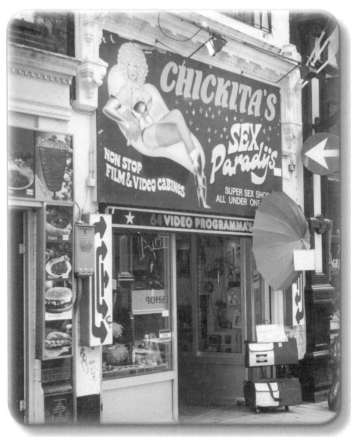

Colin White

licensed to sell beverages of an intoxicating nature, and none legally allow the sucking of straight cigarettes. From the Dutch medical point of view, soft drugs are considered harmless when compared with the more socially accepted alcoholic indulgence. Meanwhile, Holland's homegrown marijuana (**nederwiet**) has the honour of being classed the strongest in the world thanks to decades of careful cultivation. The Dutch have always been good with plants.

"Growshops" stock various varieties of seeds, weeds, soil enrichers, planting pots, and artificial sunlight devices. For the more serious smoker, proprietors are only too willing to guide customers in their purchases by process of elimination based on the anticipated growing-environment:

- indoors, outdoors, greenhouse, soil composition
- harvesting time
- direction of prevailing natural light

The existence of soft drug establishments, which were first introduced in 1975, relies on the national obsession with social tolerance being a greater force than the law. The 1976 Opium Act prohibits the importing, trafficking and possession of "soft," succulent smoking substances. However, possession and selling of less than five grams per day are tolerated.

This scenario gave rise to a neo-German invasion at Eastern border towns and cities. Two autobahns herded the *moffen* from Düsseldorf, Cologne and the Ruhr to Venlo, where columns of Teutonic tokers lined up to try, buy and fly. Then, in 2011, a national weed pass (*wietpas*) policy—which allowed locals access to the fun stuff but denied tourists of the pleasure—was introduced. The scheme was short-lived thanks to 26 out of the 100 cities with coffeeshops boycotting the plan. Within a year the *wietpas* went up in smoke and the Dutch government was forced to compensate coffeeshop owners who suffered loss of customers, *Krauts* and cash. Predictably, the EU regularly attempts to stub out the smokeshops, and always the disjointed public rise in defiance.

The soft drug industry is so firmly rooted that it is represented by three officially recognized trade unions: BCD (***Bond van Cannabis Detaillisten***) for coffeeshops, BGSD (***Bond van Groeishop Detaillisten***) for growshops, and PCF (***Platform Cannabisondernemingen Friesland***) for sellers and smokers throughout . . . Friesland.

The question arises as to how the coffeeshops restock their supplies, since no traffic jams caused by wholesalers delivering their goods in small increments are ever reported. *"I don't know,"* confessed an Amsterdam police spokesman. *"I can't tell you that,"* revealed the proprietor of one such establishment.

Local authorities keep their lenient eyes on the industry, which earns over 300 million taxable €uros per year. If a marijuana merchant exceeds the tolerance zone, the enterprise is closed down. Although ventures such as pre-cooked "space cakes" and the "Blow Home Courier Service" have been forced to close, others such as the hash taxi are encouraged to continue.

Another incarnation of the soft-drug industry is the "smart shop" which specializes in approved "magic mushrooms," mind-expanding truffles and other psychoactive substances such as "herbal ecstasy" and "ginseng-like tea."

DRUG/ II - THE HARD LINE . . .

Hard drugs are a different matter. The merchants comprise an army of solicitors of various minority groups who hustle for customers at main railway stations, monuments, parks, youth centres, red-light districts and any other public place with enough traffic to traffic to. In theory, possession of hard drugs is illegal. In practice, users are not arrested; only the (bulk) dealers are liable for prosecution.

For some years, an "innovative approach" was to give the dealers and junkies their own part of town—the Zeedijk in Amsterdam—where they were allowed to do business. The idea was to be kind and open to dealers and junkies while concentrating their activities to a specific area. The result? In the words of Eduard van Thijn, then Mayor of Amsterdam, *"We thought we could be tolerant and still control hard drugs. We were very naive."*

One of the constructive aspects of the Dutch view on the unfortunate reality of hard drug addiction is that the authorities adopt the attitude that, *"These people are ill and should be helped, not persecuted."* In support of this doctrine, methadone buses freely distribute this substance in major cities to help addicts withdraw from their dependence on heroin. The buses stop at known points in the city for about an hour and a half to dispense the drug free of charge. In an effort to rehabilitate its membership Rotterdam's addicts' union (**Rotterdamse Junkiebond**) operated an **uitzendbureau** called **Topscore** for a while. Interestingly, **Topscore** complained that they had more than enough positions available . . . but never enough junkies to fill them.

Always looking for easier means of relief, hard-drug users have taken to recycling stolen pets. An Amsterdam police spokesperson has revealed that canines leashed outside shops are fair game for junkies. If a pet thief is apprehended, he is taken to the police station, then immediately released. Meanwhile, the poached pets are sold in local drug outlets. Given the widespread Western belief that dogs and cats provide a main ingredient for Asian eateries, this "dogs-for-dope, pooches-for-pudding" enterprise could prove to be an effective answer to the previously reported pets-pooping-on-pavements problem.

"The Dutch language, in its written form, looks like someone sat on a typewriter!"

The Dutch Courier, Australia

THE DUTCH LANGUAGE

ike most nationalities, the Dutch insist that their tongue is a difficult one. It is the sixth language of Western Europe and is spoken by some 30 million people worldwide. This includes two very similar languages: Flemish (**Vlaams**) mainly in Belgium and **Afrikaans** in South Africa. The term for all three of these closely related languages is Netherlandic.

Nederlanders consider Flemish to be nothing more than a variant or dialect of Dutch that is spoken in Belgium and Northern France. And **Afrikaans** is regarded as *patois* that sounds like baby talk. Apparently some people mistake **Afrikaans** for Flemish, *"while the only real connection between the two is that for a Hollander's ear, both sound like funny Dutch."*

Dutch (**Nederlands**) is basically a form of German which borrows heavily from English and French, although most native speakers will vehemently deny it. If you speak German, you will have an easier time than most with Dutch. From a grammatical viewpoint, it is easier than German.

The abundant use of vowels (including double vowels), as well as joining several smaller words to create long words, gives the written form the appearance of being difficult. However, Dutch is very regular in its pronunciation and grammar.

Foreigners may be surprised to discover that several dialects are spoken within the borders of tiny Holland. They include **Gronings** (from Groningen), **Volendams** (from Volendam) and **Brabants** (from, believe it or not, Brabant). Lesser known (and lesser pronounceable) varieties include **Drents**, **Saksisch**, **Gelders** and **Zeeuws**. **Zeeuws** zealots have applied to the EU for full-fledged language status, with the hope of losing the country-bumpkin stigma for its million-plus speakers in Zeeland, Belgium and France—so far, to no avail. There is also a separate tongue, **Fries** (Frysk), in the northern province of . . . Friesland (Fryslân), and the Caribbean cloggies have kicked in with **Papiaments**. The Dutch even have their own sign language (**gebarentaal**), which is used by about 15,000 contortionists.

DUTCH REƧIƧTANCE . . .

Nederlands is rarely encountered abroad. Basically, there is no need for it outside of the country, especially since the Dutch are so proficient with languages (nearly 90 percent speak at least one other language). Conversely, if you spend more than half a year in Holland without learning the language, your Dutch acquaintances will be offended that you have not learned their wonderful **Nederlands**.

If you take a course in the Dutch language and finally progress enough to dare to utter some sentences in public, the persons you speak to will inevitably answer you in what they detect to be your native tongue. They love to show off the fact that they have learned one or more other languages. This sentiment is shared and echoed by just about everyone who attempts to learn Dutch:

> *"I can't even get my own husband to speak Dutch to me, and he's a Netherlander!"*

Sara Slater-Le Duc

> *"I make the effort, and it doesn't even seem to register that I've used their own language. It never fails to amuse me at their curiosity as to why I even bothered to learn it in the first place."*

Rose Atkinson

And from a Dutch perspective:

> *"Most Dutch people really appreciate the fact that you TRY to speak Dutch. They think, 'Okay, you tried it, so please stop mutilating our language now.'"*

Thomas

The more you try to learn the language, the more the Dutch refuse to speak it with you and the more they complain that you haven't learned it.

But there is good news on the language-learning front. Thanks to the **inburgeringscursus**, a way has finally been found to get at least a few of the natives (i.e. language instructors) to speak some Dutch to **buitenlanders**. The government provides Dutch lessons for many legal non-European newcomers, plus quite a few "oldcomers" who never bothered to learn the tongue.

If (more correctly, when) you reach the level of intolerance with Dutchies who overprotect their language, much satisfaction (read: revenge) can be exacted by counter-attacking on the basis of the characteristic grammatical errors that they make ("Cloglish"). Start your tirade with a modified Thomasian gambit:

> *"Most Brits/Americans really appreciate the fact that you TRY to speak English. You tried it, but please stop mutilating our language now."*

Then go on to give classic examples:

1. The most frequent and distinct error happens when translating **als** into English. They almost always mix up "if" and "when" in the translation of **als**:

Correct:	*"If you were a woman . . ."*
Cloglish:	*"When you were a woman . . ."*
Correct:	*"When the baby is born . . ."*
Cloglish:	*"If the baby is born . . ."*

2. They also botch English verb tenses, especially in the present and past. This is because there is one basic present tense in Dutch, for example **ik ga** for "I go," but in English there is also the present participle: "I am going," which has no true equivalent in Dutch. The same confusion applies to the use of past participles ("I was going" and "I have been going").

If that doesn't work, tell 'em, *"I much prefer German. It's a pure language."*

Finally, as a shortcut to quickly gain Dutch friends and respect through the use of their language, memorize this expression—they orgasm over it and feel it encapsulates their character: *Doe maar gewoon, dan doe je al gek genoeg* (Just act normal, that's weird enough).

THROAT DISEASE . . .

There are only a few difficult sounds: the gutturals (represented by the letters *ch* and sometimes by *g*); the *ui*, *ij* or *ei*; and the single-versus-double *a* (*man, maan*). If you have never encountered the language but are tempted to experiment with these examples, try reciting the list of ingredients from a soup can, with your mouth half full of syrup.

Legend has it that during World War II the secret test to prove Dutch nationality was to have an individual pronounce the name of the town of Scheveningen (which includes the Dutch guttural sound) and that foreigners failed when they pronounced it along the lines of *"Shave-a-Nigger."* An alternative version is that suspected infiltrators were made to utter this nightmare of a sentence: *"Achtentachtig schitterende Haagse grachten met Schevenings prikkeldraad"* which contains eight gutturals, some *aa*'s and translates to the nonsensical "Eighty-eight beautiful Hague canals with Schevening barbed wire."

When first exposed to any language, it is normal to match sounds and pronunciation with some words from your native tongue. This can give rise to some amusing situations:

> *"There were these words frequently used in the evening TV news, 'Koningin Beatrix.' What I heard was 'Connie and Beatrix.' Then they'd show you a bit of film of a nice lady in a big hat. Presumably this was Connie, but there was never any sign of Beatrix."*
>
> Brian Bramson

GRAMMAR . . .

There are two types of nouns. The combined masculine/feminine form uses the definite article *de.* For example, "the man" is *de man* and "the woman" is *de vrouw*. Neutral nouns use *het*, hence, *het boek* for "the book."

Nowadays there are three forms of "you." *U* is polite, formal and used in business and with elders. The use of this form of "you" shows respect. *U* is used less and less these days. If its use deteriorates in proportion to the national lack of respect, it will soon be extinct. Either *jij* or *je* can be used for the singular familiar form; *jullie* is the plural form (not a girl's name). Adults who perform menial tasks, such as rubbish collectors and toilet attendants, are addressed as *U*. This is in keeping with equality, thereby reducing feelings of guilt. *U* is used with **Sinterklaas** while *jij* is used with **Zwarte Piet**, but watch for **Zwarte Piet** to be promoted to *U* status for obvious reasons.

Another confusing feature of the language is the use of the verbs "sit," "stand" and "lie" to mean "is." Using these terms correctly is a true test of one's knowledge and skill:

> *"In English, a thing just IS. The tree IS in the garden, the sock IS in the wash, the cheque IS in the post. In Dutch, a thing never just IS. In Dutch it either 'stands,' 'sits,' or 'lies'... Deciding when to use 'stand' and when to use 'lie' is easy—it's a simple matter of orientation. The bottle 'stands' in the fridge, but the pen 'lies' on the table. 'Sitting' is a bit more complicated. Things 'sit' if they are in an enclosed space. So your keys 'sit' in your pocket. With me so far? So why, I hear you ask, doesn't that bottle 'sit' in the fridge? Because the orientation rule overrides the enclosure one, okay?*
>
> *Now the trouble is, these rules are not quite water-tight. I've been asking people about the case of a box on a table. The box 'stands' of course. But if it's a cube? How can you tell if it's 'standing' or 'lying'? 'Read the label on the box,' they say. Bit of a cop-out if you ask me.*
>
> *But the clincher is glasses. There's some debate about what glasses do on your nose. Opinion seems to be divided 50–50. Some say they 'stand' on your nose, others say they 'sit' there. So I take my glasses off and I place them on the table (careful to make no change of orientation, mark you) and ask people what the glasses are doing now. 'Lying' they say, unanimously. At this point I lose it completely and have to go lie down in a darkened room. Or maybe sit or stand there. Who knows."*
>
> Brian Bramson

The character of a people is reflected in its language. An example of this is seen in the compulsive-obsessive use of diminutives in daily speech. As a Dutch physician explained, *"Everything has to bear the stamp of the small-scale complacency, which personally I consider to be one of our most typical features."*

The suffix *-je* is the most common way to exercise this. The Dutch drink **een kopje thee** (a little cup of tea), take little strolls (**een straatje om**) and take little journeys around the world (**reisje om de wereld**).

They will tell you that they use a lot of diminutives because they live in such a small land. The use of the diminutive is an integral part of the Dutch language and usually adds a positive and cosy feeling to what is being said. But beware because the "little" factor can at times "belittle the bespoken" by denoting sarcasm, irony or anger.

A POKE IN THE ij . . .

Although Dutch spelling is fairly regular, there are some areas of confusion. One example is **ei** and **ij** which are both pronounced the same. Another problem is that the **ij** character is difficult to access on keyboards outside the country. Some people write it as a letter "y" instead of the two letters "i" and "j." Some publications place the **ij** under "i" and some place it under "y." Here is the sensible solution:

> *"Get rid of **ij** completely; its sound is already available with **ei**. I realise that this will be difficult, since in some respects the letter **ij** is the symbol of Dutch identity: the one letter that no other language has in its alphabet, the one letter that causes the Dutch language to appear in international standards for computer character sets. To appease the possible loss of National Pride that might be caused by abolishing the letter, I would propose then keeping it for two cases: the stretch of water by Amsterdam called the **IJ** (since it would cause the Dutch a double loss of pride to have to go sailing on the **Ei**), and (in order to retain a need for the lower-case letter) for the Bijenkorf and its jewellery (byoux) department."*
>
> Steven Pemberton

Much of the population likes to use modern or progressive spellings which are not yet official, such as **buro** for *bureau* or **odeklonje** for *eau de cologne*. The latter also exemplifies the battle between traditionalists, who prefer to leave "c" as "c," and those who consider themselves progressive, preferring to replace a hard "c" with "k." A cute but dying tenet of this is explained by our previously quoted language expert:

> *"The Dutch regularly have a spring-cleaning session done by a committee of wise persons. The committee is made up of representatives from the Netherlands and Belgium. A basic*

*premise for the Dutch is that Dutch spelling mustn't look German, and for the Belgians that it mustn't look French, so there are clashes which lead to anomalies such as **kopie** and **fotocopie**."*

Steven Pemberton (excerpted)

The "c vs. k" struggle is resolved in some dictionaries by a blanket statement: *"If not found here, look under 'c' ('k')."* The accepted reference on such matters, a publication called *Woordenlijst Nederlandse Taal*, aka *Groene Boekje*—"Little Green Book" or Dutch spelling Bible—attempts to konquer these kultural kalamities every ten years without kreating more kontroversie. The 2005 edition added about 10,000 new words and 9,000 spelling changes. Although it is annoying to have to relearn the spelling of so many words, the fact that it is done in an orderly and logical fashion at regular intervals makes it easier to cope. Information about the latest edition is leaked to the press in the spring, the book is released about six months later, then the new rules take effect ten months later in August of the following year. While students have to learn the new spellings to pass their exams, adults have it easier as the majority need only update their computer spellcheckers. Even that may soon be unnecessary as the publisher of the "Little Green Book" has announced plans to publish only digital editions in the future—the "Little Green Bytes," perhaps.

Abbreviations, acronyms, numbers and letters can be turned into verbs and other word forms by using an apostrophe to glue the appropriate verb/word ending. Hence, "to cc" is **cc'en**, "to desktop publish" is **dtp'en**, "little 2" is **2'tje**, a "little k" is a **k'tje**, a "little DVD" is a **DVD'tje** and a pensioner (recipient of **AOW**) is an **AOW'er**. Many imported foreign words behave the same; hence a "little baby" is a **baby'tje**. Although this process may appear simple at first glance, attempting to conjugate and use one of these in everyday speech takes a bit of practice. Take the example of **sms** (short message service) where **sms'en** means "to text":

Present	Past	Present Perfect
ik sms	*ik sms'te*	*ik heb ge-sms't*
jij sms't	*jij sms'te*	*jij hebt ge-sms't*
hij/zij sms't	*hij/zij sms'te*	*hij/zij heeft ge-sms't*
wij sms'en	*wij sms'ten*	*wij hebben ge-sms't*
jullie sms'en	*jullie sms'ten*	*jullie hebben ge-sms't*
zij sms'en	*zij sms'ten*	*zij hebben ge-sms't*

NUMBER CRUNCHING . . .

The Dutch have an amusing way of telling time, at least when it comes to reporting the time anywhere between quarter past the hour and quarter to the hour. The most potentially damaging problem is on the half hour. While "half eight" means 8:30 in England, to the Dutch it means 7:30. *"No wonder I was late for every appointment in my first year here,"* explained an enlightened British expatriate.

When relating minutes before or after the half hour—that is, between :15 and :45—the time twisting increases. In such instances, the minutes are related to the half hour:

7:20 is *tien voor half acht,* ten before 7:30—or for beginners, ten minutes before half an hour before 8:00.

8:35 is *vijf over half negen,* five past half-past eight—or for beginners, five minutes past half an hour before 9:00.

The 24-hour clock is commonly used in written form for train schedules and the like. For 17:20, *vijf uur twintig* or *tien voor half zes* are uttered instead of *tien voor half achttien*.

With spoken numbers, the rule is to reverse certain elements of a numerical expression, thereby requiring the brain to engage in binary leapfrog. Take the number 26,457,431 for example. In English, it is *Twenty-six million, four hundred and fifty-seven thousand, four hundred and thirty-one.* In Dutch (without the translation complication) we have: *Six-and-twenty million, four hundred seven-and-fifty thousand, four hundred one-and-thirty.*

Then there is the annoying habit of reversing the use of commas and decimal points as separators, so that €10,500.50 is written €10.500,50.

To round-out this numbing numerology, let's give a little space to multiples. In Holland, the billion (thousand-million) is a *miljard*, and the trillion is a *biljoen*. In the UK and France, the billion was formerly a "milliard," while in Germany, it was a million-million (10^{12}). The trillion (million-million) is 10^{12} in Britain but 10^{18} in France and Germany. We have absolute confidence that the EU will work the whole fiasco out in their own good time and issue a definitive million/milliard/billion-word ruling before €Utopia drowns in its own "naught"iness.

FOREIGNER*/* FAVOURITE*/* . . .

hallo
Don't let what appears to be friendliness fool you when you first arrive in Holland. When someone yells **hallo** at you, this is most likely not a greeting but rather an explicit expression of contempt to draw your attention to something stupid you have done. It is generally used to embarrass. This is most effective with non-Netherlanders.

ja
Ja has lots of meanings, depending on how it is used. Intonation and context can change the meaning from "yes" to "no," "maybe," "ummm," "well," "really" or "er." There are plenty of variations, including:

- The inhaled **ja** is a doubtful, distracted or spaced-out "yeah."

- The quick **jaja** means *"You're right, but get to the point! I'm in a hurry."*

- The slow **jaaajaaa** means *"Yes, but I don't believe you."*

- A **jaaa!** means *"Yes, please!"*

- The **jaaaaa** of disbelief is described in Chapter 10 – On Dutch Customs.

- A **jahaaa** means, *"Yeah, yeah, I know. You've told me a hundred times."*

- A **tja** indicates a **ja** in doubt *("yeah, right")*, can mean *"well"* or is used as a breather without any real meaning.

jeetje, jee, tjee and like derivatives
Exclamation meaning *"yikes!" "oh dear!"* or *"blimey!"* (caution: bastardization of "Jesus")

sorry
Common form of lip-service, often used in combination with "whore," as in *"Surrey whore"* (**sorry, hoor**).

SVP
The French "silver plate" (spelled *s'il vous plaît*) is often used in its abbreviated form, **SVP**, on signs and in letters as a replacement for its direct Dutch equivalent **AUB** (in full, **als 't u blieft**) or *"(if you) please."*

tje
Exclamation meaning *"wow"* or *"gosh."*

tjonge
Exclamation meaning *"Well, well, who would've thought that"* or *"Dear me!"*

KIKKERLAND KEEPERS . . .

Many unique Dutch terms are explained throughout this book. But what about the word **kikkerland**? Literally, it means "frog-land," alluding to the fact that the rainy and watery lowlands is a paradise for frogs. Despite the allusion to cold and dampness, the term is also a fond nickname that conveys a feeling of warmth. With the diminutive *je* added, the meaning emphasizes the smallness and cosiness of the country: **Wij leven in een klein kikkerlandje** ("We live in a little froggy-land.").

Typical behaviours and character traits often find their way into language. A good example is the term "wagging finger," or **vermanende vinger** (**vermanen** means to admonish). In the same vein, "mosquito-sifting" (**muggenziften**) and "ant-fucking" (**mierenneuken**) are synonyms for "nit-picking" and "fault-finding." It should therefore come as no surprise that **poldermodel** (see Chapter 7 – The National Passion) has been blessed with its very own verb: **polderen** (to discuss, negotiate and compromise cloggy-style). The polder process was born in the Middle Ages at a time when all classes had to work together to build dikes in order to survive. Another keeper is **rechtdoorzee** (lit. "straight through the sea") which means "straightforward, blunt, frank" and often refers to seemingly rude behaviour that shocks foreigners, but that is seen by cloggies as simply being honest and open.

Having previously qualified **shit**, we should now explain that swearing **(vloeken)**—native and imported—is acceptable at most social (non)levels, provided it has no religious basis (There is a blasphemy law in effect!). Interestingly, there is a League against Blasphemy and Swearing (**Bond tegen vloeken**) founded in 1917, online at bondtegenvloeken.nl, which claims to have more than 24,000 members. In 2002, the **gemeente** of Reimerswaal banned swearing in public, followed by the Bible Belt town of Staphorst in 2005, although there is no punishment for offenders.

A source of pride for tiny Holland is found in some of its huge reference works. The popular three-volume Dutch dictionary referred to as **de dikke van Dale** was first published in 1864 and is updated regularly. Another icon is the *Woordenboek der Nederlandsche Taal* (WNT) which claims to be the largest dictionary in the world. At approx. 50,000 pages in 43 volumes—stretching about three metres wide on a bookshelf—it contains all Dutch words and their origins from 1500 to 1920, plus a supplement published in 2001 with modern-day Dutch words. Perhaps most appealing to users is that it is available for free online.

Newspapers abound with articles that can be confusing. Headlines often appear to state the hypothetical as fact. These types of headlines describe proposals and experiments, and foreigners should learn not to fall for them. A headline such as *"All newcomers to the Netherlands must first learn Dutch in their native land"* does not necessarily mean that all newcomers to the Netherlands must first learn Dutch in their native land. It's more likely that this idea is being considered, discussed and debated. It may or may not be voted on in future. If part or all of it passes into law, the new law may be appealed or repealed.

Finally, the character of the land and people is revealed through many colourful idioms about typically Dutch things (wooden shoes, windmills, water, ditches, dikes, ships, sea, sand, Bicycles and flowers). For a list of these Dutch idioms, see Appendix C – A View of the Netherlands through Dutch Idioms.

DUTCH EXPORTƒ . . .

The Dutch have found their way into various languages in the form of "clognomens," or idioms, the most adopted of which appears to be "cheese head." Also popular are allusions to being tightwads. Appendix A – A View of the Dutch through the English Language, contains a list of expressions that have found their way into English. No other language has absorbed as many. To demonstrate the effect of the Dutch on languages other than English, here are some expressions about the Dutch that have migrated into Japanese:

- *daburu datchi* (lit. double Dutch) means *"gibberish."*
- *datchi akaunto* (lit. Dutch account) means *"going Dutch."*
- *datchi pessari* (lit. Dutch cap) refers to a birth control device.
- *datchi saundo* (lit. Dutch sound) refers to Dutch rock music.
- *datchi waifu* (lit. Dutch wife) refers to an inflatable doll.

GAME OF THE NAME . . .

Legend has it that when Napoleon Bonaparte absorbed *les Pays-Bas* into his vision of a European community, he forced people without a surname *(achternaam)* to adopt one. This was in order to accurately identify everyone for taxation purposes. Napoleon's first strategic blunder was to allow the Dutch to choose their own new names.

Until then, many Hollanders had used a simple principle such as [name]–[father's name] to identify themselves (as in "Jan van Piet," whose son was "Piet van Jan," whose son was "Jan van Piet" and so forth). In Noord Brabant, there were often four first names followed by the surname, thus Jan Jan Pieter Cornelis de Haen (Jan son of Jan, son of Pieter, son of Cornelis, surname de Haen). In any event, sticking with the *van* concept seemed to be the best way to continue for many of 'em. Hence "Jan van Piet" who lived in Diemen became "Jan van Diemen," and his son was "Piet van Diemen" (which resulted in further confusion rather than clarification in larger towns and cities).

Some assumed that Napoleon's surname thing would be a temporary inconvenience and that once the French had gone home, the logical "Jan van Piet" principle could be reinstated. Calling on their love of practical jokes, people concocted all manner of odd names. Alas, it backfired: Today there are families still bearing surnames such as **Hondendorst** (Dog's Thirst) and **Hoogklimmer** (High-climber); embarrassing names like **Kloot** (Testicle), **Eikel** (Penis, Dickhead), **Naaktgeboren** (Born Naked) and **Geijlvoet** (Randy Foot); or tonsil-torturers such as **Zijtregtop** and **Gezelschap**.

Multiple forenames are still in vogue. Although you will probably be asked to use a one-syllable, vowel-happy forename (Huub, Joop, Kees), the birth name is invariably a formal one, followed by 1–5 middle names and topped with a surname. In the case of married women, the maiden name is attached with a hyphen. Here are some examples:

Peter Johannes Theodorus Gustav Arnoldus de Jong
Hubertus Cornelis Johann Maria van Dijk
Wilhelmina Johanna Carola Petra Van Leeuwen-Waterdrinker

Parents can decide if their children bear the last name of the mother, father or partner until registration of birth. If married parents can't agree on a surname, it defaults to the father's **achternaam**. For unmarried parents, it defaults to the mother's maiden name. For other family situations such as lesbian parents, adoption by a mother and

Rusty Haller

Rusty Haller

How the Dutch appeased Napoleon

father or by two men, divorce and forming blended families, there are rigid rules for choosing a surname. When it comes to choosing a child's *voornaam,* the only restriction is that the name cannot be "indecent."

Selection of surnames is an important decision since it is difficult to have one's name changed in the country. Names can be changed by a confusing and expensive legal process consummated by royal decree. The only exception is if the name is truly embarrassing! Here is how the government explains it:

> *It is possible that your name is unsuitable or ridiculous; for example, the names of **Poepjes** (Poopies) or **Niks** (Nothing). In some cases a name is absurd due to someone's profession or position in society. For example: an opthalmologist with the name **Schele** (Cross-Eye) would not be taken seriously. In these cases you can request to have your name changed. The judiciary will decide whether your name is truly unsuitable or ridiculous.*

CHILDREN

"In 20 years I have never seen a (Dutch) child physically punished."

Luca Dosi Delfini,
Dutch art historian,
National Geographic, 1986

here one person views a child's behaviour as adorable and refreshing, another may view it as undisciplined and intolerable. This chapter, despite its title, is not so much a comment on Dutch children themselves, but more a comment on their upbringing.

As early as the 17th century, visitors to the Netherlands were both surprised and disconcerted by the overindulgence that the Dutch displayed towards their young. They spoiled them then and have been refining the art ever since:

> *"In all this upbringing and education, children should not be kept on too tight a rein, but allowed to exercise their childishness, so that we do not burden their fragile nature with heavy things and sow untimely seed in the unprepared field of understanding."*

Jan van Beverwijck, 1656

> *"Dutch families [in the 1600s] seem to have been much more reluctant than other contemporary cultures to relinquish their hold on the young."*

Simon Schama, 1987

> *"It's almost a caricature that [Dutch] children are the ones that decide what happens within the family. Their wishes become so strong that parents have to work very hard to give them what they want."*

Paul Vangeert,
Prof. of Dev. Psychology, 2007

KID KREATION . . .

Holland is a great place to progress through pregnancy to childbirth, as every Dutch parent will tell you. Midwives and physicians undergo thorough obstetric training and practice. Natural births are encouraged, and home is considered a good place to do it. Wherever the baby-falling (*bevalling*) takes place, a mystical atmosphere of cosiness and intimacy prevails between all present. Strangely, no fresh-cut flowers can attend. When the newborn finally arrives, it is treated with the utmost fuss and care—perhaps too much so.

The arrival of a new baby is announced to the community by various means, including outside advertising which essentially trumpets: NEW BABY HERE—ALL CONTRIBUTIONS WELCOME. The signs are in the form of storks, animals or toys. Other celebratory decorations may adorn the grounds or house too. Special treats, colour-coded to reflect the gender of the child (see Chapter 8 – Food for Thought), are served.

During the first weeks of life, baby and its mother normally face an almost continuous stream of visitors: relatives, friends, nurses, advice-givers and well-wishers. The exhausted mother may well want nothing more than privacy and quiet with her newborn, but will find she must serve both infant and intruder—and not always in that order. The new parents (like all cloggies) love receiving gifts, but this makes them beholding to the interlopers, and the cycle continues. This constitutes one of baby's earliest extrauterine lessons in the arts of independence, give-versus-take and rebelliousness.

Parents need not worry about "going without" where children are concerned. The welfare system considers minors a top priority. In addition, a generous child benefit called *kinderbijslag* is paid on a quarterly basis for kids from birth until age 15–18 years. In some situations, *kinderbijslag* is paid to families or children living abroad.

Legal ages for children in Holland are: 12 years for euthanasia; 16 years for sex and other fireworks; 18 years for marriage, drinkable alcohol, tobacco products, soft drugs and being licensed to drive cars unsupervised; and 21 years for being a prostitute and financial independence.

Laurie Boucke

**Royal Stork Airlines announces
the arrival of a new "protest-ant"**

RAIJING MODERN
DUTCHEJ & DUTCHEJJEJ . . .

There are two basic ways to bring up **kikkerland** kids:

• The commonsense way by teaching them some manners and respect (mainly found in what's left of the countryside). Polite and well-behaved children are a delight for all concerned. As they do not attract much attention by their activities, they remain to a large extent invisible to outsiders and thus are not the subject of much comment in this chapter.

- The classico-contemporary way as spoiled godlets. This category is very much in the majority and in this respect warrants further comment.

The golden rule is (and apparently always has been): Let them be free . . . free to explore and experience whatever they please . . . free to be "creative" (destructive), with little or no concern for anyone else, as long as they are not in serious danger. They must learn to be independent and rebellious as young as possible.

Speak to the little terrors in baby language and pamper them until they finish their childhood (around the age of 30). In public, suggest discipline by giving loud instructions regarding behaviour that is permitted and that which is not. Angelface will immediately disobey by testing the instructions, whereupon cherub's activities are ignored.

Throughout the period of infantile pampering, training aids are strategically introduced. The first, a ball, is presented before the art of walking has been mastered. The second, the Bicycle, is introduced shortly thereafter. By the age of three, most mini-Netherlanders can ride a two-wheeler competently. Around this time, children are awarded their first pair of ice skates, which are thereafter renewed annually.

By far, mother's greatest gift to herself and to the child in the early years is the *crèche* or nursery/day care for Neder-nippers from 2–3 years. Having managed to secure a place in one, the quality of care is usually excellent. The problem is that the hours of available care are both limited and expensive. The waiting lists can be long and the rules of engagement a deterrent. For example, working mothers receive priority, but how can a new mother find or start a job with a toddler in tow? Childcare (**kinderopvang**) hours can be inconvenient in that you may only be blessed with three half-days a week.

BATTLE OF DE WITS . . .

If you visit a Dutch family, abandon all hope of being able to hold a reasonable conversation. A loudmouthed child will inevitably:

- place itself between host(ess) and guest, where it will dance, stomp on your feet and chatter to get attention

- cuddle up to mother, stroke her face and hair or wriggle around in her lap, continuously asking stupid and unnecessary questions

- sit between you both, stare at you, and imitate your every facial expression and movement

The indestructible public playground (**speeltuin** or **speelplaats**) is a thing to be admired in terms of ingenuity, entertainment and temporary relief. Happily for parents and baby-sitters, there seems to be a playground within a short distance of nearly every residential street. Many large shops have an indoor version called a **speelhoek** (lit. play corner) where parents can leave their little treasures (**schatjes**) while they go shopping. Sometimes the temptation of free childcare is just too great, and some parents abuse the privilege by leaving their kids in the **speelhoek** unattended for hours on end.

When the toddler years come to an end, toddlerhood starts in earnest. Here are some true examples of what to expect from this growing bunch:

1. When mother notices that a visitor is about to leave because of her sweet child's behaviour, she will tell the child, in her sternest voice, to go away and *"let mama talk."* The child will ignore her until the command has been repeated at least three times. Within a few minutes, the child will return. The mother will be delighted to have her free, little angel back (totally forgiven and welcome to continue its previous activities).

2. Two mothers board a metro train, along with five small children. One of the children places her dirty hands on a gentleman passenger's bag. He asks her to stop. The mother, very shocked at the man's behaviour, explains (at great length) the importance of freedom for little children.
   As she continues defending her child, the metro arrives at a station, the doors open, and one of the children steps from the train. The doors close and the train pulls away. As it is about to enter the subway tunnel, the woman notices the child is missing and pulls the emergency stop lever.
   The recently rebuked passenger smiles and remarks, *"But the child was only being free . . . !"*

3. As mother and five-year-old child walk past a display of kitchen units, the child heads for the units. Mother says, *"Don't touch the cupboard drawers."* The child continues towards the display. Mother says, *"Don't touch."*

The child arrives at the display. Mother walks past the display on her way out of the shop, saying, *"Hey! Hallo!"* The child opens and closes doors and drawers (as loudly and clumsily as possible) a number of times as mother does nothing to discipline her child for not obeying her, satisfied that the adorable one is free to touch and experience the cupboards.

4. In a supermarket, as mother is paying for food, her child spots five-cent plastic bags hanging by the counter. The child helps itself to a bag. There is no reaction from mother. The child carries the bag to mother and says, *"Mama, I have a bag for you."* Mother explains, *"That's not allowed"* (the popular **Dat mag niet**). Mother and child ignore each other. As mother packs her purchases away, cutie again offers her the bag. Mother explains further, *"That's not allowed. THOSE COST PENNIES! That's why mama brought her own bags."*
    After another round of mutual ignoring, mother advises that the new bag cannot join the family. Angel begins to cry and eventually drops the "stupid bag" on the floor. Mother and her (still) screaming child walk away. The bag is left on the floor. No attempt is made by mother to return the bag to the hanger.

5. A mother and young daughter travel to the city market by bus one winter morning. A group of local youths pelts the bus with snowballs, almost breaking the windows. *"**God!**"* sighs the girl who then turns to her mother and announces, *"**Dat mag niet!**"* Mother smiles her retort *"**Waarom niet?**"* (Why not?).

Other favourite antics for this age group are to yell, scream, fight, cry, run around the room, climb all over the furniture, slam doors, bump into you—again, anything making it impossible to converse.

This attitude of parent and child continues in public: waiting rooms, transport, schools, streets, restaurants and shops. Above all, beware of the cinema syndrome where the combined traits of adult, adolescent and infant cloggies merge into three hours of sheer hell (see Chapter 10 – On Dutch Customs).

The polder **puber** (adolescent) does not vary strikingly from those in other societies (except perhaps in volume level) since the characteristics of this species seem to be fairly universal. The local environment typically dictates the type and level of mischief. For example, Dutch *pre-pubers* as well as *pubers* excel greatly where Bikes are concerned and are able to repair a puncture in gale-force winds, or completely dismantle any model in five minutes flat during a hailstorm. In the seaside resort of Katwijk, authorities have defined a "vandal zone" on the beach in an attempt to reduce the degree of destruction within town. Unfortunately, the zone is closed at high tide.

A Nightmare on Elmstraat:
Urban scholars perfect the art of Bicycle destruction

One current quirky conundrum that may be unique during adolescence is the high level of debt incurred by Dutch youth. Many obtain credit cards and load them up with designer clothing or the latest model of mobile phone *met* hefty and cool *abbo's* (*abonnementen* or service plans).

SCHOOL DAZE . . .

The school years that follow the carefree *crèche* days continue to shape the worldly views of the youth. Parents may select the school(s) their offspring attend. The choices available are based on classical education, philosophy and religion. Classical education teaches the children to be "streetwise." Education based on philosophy is for *avant-garde* parents and has its roots buried in freedom of expression (with obvious results). Selection of a Roman Catholic or Protestant school enables parents to segregate their children from Turks, Moroccans and other imported pupils. Even so, there has developed an unofficial definition of schools as "white," "mixed" or "black" based mainly on pupil ethnicity. This is deemed not to be racist as long as the white kids and the little **allochtonen** are taught at the same level.

The Dutch Constitution (yes, they've got one too) guarantees citizens the right to freedom of education. About one-third of children attend public schools, and two-thirds go to private schools; both are financed by the government. Parents are welcome to participate in decision-making on all levels by joining various councils and committees, and are advised, *"If you want the school to take account of your wishes and ideas, exercise your right to do so."* And of course, every school has a complaints' committee or is affiliated with one.

With so much choice available and with the never-ending cacophony of discussions, complaints, committees, hearings, policy-making and policy-revamping, it naturally follows that things are going to get out of hand occasionally. In 2005, things came to a head between a **basisschool** in Zuidhorn and an over-protective mother after the school declared that the woman had overloaded their resources with her incessant stream of questions, comments, complaints and other protestations regarding her daughter's education. During the previous school year, mum-knows-best had reportedly:

- Sent 50 e-mails and written 20 letters to the school
- Made 9 personal visits to school authorities
- Written 29 letters to the school board
- Written an unspecified number of additional letters of complaint to the media, the National Complaints Commission, the Labor Inspection Service, the Educational Inspection Service and to the Queen's Representative to Friesland.

In order to shut her up, the Groningen District Court rationed her to what she could get on a single sheet of paper once a month and banned her from any physical contact with the school, its administrators and teachers for at least one year. The woman is, of course, protesting this.

The Dutch school system is baffling at best. A few common threads running through it are:

- Limited school hours. For example, in some areas, school children have no classes every other Friday and are free every Wednesday afternoon.

- The dreaded lunch break. During this time, parents are supposed to collect their darlings and take them home for lunch. In practice, most opt to leave their kids on the school grounds, even though they have to pay a communal child-minder to do so. It's worth it to have a break from the lunch break.

- Insurance policies. To better sleep at nights, parents are strongly urged to have one or more insurance policies in place, should their offspring decide to frolic a little too wildly. In this respect, it is wise to have third-party insurance (*WA-verzekering*), window insurance and a few other supplemental policies for good measure.

- Summer holidays. The length is six weeks. In order to avert a mass exodus from (and return to) the lowlands, the country staggers the summer recess dates over three regions.

The school system starts out simple and innocent enough, then progresses to a confusing mess. Education is compulsory from age 5–16 if a diploma is earned, otherwise until age 18. Here is a synopsis of the current levels of learning:

1. Kindergarten *(kleuterschool)*. Required by law to attend at age 5, but fortunately kids can start at age 4. In some situations, a *crèche* is affiliated with a particular school and kids don't have to change schools at this time.

2. Elementary school *(basisschool)*, age 5–12 years. In addition to "clognitive" skills, facts and figures, primary schools are required to *"foster the development of social, cultural and physical skills. This includes learning to speak up for oneself"* (which explains a lot!). An example of a

Rusty Haller

goal in physical education is learning to use climbing equipment (no comment).

3. Junior school or junior high *(onderbouw van de middelbare school including brugklas,* classes 1–3)*,* age 12–14 years. The confusion starts here with the offering of several different types of school. All pupils receive a basic secondary education which in theory is the same, but the level of learning varies, depending on the type of school.

4. Comprehensive, grammar or high school *(bovenbouw van de middelbare school,* classes 4–6)*,* age 15–18, but can end at age 16 and/or continue to age 20. More of the same of the first round of *middelbare school,* only with more choice, more decisions, more pressure on all concerned. Consult your psychologist for more.

Despite all the school freedom and fascinating topics on offer, truancy *(spijbelen)* is high in the lowlands. All sorts of innovative approaches have been taken to deal with truants *(spijbelaars)*, including a truant bus service *(spijbelbus)* offering coffee, shelter and counselling; community service; written reprimands; jail threats (rarely acted upon); and fines. Fines as high as €2,300 haven't made much difference and have led the teachers' union to conclude, *"Give a truant a high fine and all you accomplish is that he returns to school with deep resentment."* The National Parents' Association for Special Education or LOBO (Landelijke Oudervereniging Bijzonder Onderwijs) had this to say about *spijbelen*:

> *"The blame is placed on the pupil, but good instruction must be given and motivate the child to go to school. If a school doesn't do so and the pupil continues to skip classes, then you have to ask yourself if the school shouldn't also be fined."*

Dutch school kids experience the same share of bullying *(pesten)* as other Western nations. What differs is the manner in which it is addressed by those in authority. For many years the policy was to re-educate/punish the victim—not the bully—in the hope that the over-meek "cloglet" would become more assertive and "in your face" to fend off bullies. Eventually it was discovered that the bullies were part of the problem and they too should be part of the solution. Thus, schools are now required to "deal with it." Some suggested means to combat bullying include:

- Talking about bullying and teasing.
- Executing a contract between bully and victim.
- Posting a list of (anti-bullying) *regels* in the classroom and making everyone sign it.

The ultimate punishment for any school crime is, of course, to remove the source of the problem . . . the pupil. Expulsions do take place but not without a lot of effort on the part of school boards. An explanatory letter must be sent to the pupil and parents who may then (you guessed it) appeal against this dastardly decision within six weeks. The school board then has four weeks to give its next decision. If the board still wants to expel the pupil, the parents can go to court to appeal. By this time, the kid has finished the school year and is *op vakantie*.

Understandably, teachers take more sick leave than members of any other profession. Although this costs society about 25 percent more in sick leave and disability payments, there is sympathy. A large number of teachers remain home when they are *overspannen* (stressed out), with the "psychologically fallen" (*psychische gevallen*) accounting for a healthy share of the nation's medical payments. But an increasing amount of the harm suffered by teachers is of a physical nature, perpetrated by parents and pupils alike.

Nothing would be complete in the Netherlands without the possibility of free finances. Low income parents of secondary school pupils have the right to receive study costs, while all students receive "*stufi*" (student finance) based on their parents' income level. These may sound like the same thing to the untrained ear but are not. Study costs go towards school fees (which are mainly paid by the government) and "other costs of study." Student finance kicks in after *middelbare school* and funds higher professional education *(hoger beroepsonderwijs)* and university studies. At this level, all students are entitled to a performance-related grant. Clear as mud.

When full-time education is finally completed, the Dutch are suitably prepared for welfare or work, and parental pampering diminishes as the school-leavers continue their magical mystery tour of life.

GEZONDHEID

BACK TO THE FUTURE . . .

Despite all the boasting and bragging about the Dutch healthcare system (the Euro Health Consumer Index awarded Holland the highest score in 2008 and 2009), hospitals are not always a good place to turn to if you want to get well. Many are typically overbooked and understaffed. One in twenty hospital deaths are the result of mistakes, and every year, around 20,000 ambulances arrive too late to save the stricken. At the same time, a recent survey of seven academic hospitals revealed that up to 30 percent of surgical capacity is unused. The situation is contagious, and the disease is spreading to other hospitals. The result is an increase in deaths and post-surgical complications. To combat complaints and apportion blame, hospital health experts have started to point their latexed fingers at (believe it or not) flowers and house plants as a cause of infection and have begun banning vegetation from bedsides. This atypical act of **bloemenverbod** naturally causes many Dutch patients (and local flower vendors) to wilt into depression. After serious study and debate, the best solution to date has been for a visitor to bring gifts of flower vouchers to cheer a patient up and allow him to re-infect himself when he gets home. In an attempt to keep the customers (i.e. patients) coming, hospitals include French fries, **kroketten**, chocolate and whipped cream on their menus, arguing that the inclusion of these healthy morsels aids patient recovery and allows them to check out sooner (one way or another).

Hospitals have increasingly resorted to "creative accounting" since new administration systems were introduced in 2012. The NBA (**Nederlandse Beroepsorganisatie van Accountants**), in a classic case of "cover your **billen**," encouraged its members to refuse to sign-off on ALL hospital accounts due to a *"lack of clarity in the interpretation of the rules."*

When it comes to orthopaedics, people really feel out on a limb. Knee and hip surgery patients typically wait 32–52 weeks for an operation. Sufferers have started to limp to Spain (and other sunny, potato-starved destinations) to exact relief. Insurance companies generally go along with overseas procedures, possibly to deny potential accusations of "cruel and unusual punishment" (i.e. the inability to ride Bicycles).

On the home front, the quality of care and service offered by GPs (**huisartsen**) has been ebbing for years, with some disconcerting and strange outcomes. It is not uncommon for a diagnosis to be made over the phone, without ever meeting or examining a patient. Likewise, medicines are prescribed by phone without consideration of a patient's medical history or allergies. Doctors sometimes even ask patients to recommend a course of treatment since most Hollanders "don't like to be told what to do." Younger patients claim it is their right to take any medication they please and tend to "cause problems" if they don't get their own prescribed fix. Thus some GPs just give in to the self-proclaimed experts rather than doing battle, Dutch style. In other situations, doctors refuse to speak to or see a patient for several weeks and instead instruct the receptionist to tell the patient to call back if the condition remains after a month or so. An expatriate in Groningen illustrates the problem as follows:

> *"My doctor prescribed stuff for me over the phone while I was on vacation here and wasn't even his patient yet! . . . I've found one great doctor but she's on the other side of town, so I can't go to her because there's some rule that I have to go to a doctor in my neighbourhood."*
>
> Barbara Neimeister

Huisartsen have their excuses for the doctored services they offer:

- There are too many patients.
- There are not enough doctors.
- There is little incentive to open a practice due to low salaries, high workload and the costs of managing a practice.

- More people have no medical insurance.

- The increasing elderly population is demanding—with many old-timers becoming demented, more than 80 percent of home visits to them are "for no good reason."

In essence, everyone has become so "cheesed off" with the situation that the Dutch Federation of Patients and Consumers (*Nederlandse Patiënten Consumenten Federatie, NPCF*) has resorted to inciting doctors, dentists (who say they are paid less than plumbers), physiotherapists and kitchen staff to adopt French blockading tactics—hence protest marches, strikes, placards and other such Dutchery.

Holland's senior citizens are particularly affected by rising healthcare costs, cutbacks, administrative malingering and widespread fraud. A Health Inspectorate investigation has exposed rampant neglect in the managed care of old people, including inadequately trained staff tying patients to their beds and denying them adequate washing arrangements. Some other examples:

- A retirement home in Boxtel, having already purged its bathrooms of luxuries such as soap, toothpaste and shampoo, advised its 70 residents that toilet paper will no longer be supplied *gratis*—they must make their own arrangements. In that way, the home could continue to provide three meals a day, and the old folks could continue to go to the toilet when nature called, rather than be forced to go at specified times. When news of this reached the press, a horrified Holland united forces in hopes of providing relief. Shortly thereafter 5 pallet loads of toilet rolls were delivered to the home, narrowly diverting another disaster (if only temporarily).

- In 2008, the Consumers' Association (*Consumentenbond*) busted 22 hospitals for denying patients some change for supermarket-like coin-operated wheelchairs.

- Four years later, Holland's nursing homes and senior care facilities were still over-feeing the feeble with charges of €32 for washing clothing and €50 for walking with a caregiver. Other billable "special activities" can include such luxuries as taking an extra shower, providing a second *kopje koffie*, and the provision of disinfectant and disposable gloves for staff members.

Considering all of the above plus the fact that many Dutchies somehow manage to feel lonely and isolated in their overcrowded country, is it any wonder that one of the leading causes of death in the Netherlands is suicide . . . or that one out of every 18 Nederlanders devours anti-depression pills on a regular basis?

On the topic of mental problems and isolation, the government is going national with a policy of caging asocial citizens (***tbs'ers,*** derived from ***terbeschikkingstelling***—a law for mandatory psychiatric treatment) in iron huts constructed from shipping containers. The new homes are welded into dedicated city suburbs. And how do the delicate Dutch define "asocial" behaviour? *"Troublesome tenants who break the **regels**, make too much noise, cause unacceptable odours, use and sell drugs, grow cannabis, prostitutes and people who cause domestic problems"* (which in Holland includes just about everyone). How long has this been going on? Surprisingly, before World War II every city in the pacifist, liberal-minded Netherlands had a special area for this scum of the earth. The practice was discontinued in the 1970s when it was deemed asocial to use asocial shipping crates. Now that they are all back shouting, stinking, doping and copulating away in normal neighbourhoods, studies have re-evaluated the situation and decided that it was not such a bad idea after all. Just don't mention the terms "mental asylum," "gulag" or "trailer park trash," please.

TALKIN' TRA/H . . .

Little is more threatening to a person's health than a pile of stinking, rotting, rat-infested garbage sitting for days in the kitchen and then transferred to the doorstep. Yet that is the conventional way to collect household rubbish in the Western world. In Holland, the problem is compounded since ownership of the material transfers to the Crown as soon as it is placed outdoors. If on royal-rubbish collection day your bundled waste has not been removed, the reason must be that either: (1) Their Majesties have sufficient stocks of rotting kitchen waste and the like to last until next collection day; or (2) You have been officially honoured by the Crown, who have decreed that you may keep that week's tribute as a royal bequest. However, you have some possibilities concerning the immediate problem . . .

1. Leave the rubbish where it is and expect problems. The neighbours will probably write you a nasty note or come to your home and complain about THEIR King's

Rusty Haller

Asocial accommodation

garbage that YOU left on the street. Children, dogs, cats, birds and vermin will rip the sack open and spread the contents about (reaction from neighbours as above). The garbage cops (*reinigingspolitie*) will notice your rubbish and will most likely fine you.

2. Remove the rubbish to a skip, a rubbish heap, waste gathering site (*afvalpunt*) or another street where the palace has yet to make its collection.
   The *reinigingspolitie* are a bored species and will inevitably search through the container(s), looking for clues of ownership. If a bag is hiding any items which include your name and address, you can expect to receive a photocopy of the evidence, along with a fine and, worse still, a letter from the *gemeente* calling you an evil "rubbish offender" (*huisvuilovertreder*). Some authorities place camouflaged cameras at strategic locations to identify rogue residents who release rubbish by the road.

No discussion on rubbish collection can be complete without a mention of the Rampant Recycling Rage. The Dutch have long given up on using household refuse as a means of elevating their ground level and have embraced recycling with vigour. Villages, towns and cities alike have embarked on various complex schemes in an attempt to out-recycle the rest. Peter Spinks, a writer for *New Scientist* magazine, summed up the situation admirably in his exposé of the recycling effort in his adopted town of Egmond:

"Each household has a set of green and grey bins with black plastic wheels. They are emptied at bin stations, on alternate weeks, by a hulk of a yellow and red refuse truck with flashing lights and an automated bin lift. By the time the truck arrives the refuse has, in theory at least, been separated into recyclable parts. Vegetable peelings, uneaten food, plants and garden debris go in the green bin; plastics, metal, hardboard and the like go in the grey one. Glass bottles, which are not deposit-refundable, must be taken to the communal glass dumps. Newspapers and magazines are collected monthly, with luck, by schools; string, ribbon and old clothes are collected twice a year by the Salvation Army.

For a start, paper collection, a dire necessity for newspaper-accumulating journalists like myself, requires the patience of Job and the logistics of a Stormin' Norman-style strategist. The schools, which regard paper collection as less a profession than a charitable hobby, make their collections the first Wednesday of the month, unless that is a public holiday, in which case they collect on the second Wednesday. Neither advance warning nor a calendar of collections is given to households, who need to keep track of 'paper days.' The bins, too, require constant attention. In winter, to loosen garbage frozen to the sides, householders are advised to place bins in the sun, if and when it shines. Come summer, the decomposing contents of the green bins should be emptied, with noses pegged, into the grey bins, thus rubbishing the whole idea of separating refuse.

Not that the separation process itself is exactly straightforward. Take the supposedly simple tea bag, for example. To be religious about it, as the largely Calvinist Dutch are about most things, the wet tea leaves should be removed from their filter-paper bag and deposited in the green bin. The bag, once ironed dry, should be put aside for the infamous paper collection, along with the tea label (after removing the metal staple, which goes in the grey bin) and the piece of string, which is rolled up for the Salvation Army.

To keep separators on their toes, compliance is monitored by a petty-minded bank of bin inspectors, who police the streets armed with indelible red pens. Their brief is unenviable but clear: to ferret around, elbow-deep, in bins whose owners can be identified by prominently displayed numerals indicating house numbers. The bins of first-time offenders are marked with warning crosses; those of second offenders, horror of horrors, are not emptied.

Transgressions are easier to detect in green bins. Therefore the rule of thumb is: when in doubt, go grey rather than green. This is what many Egmonders now do, even when not in doubt. The practice explains why fewer and fewer bins appear on 'green weeks' and why grey bins invariably overflow, leaving a smelly mixture of rubbish strewn across the once-spotless streets."

Recycling confusion is also responsible for clandestine dumping. People sneak out at night and deposit sacks of smellies in neighbouring towns, parks, forests, lay-bys and even across the border into Belgium and Germany—another point scored for the environment. On a much grander scale, a Deventer family made greedy "green" greenbacks in 2009 by sailing off to Africa with thousands of domestic appliances on which consumers had paid a recycling fee. On arrival in Ghana, starving children stripped the refrigerators, washing machines and TV sets of copper (and other valuables), and left the hulks to leak toxic substances into the air and ground—not quite the level of waste management that the EU expected.

THE SMOKESCREEN . . .

For decades, an obvious symbol of "Dutchman in the house" was the open display of the characteristic blue, plastic envelope of dried leaf shreds (**shag**), placed strategically in front of its owner. Expressions such as **een shagje draaien** (roll a cigarette) and **effe een sjekkie rollen** (how about a roll-up?) were an integral part of the **gezelligheid** equation.

Now Holland marches in lock-step with the rest of the Western world, having outlawed smoking (**roken**) in shops, businesses, public transport, cinemas, theatres, and even on open-air train platforms (where silly, painted **pafpalen**—"smoking poles"—announce the odd square-metre of **shag**ging space). Surviving vending machines require special payment methods and/or AgeKeys, and Dutch smokers are now (to quote an old Dutch idiom) *schijten peuken* (running scared, lit. shitting cigarette butts).

An unforseen consequence of the ban is that some establishments now reek of putrid pongs such as armpit odor, sweaty feet, stale beer and stagnant canals . . . the sweet scent of smouldering tobacco having been extinguished.

CLOJING TIME . . .

Some unique aspects of the tragic topics of death and dying warrant a mention here. The Dutch have found some interesting ways of handling both.

Although euthanasia has been practiced in the Netherlands since the late 1980s, Dutch parliament enacted and refined the current law in 2001 and 2002, making Holland the first country to legally allow it. Euthanasia is mainly performed by lethal injection and stopping medical treatment (*passieve euthanasie*). In addition to letting the terminally ill die peacefully, Dutch doctors have also been known to "assist" babies and children as well as patients who are not ill but who are "suffering from life" (calamitous cloggies). As an exquisite example of legal double-Dutchery, euthanasia is both illegal (inasmuch as it is a punishable offence) and legal (since the perpetrator cannot be prosecuted if lawful prerequisites are met). For euthanasia to be legal, a candidate must be in unbearable and incurable pain; make a voluntary and informed request, with family consent; be aware of any and all other options; and seek a second medical opinion. These conditions are not always met, yet there are few prosecutions even though physicians must report euthanasia deaths to the public prosecutor. The Dutch association Right to Die-NL (*Nederlandse Vereniging voor een Vrijwillig Levenseinde* or NVVE) which boasts 143,000 living members—and growing—has a website that advises those who do not qualify for euthanasia how to commit suicide with dignity to avoid messy endings such as self-immolation or jumping in front of a toiletless train.

A Dutch funeral (*uitvaart*—be careful with this word) is an occasion where the Dutch really excel at money-related cold-mindedness. A recently bereaved spouse or parent must be ever-cautious to the profiteering of funeral organizers. In the event that you are unfortunately placed in this position, recruit the aid of a cloggy. He/she will guard you against:

- overpriced floral tributes (expect a 200–300 percent price hike on cheap bouquets of flowers when ordered for funeral purposes)
- overpriced coffee (while your only thought is to lay your loved one to rest with dignity and respect, your aide will embark on a debate over the funeral arranger's price-per-head for coffee and cookies, compared with the local *café*)
- choosing the wrong day (funeral charges are higher on Saturdays, and burials are banned in most places on Sundays)
- paying extra for piped music if you think nobody will listen to it.

After the formal ceremony, the whole congregation adjourns to the abode of the next-of-kin for a drunken and relentless round of bickering and bartering over the spoils.

Thoughtfulness and consideration are also not the strongest properties of funeral organizers. A funeral in Zwolle was cancelled on the scheduled day of interment when management suddenly decided to send the grave diggers away on a training course. Concerned city officials conceded that the ceremony could still take place . . . if the family paid extra. Conversely, when postal carrier PostNL announced the cancellation of Monday regular-mail deliveries in 2013, the company excluded condolence cards (**rouwkaarten**) from the list of nondeliverables.

Traditional graves are rented for 10 or 20 years, then the tenants are either left in place (as eternal **krakers**) or evicted to a mass grave called a **knekelput**, and new renters are found for the dwellings. After expiration, it is possible to negotiate an extension of the original lease, but expect the price to be higher. Each grave holds a maximum of three coffins, stacked vertically. Fortunately, the Dutch have made sure that graveyards are always above sea level; in some areas the highest ground around is the boneyard, artificially raised by around two metres to keep the coffins above the water table.

Recent statistical analysis has confirmed the obvious: after centuries of packing posthumous people inside polders, there ain't much space left for many more of 'em. Even with cremation becoming increasingly popular, time (and space) is running out. Fortunately, a number of alternative solutions are under study, including the following:

- The Freeze-Dry Funeral. Your dead body is reduced to a temperature of 18°C over a 10-day period, immersed in nitrogen and then shattered. The resulting pile of person pieces is then dehydrated to form a powder.

- Wall-to-Wall Storage. Your body is prepared for interment in the conventional fashion, but instead of going down you go up and along. Specially constructed walls will house hamlet-fulls of Hollanders, whose souls can discuss and debate away in a Feboesque environment. One suggestion was to build the things on ground currently occupied by churches that have lost their licence to lecture. *"It's better than building another dance club or coffeeshop there!"* suggested one enthusiastic supporter.

  This is the method of burial popularized by the late Pim Fortuyn, who found the thought of a corpse being eaten to death by worms distasteful.

Today's **kikkerlanders** have the opportunity to digitally inter their late loved ones, or even themselves. There are two basic programmes available . . .

1. The virtual grave, which consists of nothing more than a high-priced Internet web page with all the emotional and sentimental elements in place. The final resting page can be linked to a live Internet cremation where the funeral can be attended through high-quality webcam video.

2. The digital gravestone. Depending on how much cash the bereaved want to waste, the digital gravestone can incorporate such important features as a shatterproof screen, incoming and outgoing e-mail, audio-video clips of the deceased and special access provisions. One such digitally desirous Dutchman requested a special PIN code to be embodied, so that only his mistress could access risqué photographs of himself in a stiff condition.

. . . or if this is too high tech, they can just pedal the corpse along to the **uitvaarthotel** on an **uitvaartfiets** (a **bakfiets** whose trailer is designed to carry a coffin). A funeral home in Hedel, Gelderland, incorporates hotel accommodation in the package so that relatives can spend the night in a room next to the dearly departed, prior to planting.

Rusty Haller

A 64-bit telepathic iGrave

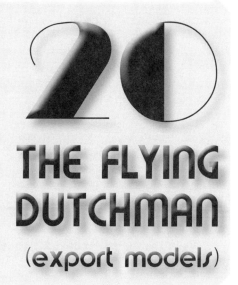

THE FLYING DUTCHMAN
(export models)

> "I only miss Holland when I'm in Holland."
>
> *Paul Verhoeven,*
> *Film Director, 1992*

utch persons migrate. They have to. If they didn't, they wouldn't all fit in Holland. When they migrate, they take their "Netherness" with them and shed it kilo-by-kilo as their newly adopted culture requires, with a pinch of protest thrown in for good measure. Some traits persist; some are relinquished willingly; others begrudgingly. It all happens instinctively, without the **regel**-mad **buro**clogs imposing a compulsory **uitburgeringscursus**.

They migrate through an osmosis-like process whereby they assimilate into their new-found culture so easily and so well that even they at times appear to forget their roots. But they rarely lose their heritage and revert to type whenever convenient or satisfying for the ego.

THE WORLD ACCORDING TO JAAP . . .

To the uninitiated, the reasons Hollanders emigrate may appear rather illusive. Dutch immigrants like to make reference to profundities such as: *"for certain reasons," "for my own choice," "because of various things that are important to me,"* but will rarely tell you WHY. It soon becomes apparent that the main factor for leaving heaven is MORE: more money, more living space, more freedom from domineering relatives, more opportunities. In terms of emigration for economics, the Dutch are no different than anyone else. When it comes to crowds and nosy, interfering relatives, they have more to escape from than most. Emigration allows them to shed those properties that they felt compelled to conform to as a part of their devout Dutchness.

They take refuge in such places as Australia, Canada, New Zealand, South Africa, Spain, the USA and their ex-colonies. The wooden shoes, windmills, dikes and so forth, are packaged and go with them. These symbols are subsequently summoned to perform services, as required. Once successfully migrated, the post-Holland Hollander will immediately pronounce *"Ja! I am Dutch, but I am not like the others. I would not be here and now if I was!"*

When challenged, many view their homeland as utopia corrupted: *"How Holland has changed since I was there!"* It is as if THEIR parting has turned Someren into Sodom and Groningen into Gommorah.

They love to BE Dutch and to "knock" it at the same time. They abhor the image of the three W's, tulips and blond-plaited maidens in traditional costume and rigorously reprimand their unwitting hosts who (dare) associate these superficial symbols with Holland. Yet when the same people need some heritage or history, out come the wooden shoes, windmills, tulips and feigned costumes.

The break is not always complete. Friends and relatives flock to the new nest. The prospect of a cheap vacation and visiting a foreign land without the encumbrance of travel inconveniences is irresistible to those left behind. Although such rekindling can be *leuk* where (grand) children are concerned, it also volunteers to be a pain for the re-liberated emigrants who have to be constantly reminded of WHO and WHAT they are, and from WHENCE they came:

"The Dutch people I know come to visit from Holland, uninvited, for 12 weeks or so. During that time, they expect more or less to be catered to, to be driven around and expect you to tour with them whether you have work to do or not. They don't think they have to help with the grocery bill, but they will tell you when the beer is gone or there are no more chips. Only in the last four years have I come to think of this as imposing on people in a major way."

M. Mol, British Columbia

Colin White

A Dutch heritage festival in California

The degree to which the immigrants retain or relinquish specific values varies from land to land. In some cases, local politics and/or economics have eradicated certain of the most beloved behaviours. The influence of the local culture and customs, and freedom from former social and bureaucratic pressures, also play a significant role in this reshaping process. One factor in the equation appears to be the size of the country in question. In this respect, the general rule seems to be:

Shedding the image

*Retention of national nature
is inversely proportional to the size
of the adopted land mass.*

A common factor is that the immigrants feel no compunction about enlisting the local labour as servants whenever and wherever customary. Far away from their homeland, they feel no guilt or remorse at "exploiting" their fellow human beings in a way that would cause widespread disquiet back home. It appears to be justified by:

- The old adage "When in Rome . . ."
- We help the economy by providing employment.
- We treat them well.

Of late in some countries, there is a growing trend to reduce the number (or completely eliminate the use) of servants, but only *"because they are becoming more and more expensive. You must OVERPAY for their low productivity."*

THE RIGHT STUFF . . .

When abroad, all nationalities are drawn to memories of home, hence the success of English fish-'n-chip shops, American hamburger joints and oriental restaurants.

Understandably, the Dutch cuisine is not so represented, but another lifeline is: Beer. Usually paraded as "HEINEKEN EXPORT— brewed in Holland" or the Amstel/Grolsch/Bavaria equivalent, renegade Hollanders will flock to the stuff like iron filings to a magnet and orgasmically utter:

"Ahhh! [BRAND NAME]—so much better than [LOCAL BREW]!"
and then confess:
"But this is entirely different to what is sold in Holland."
On realizing what they have just confessed to, a qualification is added:
"I think it is better. Only a Dutch brewery could do something like this!"

This attitude is strongly endorsed by the breweries themselves. In the words of the late Alfred Lord Heineken, *"We are a Rolls Royce abroad, in Holland just a normal beer."* Oh, the humility of it all!

Laurie Boucke

**Uses for Rolls Royce packaging –
native doll's house . . .**

Laurie Boucke

. . . the coconut cupboard . . .

Nowhere is the concept of cloggy camaraderie more pronounced than in the seemingly endless supply of overseas Dutch clubs, friendship societies, newspapers, newsletters, gourmet shops, tulip festivals, "heritage days" and the inevitable King's birthday celebration. The latter events provide an excuse for genuine Dutch immigrants to

Laurie Boucke

. . . monkey cage cover

dust off all the Neder-paraphernalia and related junk that they imported under the guise of "household goods" and display it with gay (old definition) abandon as part of their heritage, tradition, etc.

Dutch fraternity is focused on just about anyone with a *van* or *de* in their name. The fate of these identity prefixes is interesting in itself. **Van de** and **Van der** either become a single prefix (Vander Meulen) or no prefix at all (Vandergronden, Vandenberg). The *ij* becomes a "y" (Wijnbelt to Wynbelt). The spellings of some names are changed to facilitate pronunciation (Geert and Gert melt into Kert, then Curt). This process of identity preservation-integration is epitomized in a plea from a newsletter published by the New Zealand-Netherlands Society Oranje

Auckland, Inc., which published a request for readers to submit ideas for a society logo. The plea gave the following suggestions:

> "... A coat hanger with a pair of clogs hanging from it? An outline of Rangitoto Island with a windmill on top?"

Flower fascination is not forsaken abroad. lowland-leavers lavish love upon their favourite bulbs and bushes in every corner of the world. When they leave Holland, they are absolutely delighted to find themselves surrounded by relatively enormous garden plots (and usually more sunshine) in which they can grow an abundance of flowers—or even better, fields of wildflowers, thereby saving on florist bills. In an inherently efficient manner, many take their cultivation-cunning with them and frequently engage in entrepreneurial and lucrative greenhouse and nursery ventures. Those who are fortunate enough to own and operate their own retail outlets subtly hint at the source of their superblooms, as shown opposite.

The Dutch have been highly successful in farming. Not only are their farms very productive, but their flexibility and ability to migrate have also added to their earnings. For example, they have been known to purchase large areas of fertile land, convert them into profitable agricultural regions and later sell the whole thing for a "small" fortune as prime real estate.

Further fundamentals include *koffie, gezelligheid* and thriftiness (to the point of continually coveting *koekjes*). One of the first things to be perused is the quality of the local coffee. If it is undrinkably weak and tasteless (as opposed to customarily weak and tasteless), then *koffie* will be placed on the lifeline supply list. Other essential items include *erwtensoep, dropjes* and, of course, *jenever* (gin).

They have anchored their architecture wherever possible throughout history. Their famous gables, drawbridges and windmills are often found where they have reigned or prospered. Large and luscious *landhuizen* (manor houses, plantation homes) of old are the subject of renovation around the globe. In more recent times, quaint shopping streets with storybook facades as well as windmill restaurants and souvenir shops have been built or restored as major tourist attractions.

Perhaps the most important ingredient that kept early immigrants united and determined to succeed against all odds was their religious conviction(s). With the passing of time (and with a few classic exceptions, such as some Dutch Reformed Church/Calvinist elements), most of the devout religious communities have since disappeared.

Complaint and criticism prevail, albeit in a diluted form (gone is the thirst for protests and demonstrations). Dutch immigrants criticize life in their host country, comparing it to their wonderful Nederland. Things perceived as being better than in Holland are not generally acknowledged in the new land, but are held in reserve for the next visit home. This is necessary as their absence will have prevented them from keeping abreast of current complainable topics. Thus the only way to maintain a homecoming conversation is to neutralize the nonsense by bragging about their wise move abroad, the relative cost of things (necessary to prevent alienation), the freedom from governmental regulations and the abundance of space.

Somewhere along the path, some of *The Right Stuff* becomes the wrong stuff. The main victim appears to be the Bicycle, which is tragically disowned in the most stressful and traumatic parting ever experienced by a cloggy. The Bicycle as a protected species, having survived the perilous journey to foreign lands, cannot cohabit with cultures which do not understand the necessity for the *fietspad*, riders' rights or Bike hospitals/hostels. Ironically, the final blow to the devices is served by the immigrants themselves who put the contraptions to shed because of the reasons they deserted their homeland:

DISTANCES – having escaped the cramped conditions in Holland's towns and cities, there is now too much space to contemplate cycling everywhere over heretofore unheard-of distances.

CLIMATE – favourite lands to adopt typically enjoy hot summers and/or violent winters. Dutch pedal power soon exhausts itself under these generally uncomfortable conditions.

TERRAIN – the addition of a vertical component to the landscape (mountains and valleys) introduces rugged, steep roads and generally unfriendly conditions.

Another casualty is language, unless both parents make a concerted effort to speak Dutch at home. This is rarely the case.

COLONIAL CLOGGIES . . .

The Dutch colonized part of the East and West Indies for about three centuries. In general, their behaviour was much the same as that of other colonizing nations—a general plundering of land and people. The attitude, however, was coloured by their Calvinistic heritage:

- On the one hand, they would not allow extreme poverty, hardship or cruel rituals to persist.

- On the other hand, they kept themselves remote and somewhat aloof from the entirely different mentality of the colonized populations.

Indonesia

Great difficulties in the Dutch East Indies were caused by Netherlandic ambivalence towards the old Indonesian rulers who were allowed to continue to reign, but under strict Dutch regulations. The East Indies were a source of great wealth and aided Holland during the economic crisis in the 1930s. World War II and the Japanese occupation contributed to the cultural chaos in the region's post-war period. Holland experienced untold problems in reasserting authority. A premature independence came to Indonesia in the late 1940s, causing a forced mass migration of not only the true Dutch but also some 500,000 Eurasians whose only sin was that of their parents' desires.

Nowadays Dutch involvement in the country is reversed. They are generally short-term residents involved with aid/agricultural projects or similar programmes, and of a generation who feel a certain guilt over their forefathers' activities.

They are in their element as far as creature comforts are concerned. The local coffee and tea are *lekker*, cheap and abundant. Many of the older houses are typically old-Dutch style, and the popularity of the local food (at far less than Dutch prices) goes without saying. Typically, the Indonesian language is mastered in no time, even

John Elston

John Elston

"Modest" Dutch homes in Indonesia

for the lesser-educated Hollanders whose pre-arrival skills tend to be limited to the vital **bami goreng**, **loempia** and **saté**.

Many of the Netherlanders are perceived by others as *"the typically loony/aging hippy types and not the highly sophisticated types."* Whatever type they may be, they throw themselves into the community and seem to love every minute of it. This Indonesian immersion applies to those who elect to remain on a permanent basis to such an extent that they almost stop being Dutch. However, offspring are commonly cursed with pressures to develop the forceful personality of the true cloggy.

Lumps of Lesser Antilles

The Kingdom of the Netherlands consists of three Caribbean islands (Bonaire, St. Eustatius and Saba—all located in the Lesser Antilles) and the Netherlands itself. Aruba, Curaçao and half of St. Maarten were also part of the Kingdom until The Great Dutch Downsizing of 2010.

Hollanders grabbed the Antilles in the 17th century. They had found their tropical paradise:

- lack of size (islands range from 5–180 sq. miles)
- abundance of water
- lack of elevation (only one proper hill, plus one volcanic rock)

IT WAS PERFECT.

In true European style, they then spent the next century or so spoiling it. At first came the "gingerbread houses," slave huts, drawbridges, canals, ports and prostitution. Later, the need for lego-roads, banks, road roundabouts with traffic lights, **Sinterklaas & Zwarte Piet**, **Koningsdag**, lotto and topless sunbathing beaches was satisfied. The official languages are Dutch, English and **Papiaments**; the local currency is the (Netherlands Antilles) guilder; and hotel/restaurant food is bland and boring. The result is a tropical home-away-from-home which can act as a tax haven for the rich and an exotic Caribbean **kikkerland** getaway for the rest. All of this, of course, has been achieved by reprogramming the native population.

The tourist industry preys heavily on the cloggy connection. Thus, top priority is given to renovating, decorating and constructing traditional quaint structures. All the basic souvenirs—Delftware, wooden shoes and lewd T-shirts—are on sale, in addition to the local island goodies. Resident Dutch merchants readily admit that they prefer American tourists to their own kind since, *"A tourist tends to buy the same overall amount of souvenirs during a visit, whether spending one week or one month on the islands."* And with their generous holiday allowance, the Hollanders spend a minimum of three weeks on the island(s) and tend not to buy souvenirs imported from Holland, whereas Americans do so in excess.

Laurie Boucke

Antillean Noordwijk

To the Dutch residents, island life is at times reminiscent of village life back home. On the glamorous side, life can be cosy and secure with a fixed daily routine, favourite hang-outs, familiar faces, *koffie uurtjes*, visits to the local baker, etc. But with the mentality of a small village come the usual problems of nosy neighbours, false friendliness, excessive envy and gossip. Add the element of foreign territory and you get the usual boasting ("my pool," "my housemaid," "my suntan") and complaining ("too hot," "too many insects," "too primitive"). The compulsory clique who miss everything about Holland take no comfort in the fact that the local supermarket imports most traditional tasty treats.

Laurie Boucke

**Windmills, cacti & palm trees – home away from home
(Netherlands Antilles)**

The never-say-no mindset of the natives is a truly trying experience with which the straightforward Hollander has to come to terms. Antilleans consider it polite and proper to say "yes" (and thus make impossible promises) and rude to say "no." Merge this with the regional *mañana* mentality of being late by several hours, days or weeks for appointments or whatever, and it is enough to make any self-respecting Netherlander high-tail it home to show off his tan in the civilized world of Chapters 2 through 19.

Laurie Boucke

**Joop performs the Aruban Rumba as reinforcements of
Rolls-Royce Dutchness arrive in Curaçao**

For over half a century, the **moeder**land and its Antillean vassals squabbled about autonomy, and each time it came to giving up financial aid, things would quiet down for a while. Eventually, everyone got sick of the same old argument and the inevitable dissolution was decreed. Unfortunately for Holland, the indications are that the unshackling does NOT include an un*shekel*ing. Even though Aruba, Curaçao and St. Maarten are now "countries," their estranged parent still gets to poke its euronose into finance, defence and foreign policies. The other islands are "special municipalities" (**bijzondere gemeenten**) of the Netherlands (adopted by the homeland province of North Holland), thereby setting up a potential paradox regarding EU membership . . . and thus likely to be re-re-defined (again).

Suriname

Originally sighted by one of Columbus's crew, Suriname came under Dutch control in 1667. It officially became a Dutch colony the same year when the English gave up their claims to it as a consolation prize for the Dutch loss of the state of New York, then New Amsterdam (see "New World Netherlanders," this chapter).

Suriname was, and is, Holland's answer to America's Deep South—a territory where white entrepreneurs used African slave labour to cultivate specialized crops (one of the most important here being coffee). The set-up was Calvinistically correct, provided slaves were not sold to Iberian customers. (Such a trade would have exposed the merchandise to *"the abuses and perils of popery."*)

For years the Netherlanders secretly cultivated coffee in Suriname. They took great care to prevent Brazil (known in part as "New Holland" until the Dutch were expelled) from acquiring any beans. The whole enterprise foundered when a Brazilian espionage mission managed to smuggle THE BEAN out of the country. This broke the Dutch monopoly and gave rise to the Brazilian coffee empire. The Surinamese economy crumbled further when slavery was abolished.

Suriname remained a Dutch colony until 1954 when it became a self-governing state within the Kingdom of the Netherlands. In 1975, it became the independent Republic of Suriname. At this time, large numbers of Surinamese immigrated to the Netherlands, causing a shortage of skilled labour. This is cited as a reason to frequently ask for financial help from Holland.

Cruelties on the side of an absolute military regime in the early 1980s led the Dutch to stop financial aid, and the country economically went to shambles (again). The political situation has improved somewhat, but the Netherlands government still has doubts about granting financial aid to a third-world country whose natives basically behave the way they were taught. The Surinamese understandably use the word *patata* (potato) to refer to their ex-masters. The overall situation is basically a disaster as far as the modern-day Dutchman is concerned.

The native population is around 560,500 while there are around 350,000 Surinamese in Holland. Tourism in Suriname is almost non-existent. It comes as no surprise that the country is not a favourite location for contemporary cloggies, except for those with family or business ties—and the adventurous types. But Suriname is doing its best to lure skilled Dutch farmers. *"When the new **mest** laws cost 6,000 Dutch farmers their jobs, perhaps they'll want to go into exile abroad. They are most welcome in Suriname,"* the Surinamese Ambassador to the Netherlands announced.

PRETORIAN DISGARD . . .

Contrary to popular belief, South Africa was never a Dutch colony or territory. Holland first infiltrated the region in 1652 to establish supply routes and rest stations. In order to break away from English colonizers, the Dutch explored the unsettled northeast where they founded the independent republics of Transvaal and the Orange Free State. They considered themselves Afrikaners. The final severance of bloodline bonds came when Holland declined to support them in the Boer Wars.

The Afrikaans language developed from 17th-century Dutch. The first Dutch settlers spoke country dialects and often wrote phonetically. Many cloggies consider Afrikaans to be a form of pidgin Dutch or a mere dialect. In 1925, Afrikaans replaced Dutch as one of the country's two official languages—English being the second—and remains the native language of much of South Africa to this day.

As time and politics progressed, the region came to define two distinct breeds of Dutch extract:

- **AFRIKANERS:** Born in the country; despite their Dutch descent, strongly consider themselves "white" Africans, with no feeling of being Dutch.

- **HOLLANDERS:** Immigrants; will never be considered Afrikaners. They are nicknamed *kaaskop/kaaskoppe* (blockhead—lit. cheese head—there is even a Dutch company using this name) and *Japie/Jaap* (lout or simpleton).

Holland's interest in South Africa has had many peaks and troughs. Discovery of gold and diamonds (1870s) was an obvious peak, and the introduction and continued practice of apartheid (1948–1992) was definitely a trough. When the country returned to mainly black control, Hollanders faced a tough choice, summed up here:

"My friend in South Africa has definitely scrapped his plans of moving back to Holland. His wife threatened him with divorce if he should insist on leaving. My colleague seems to have forgotten that a housewife in South Africa is used to having an elaborate domestic staff of natives and would never get used to a modus vivendi in which she should (for the first time in her life!) have to do everything in and about the house herself."

and here:

"The Dutch get along fairly well with the blacks, but the blacks have an entirely different mentality. This is something that is not realized overseas. The blacks come out of a tribal existence. When the world says, 'You must have democracy in South Africa,' the blacks don't understand what democracy is. They are used to one leader or chief who tells them what to do. When they have the power, as in other African countries, they become very autocratic and corrupt, and just a few people prosper while the rest suffer and/or starve."

Yet some of the Dutch do leave, but not without trouble adjusting to the reality of their new situation:

"I would cry if the wooden clog was the symbol of Holland!"

DOWN-UNDER DUTCH . . .

It is difficult to imagine water-denying dikes constructed in the parched outback of Australia, or tulip fields invading the rich sheep-grazing areas of New Zealand, but the purveyors are there. In general, they are a well-respected, hard-working bunch.

Australia

Hard-working and hard-playing—this is exactly the image that Australia likes to portray. Here we have perhaps the most successful Dutch integration of all the lands discussed in this chapter, but not without a rocky beginning. The invasion began after World War II, when false promises of paradise were used to lure unsuspecting Dutchies into making the long journey. Too proud to admit they had been duped by propaganda, they fuelled the myths which continued to bring boatloads of their compatriots.

The flood peaked in the 1950s and early 1960s with the support of Dutch religious and governmental organizations. Today Australia is once again viewed as a nether-utopia. There are 24 Dutch language radio programmes around Australia, and weekly and monthly newspapers, plus many social, community and religious clubs. Dutch press scoops include world-shattering news items such as *"Tasmanian cows give more milk than their interstate cousins,"* and *"Philips light bulbs illuminate the Sydney Harbour Bridge."*

Anthony Vandewerdt

A Dutch windmill-lighthouse in Western Australia

To the Dutch-Australian, the most beloved person to have ever set foot on Australian soil was the little-known navigator:

ABEL JANSZOON TASMAN

Apparently, Lutjegast-born Abel discovered the lump of land at the bottom right of Australia in 1642 on orders from then Governor of Java, Anthony van Diemen. Abel named the place after Anthony, Anthony said **bedankt**, and Australia renamed it Tasmania ("Tassie" or "Tas" for short). And so that is what it has since become to the Hollanders that live there: Tas-MANIA.

To celebrate the Tasman Trip's 350th anniversary, Dutch-Australians conspired to give Abel his well-deserved recognition (although he sailed around Australia without even seeing it) by organizing, amongst other things:

- a year-long Abel Tasman Festival (in Hobart)
- the Dutch-Australian Society "Abel Tasman," Inc.
- the Abel Tasman Commemorative Medallion
- unveiling of an Abel Tasman coastal monument
- the Circumnavigation of Tasmania yacht crews

- the Abel Tasman Blue Water Classic Yacht Race
- the Abel Tasman Yachting Cup
- guided heritage (?) tours to the Abel Tasman landing site
- Dutch civic visits including the Mayor of Grootegast and the Governor of Groningen.

Tasman gave the Australian continent its first European name: New Holland (original, huh?). As if this isn't enough, more of the Abel aftermath of discovering the southern hemisphere Holland includes:

- tulip festivals that attract thousands of visitors
- *oliebollen* festivals that attract thousands of visitors
- infestation of Dutch-sounding or -looking place names, such as Zeehan, Geeveston, Schouten and Maatsuyker
- world record for Tasman-named names (e.g. Tasman Sea, Tasman Basin, South Tasmanian Rise, Tasman Hills, Tasmanian wolf (or tiger), Tasmanian devil).

Australia has a permanent effect on the Dutch who have lived there. One settler who returned to the Netherlands had this to say about her rediscovered homeland:

"When I returned to Holland from Australia, I found it was difficult to adjust to the lack of nature and space, and also lack of clean bodies of water.
The Netherlands is regulated to the extent that it breeds resistance. Opening hours for shops are very restricted. Swimming pools open to "outsiders" (non-ethnic, male, singles, etc.) during certain hours only. There are waiting lists for many things, especially accommodation. If you don't fit in an "urgent" category, you have to wait years.
There is racism and people of colour are not treated as citizens. It is hard to make friends. It entails responsibilities, involves keeping in regular touch, a keen interest on both sides. Thus one can spend many hours on weekends travelling to and from friends to satisfy the moral obligation."

This attitude from a repatriated Hollander seems hard to understand, until one considers that perhaps the reason for the venomous voice is because she no longer qualifies for preferential treatment. Maybe Dutchness ain't so dead in Australia after all!

One thing that will never die is the stubborn adherence to one of the strongest hereditary weaknesses known to "clogdom"—the rivalry between their best-loved brews: Heineken and Amstel beers. But here the two have learned the art of **samenwonen** and live peaceably in sin in beach-front bliss in areas where their patrons are plentiful and well out of sight of their "Fosters parents."

Bruce van Uitbak

A Dutch "kroeg" – Australian style

new Zealand

Originally named Nieuw Zeeland by its discoverer who never landed there (you guessed it—Abel Tasman), the country was renamed New Zealand by its British owners (who kept the "Z" to keep the leftover lowlanders happy). Before we discuss the New Zealand Netherlanders, let's get the Abel-worship out of the way. The year 1992 marked the 350th anniversary of "the sighting" and was of course designated Abel Tasman Year, as defined and reflected by the:

- New Zealand Abel Tasman 1992 Commission
- Auckland 1992 Abel Tasman Memorial Fund
- Abel Tasman Commemorative Stamp
- Annual Tulip Queen & Abel Tasman Competition
- Abel Tasman tulip field dedication
- Cartography exhibition
- Dutch Food and Fashion Festival

- Books, TV documentaries, sports events, etc.
- Closing Abel Tasman Year Function

    (Here endeth the lesson on caning Abel.)

Cloggies complain that New Zealanders are too English:

"The New Zealanders are more English than the English. They haven't got their own identity yet. This irritates us. They are too reserved and are not open. In Holland, we got to know our neighbours, but not in New Zealand. The people are too polite to tell you what they really think."

In New Zealand more than in any other country the Dutch regret giving up their passion to protest for pleasure and possession:

"I really accuse [my fellow] Dutch people of being too quiet and too polite here. We should have made waves because other groups did and got something for it."

Although NZ-NL'ers boast, *"We are well known for our great integration skills in this country,"* they afford perhaps the greatest living example of the perseverance of "The Dutch Way" overseas. There are not many of 'em there, but NZ-NL'ers will not compromise their position or attitude for any reason:

- In 1967, two opposing factions of the Dutch community started to war over the rights to a publication title. A mere word or two relating to clogdom is apparently so important that by 1973, the issue had reached the Privy Council in London, England (the gloriously highest court in Her Britannic Majesty's Commonwealth of Great Britain and Northern Ireland). Despite a definitive ruling, the parties are still at odds over the issue. The wording in question? THE WINDMILL POST.

- A community radio broadcaster in Auckland is operated by a group of young Dutch immigrants. The station has refused to acknowledge this book as the origin of the name of their nightly programme, pleading, *"Our programme is called 'RADIO Undutchables' not 'THE UnDutchables' so there's no total usage of your book title. We receive no remuneration whatsoever so there is no commercial gain,"* rather than submit to common decency and give a 10-second acknowledgment on the air. So much for the importance of originality in Netherlandic titles when an outsider is involved.

Many immigrant NZ-NL'ers are disillusioned by what they feel is job discrimination against the Dutch:

"In New Zealand, hiring is by nationality and not by qualifications. The best jobs go to native English speakers: The English, then the Americans, then the New Zealanders. It is hard for the rest to get good jobs here. We are considered foreigners."

A Dutch retirement community has grown up amongst the wilds of the Auckland suburbs. Built and managed by an outfit called **Ons Dorp** (Our Village), the community consists of 70 houses bedekked with **klompen met bloemen**, milk cans, and Delft-blue planters with miniature windmills along a stretch of road officially called "Willem Straat." Here, blue-haired and wrinkled Hennies and Henks live in peace and tranquility speaking Dutch, thinking Dutch, looking Dutch and celebrating everything that could be remotely described as **Nederlandse gezelligheid**. The idea and intent is to provide an atmosphere of comfort-through-familiarity to the old folks (some of whom may have actually met Abel Tasman) in their twilight years.

NEW WORLD NETHERLANDERS . . .

In its early colonial years of the 17th century, the New World of North America opened its arms to the Dutch nation. This gloriously unspoiled and uncivilized land was badly in need of an injection of tulips and Calvinism, and who better to give it to 'em than the Dutch.

The colony of New Netherland covered most of the now densely populated northeast corridor of the United States, starting in 1609. There were many encounters, both friendly and violent, with the Indians ("Native Americans"). Many settlements were wiped out, and often the Hollanders massacred the natives. Immigration to Canada began much later (1890s) and occurred at a much slower pace.

Early colonial achievements included Peter Stuyvesant's heroic loss of New Amsterdam to the English in 1664. (Unbeknownst to Stuyvesant, the two countries were at war at the time, so when an English naval vessel sailed into the harbour, Peter rushed to greet them, whereupon he was immediately fired and the place was renamed New York.) As the area was originally purchased from natives for blankets, kettles and trinkets worth a few florins at the most, the affair was an overwhelming financial disaster as well as an embarrassment. (Although the area was reconquered in 1673, it was permanently

GIVEN to England one year later.) Peter has subsequently tried to re-habilitate himself among his countrymen by using cigarette packaging to advertise himself as the "founder" of New York. Some links to New York's Dutch heritage are still present (for example, the present suburb of Brooklyn derives from the earlier village name Breukelen), although much has been corrupted by the overbearing English inheritance.

Holland's most identifiable contribution to the emergent continent, however, can be felt this day in the State of Michigan where large concentrations of Dutch-Americans (the Michi-Dutch) have inhabited the picturesque landscape and infested it with tulips, (mock) windmills and other Dutch structures. (The more famous Pennsylvania

Rusty Haller

Peter Stuyvesant's grand design for New Amster-York

Dutch are not Dutch descendants at all, but German—an example of history's corruption of *Deutsch* into "Dutch.")

Unlike the Dutch Dutch, the MichiDutch haven't changed much over the past 150+ years. They deserted their lowland land to escape the then progressive penchant of the Dutch Reformed Church. As staunch churchgoers and moralistic merchants, they believe they are THE true Dutch. In the same way that Californian vineyards claim their *Sauterne, Cabernet Sauvignon* and *Pinot Noir* to be more French than the French varieties, the MichiDutch perceive themselves to be superior stock to European Dutchies. They do not merely think that they are better than the Dutch Dutch—they KNOW they are better. Thus, we have this curious phenomenon:

The Dutch above the Dutch
disown the Dutch Dutch.

The elders of the region are embarrassed by many of the current Dutch Dutch traits and customs. As one MichiDutch businessman advised, *"We're conservative here. In Holland they don't give a hoot about their image. We don't want to make that impression here."* Many of the second- or later-generation Dutch in western Michigan have little or no idea what the real Holland is like. They are appalled to discover what the natives (the Dutch "over there") wear (or don't wear) at the beach and at the "window shopping" in certain cities in Holland. At home, they view Dutchness only from within their safe cliques and prefer to marry others of Dutch descent.

The younger variety are protected against their origins and fed on the heavenly dreams of their fathers. When they peel away from their paternal protection and venture out into the real world, the bubble bursts. Those who escape the strict community and become more Americanized would at times rather not admit to their Dutch background (variation on the theme of Dutch disowning the Dutch). Most second or subsequent generation Dutch tend to shed their Michi-Dutchness once they leave their sacred pastures.

Canadians have a similar situation with their Calvinist Dutch who retain many of the old practices and traits of their ancestors. They are rather conspicuous to outsiders through their churches:

"In one small town there are five, six or even seven such churches close to each other, and each one holds to a slightly different belief, so that they are all at odds."

Janny Lowensteyn (Quebec)

The rest of the New World Netherlanders have integrated to the point that they are hardly visible, although they still observe the Americans and Canadians through their original moral eyeglasses. They view their hosts as somewhat slow, "laid-back" and passive, traits which the Dutch find to be irritating: *"They never seem to protest, but just accept most things,"* complain the cloggies as they themselves abandon the protest practice.

In general, Americans are perceived to be more "open" than Canadians, but not nearly as "open" as Hollanders.

"It is hard to get close to Canadians because they are reserved. They are always helpful in emergencies, but then they go back in their shell and want to be private. We Dutch are very open and always ready with comments, criticism and advice. We're not afraid to come straight out and ask, 'How much money do you make?' The Canadians think we are rude for this."

Newcomers go through the usual frustration and comedy of adjusting to a new mentality and to different customs, as exemplified by one such immigrant:

"The first time my wife had to go to a doctor, she was told to undress in a little room and to wait until the doctor would come. Although she noticed those gowns in the room, she did not put one on (nobody told her about them). When the doctor came in, he was quite shocked that she was lying there au naturel.
A friend of ours was told to put one of those gowns on, but she thought that it would be more practical for it to be open at the front instead of the back. Again, that doctor probably thought that most Dutch women are so liberated that they do not mind to walk around naked!"

Those Hollanders who elect to ride Bicycles find themselves part of a brave new world. *"People dress up in special outfits, helmets, etc., like they are going to the Tour de France. They are over-concerned about safety and liability."* The gear is ridiculous—and even worse, it is EXPENSIVE.

The Dutch who emigrate to the New World are relieved to find that the taxes are not nearly as high as in Holland. While enjoying the relatively low tax rates, they strongly criticize the sometimes tragic events that (in part) stem from this. One especially exciting tax break exists in British Columbia where there is no provincial sales tax on children's (under 16) clothing.

> *"Of course, you cannot tell if a fairly large T-shirt is for an adult or for a child. So you know what we Dutch answer when the lady at the cash register is asking that question!"*
> Jurrian Tjeenk Willink (British Columbia)

It is easy to track Hollanders' progression across the USA. They deposit a town called "Nederland" or "Holland" wherever possible. "Hollands" can be found in 28 states: Arkansas, Colorado, Florida, Georgia, Illinois, Indiana, Iowa, Kansas, Kentucky, Massachusetts, Michigan, Minnesota, Missouri, Montana, Nebraska, New Jersey, New York, North Carolina, Ohio, Oregon, Pennsylvania, South Dakota, Texas, Utah, Vermont, Virginia, Washington and Wisconsin. Canada has a few, too. There are also a fair number of derivatives, such as Hollandale, New Holland, Holland Pond, Hollandtown, Holland Marsh and Hollandsburg. Perhaps the best and most honest example of leaving a legacy by way of place names is a small city in the state of New York called . . . Guilderland. As a further token of their **heimwee** (homesickness), there are around 1,260 streets named Holland in the USA.

In California, there are so many strains of lifestyle and ethnic cultural diversity (all fighting for their share of the current sensitivity and victim boom) that even the highly devout Dutch would have difficulty in raising support for Bicycle paths on freeways. Instead, they satisfy themselves by reasoning that tragedies such as the abuses of local law enforcement are none of THEIR doing—none of THEIR doing and therefore none of THEIR business. They simply go about THEIR business and occasionally spoil themselves with a personalized car licence plate or an illuminated windmill on the front lawn.

Here is a lifestyle and mindset as divorced from the original as the quintessential **Vrouw Antje** (*Frau Antje*) is from those rights-swirling feminists and freedom-obsessed patriots, sliding raw fish and apple pie down their gullets, and pedalling to the bargain bread shop three miles up the road, stopping only for flowers and (free) coffee en route.

According to K.A. Carroll, an Internet correspondent, Holland/ Dutch can be compared to USA/Americans as follows:

- The Netherlands is as flat as Kansas.
- The Dutch are as blunt as New Yorkers.
- Hollanders are more attractive than Californians . . . but they drive worse than Texans.
- The food is like the Midwest—nothing to write home about.
- They live in row houses like San Francisco.
- Everything is as neat and proper as Maine.
- Cloggies are the opposite pole from the big spenders in Las Vegas . . . but as festive as people in New Orleans.
- The weather is as wet as Washington.
- The Dutch are as loyal as people in Montana . . . and complain like the people in Washington, D.C.

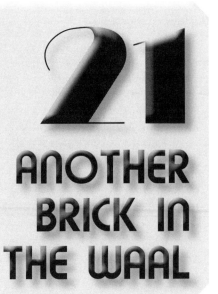

21
ANOTHER BRICK IN THE WAAL

DIKE-OTOMY OF A DISASTER . . .

Every state has its ultimate, unthinkable disaster waiting to happen, natural or otherwise. In California, it is the "big 'un" earthquake that will plop half of the place into the Pacific Ocean (arguably, to the benefit of the rest of the world). In the United Kingdom, it is the destruction of the monarchy (more likely through the spread of sexually transmitted diseases than through revolution). In Germany, it is the resurgence of Naziism. In France, it is the extinction of certain species of vegetation: the onion, the garlic clove and the grape. In Holland, it is The Atlantis Effect: the reclaiming of land BY water.

In 1995, it nearly happened—again. In a Maginot-line scenario, the threat appeared not from the raging North Sea, but from rivers feeding the Netherlands from its neighbours: the Rhine to the east and the Maas to the south. Never before had the water in Dutch rivers been so high. A quarter of a million people were evacuated, the largest upheaval since the 1953 flood. A million cows, pigs, sheep and fowl were evacuated, as were countless Bicycles, plants, flowers and secret money stashes. A university psychologist psycho-babbled about Dutch solidarity, *". . . the element of lack of control, the feeling of the strength of nature creates a kind of solidarity."* More like plain old survival, banding together in the face of danger.

The cloggiesque essence of this whole event brings to mind the story of "The Hero of Haarlem," a quaint vignette included in a children's book *Hans Brinker*, by Mary Mapes Dodge, first published in the late 1800s. The "hero" is the eight-year-old son of a Haarlem sluicer. According to preposterous foreign folklore, this boy saved the entire country of Holland by plugging a dike with his little finger until help arrived the following morning, the moral of the story being that, *"Not a leak can show itself anywhere, either in its politics, honor, or public safety, that a million fingers are not ready to stop it, at any cost."* The story is neither popular nor widely known in Holland. This, then, is our updated version, which takes place in the south of the country in modern times and incorporates real-life events from the 1995 disaster.

HAN/ VERDRINKER . . .

In 1995, there lived in the Land of Maas en Waal a sunny-haired boy, Hans Verdrinker, whose father was a farmer by profession and a "black" dike-*kijker* on the side. That is, he kept a watchful eye on the water levels and the condition of the double and triple river-dikes, many of which had fallen into disrepair over the years.

February 2nd was a typical day of torrential rain, and the boy put on his rain gear in order to take some space cakes to a gay couple who lived in the countryside. After spending an hour with his grateful friends, the boy started on his homeward trek. Trudging stoutly along the river, he pondered how German, French and Belgian canalization, melting snow in the faraway Alps and prolonged rainfall throughout northern Europe had swollen the waters. Towns in Belgium, France, Germany and Holland had been flooded. He thought about the recent voluntary evacuations from Limburg and Bommelerwaard and all the fuss and bother in his own village.

It had been painful to move the Verdrinker furniture and carpets upstairs. They had to shove and carry everything up the typical winding, narrow staircase. And his visiting **oma** made a huge fuss about saving the *vitrage* and ugly, dusty orange blinds since she had paid for them as a young wife and didn't want her fond memories washed away in a flood, although a good washing was certainly what they needed.

Hans remembered how his **opa** had bossed everyone around while having a good time doing nothing himself. *"Is there a wave* *coming? If only it could be a heat wave,"* he joked to one of his older friends. *"I don't want to live here anymore. I got seasick from all the water,"* his friend had joked back. And the pair knocked back some bottles of beer and smoked cigars while bragging about how hard life had been in their youth.

Hans thought of how his father had screamed at the evacuation authorities, *"I have hundreds of cows and pigs. I am staying put. You don't get me out!"* Yes, Hans felt he was indeed lucky to be part of such a cosy family. While humming his favourite street-organ medley, the boy thought of his father's moonlighting activities: *"If the dikes break, where would father and mother be? Where would the **zwart geld** be?"*

It was growing dark and he was still some distance from home. With a beating heart, he quickened his footsteps in the pouring rain. To lessen his fear, he began practicing the Dutch art of finger-pointing that had been passed down through the ages. First he rehearsed the vertical-and-oscillating manoeuvre, where the index finger points directly upwards and the forearm swings back-and-forth (to emphasize a philosophical ideal or point of view). Next he practiced the horizontal-poking manoeuvre (traditionally used during arguments). Just as he was bracing himself for a subtle manoeuvre-change, he heard the sound of trickling water. Looking up, he saw a small hole in the dike. A tiny stream was flowing through the barrier. The small hole would soon be a large one, and a terrible flood would result.

When Hans leaned forward to inspect the leak, his foot slipped on a damp, dank dome of dog dung. *"**Shit!**"* he yelled. As he fell forward, his outstretched finger rammed into the hole of the failing dike, effectively sealing it. His finger was stuck solidly, and the flow of water stopped. *"**Zo!**"* he thought, *"Another use for the eternally pointing finger of the Dutchman. And Holland will not be drowned while I am here!"*

He thought about the 100,000 people who had been evacuated from Tiel and Culemborg a few days ago and wished they could see him now. Images of metre-high inundations in Borgharen and Itteren haunted him. He was determined not to let his town be flooded (not that he had much choice in the matter).

He smiled as he thought about the prison in Maastricht that had been evacuated. The guards feared that groundwater would short-circuit a computer located, of all places, in the cellar. The computer controlled the locks on cell doors and a Maas escape of prisoners was anticipated.

He was proud that his little lowland country was back in the world news, even if it was because of a disaster—*"We count again!"* seemed to be the general gist. Most local reports were about the solidarity, bravery and generosity of the Dutch. Indeed, €15 million had been collected by the Nationaal Rampenfonds in just one night—big money for such a small country. But a Belgian newspaper, *De Morgen*, pointed out:

> *". . . The horror is high in the land that always thinks itself to be safe among the tulips and hashish. Proud of their dikes and their mastery over water, the illusion has now been washed away."*

Hans was determined to disprove this Flemish flotsom! And then there was that British journalist who mistranslated **kwelwater** into "torture water"—the Brits never were very skilled when it came to foreign languages, but Hans was beginning to think that this wasn't such a bad translation after all.

The boy looked up and down the dike for rescue and spotted a gaggle of his contemporaries pedalling their way down the dike. He called frantically for help. *"Kijk es! It's Hans. Why are you leaning on the wall, Hans? We are escaping from the evacuation. The army is chasing us. See you!"* was the reply. And with that, they disappeared to the clatter of multiple rusty Bike chains.

This plunged him into a gloomy mood and soon he was thinking of stories his **opa** told him about the horrible 1953 floods that had claimed 1,835 lives. Dikes in 400 locations had broken during a storm, exactly 42 years ago to the day. Hans was proud to have his finger in the dike and wished his Queen could see him.

He frowned as he thought about vandals kicking in some of the emergency dikes, resulting in all-night patrols by beefy farm women armed with baseball bats in some areas. Or how about the poor saps who heard a prank radio broadcast telling them to evacuate, only to later discover their homes had been plundered during their absence.

Night fell rapidly. Our little hero shouted loudly, but no one came to his rescue. He shouted again, *"Shit! Will no one come? Mama! Mama!"* But, alas, his mother worried not about her son—she respected the young boy's right to freedom and privacy. Then he called on God to consider possibly helping him, if the angelic flock agreed and there would be no **borgsom** involved. The answer came, through a holy resolution, *"When I am rescued, I will charge the Rijkswaterstaat* *a dike-**kijker**'s fee, plus an outrageous bonus for temporary repairs!"* And with that, he fell into an uncomfortable sleep leaning against the rain-soaked dike.

Hans awoke the next morning to the familiar sound of mooing, belching, flatulating cows. *"Mama, papa, you have saved me,"* he mumbled hoarsely, for he had lost his voice in the damp, cold night. As he peered over the dike, he saw a strange sight—barges of cows being transported to safety. *"**Godverdomme!**"* he thought, *"I must be hallucinating for lack of food. What I wouldn't give for a soggy **uitsmijter!**"*

A loud ruckus nearby suddenly caught his attention as an army patrol vehicle came to a halt along the dike. It was the platoon commander, a long-haired, lanky lad from Friesland, assigned to the area. Our young hero could hear loud voices in the distance as the commander spoke with some townsfolk who were debating whether to evacuate or stay put. *"In my mind, the situation is not life-threatening here. As far as I'm concerned, you can just stay,"* said the commander.

In the meantime, his squad of soldiers was building an emergency dike with sandbags. Hans heard both laughing and complaining emanating from the ranks. *"It's hard work, filling up the sandbags, and long hours. We must talk to the union about this,"* was the crux of the complaints. Hans learned that each bag weighed about 15 kilos, so in one day, several thousand kilos would pass through each soldier's soiled, sweaty hands. *"The coordination and safety aren't the best. It's good that the work inspectors can't see this. Ha ha,"* was one of the jokes Hans could hear. The exercise was very important for the townspeople, since word had reached them that Heerewaarden was charging €2.25 for a solitary sandbag, instead of issuing them free.

The commander and residents were still discussing matters when the mayor suddenly arrived on his Bicycle. *"What are you doing here? All you people have to evacuate immediately!"* he bellowed. *"**Ja**, but the riot police (**mobiele eenheid**) don't agree,"* replied the commander. The mayor burst into anger and retorted, *"The riot police are completely wrong. Everyone has to get out. It's time for the police, riot police, volunteers, demonstrators, protesters, environmentalists, firemen, farmers, **vrouwen**, **flikkers** and everyone else to . . . OBEY ORDERS!"* As the mayor and the military squabbled over power, the townsfolk quietly slipped away to carry on with their lives: The concept of "orders," and the obeying of them, was something they would rather not contemplate.

In the end, the mayor won, as evidenced by a stream of traffic crawling slowly across the distant bridge later that morning. Hans recognized people from his own town in what looked like an endless gypsy caravan, with furniture, suitcases, Bicycles, chickens, toys, pets and potted plants stuffed in cars, trucks, tractors and buses, or piled high on the roofs of the vehicles. The ever-present wind shifted direction and Hans heard the angry voice of a neighbour exclaim, *"Unbelievable! We are fleeing for our lives, yet we still have to pay the toll for crossing the stupid bridge!"* Everyone was leaving while Hans the saviour was stuck in the source of the scourge.

Rusty Haller

Obeying orders

A rustling noise at his feet startled him, and he looked down in dismay. A rabbit was tunneling into the dike that he was trying to save! *"Sodemieter op!"* he croaked at the creature, wondering what he could use to plug this potential breach. Just the other day, he had seen a group of men from the Royal Hunters' Association paddling around in boats, trying to rescue rabbits and other wild creatures from various dry havens such as trees, so they could hunt and shoot the critters after the flood.

His thoughts turned again to the evacuations. In Gameren, forty gardeners had remained in their nursery, refusing to move. On the island of Nederhemert, everyone remained at home. Even the replacement dike master of Groot Maas en Waal stubbornly stayed on evacuated territory. So why was Hans so alone now? He thought that maybe it was the dreaded riot police that were responsible for his isolation. Typically, fugitives were collected by such patrols and escorted to emergency relief camps—a few hours later, many would be back home again, having escaped from the confines of safety. He comforted himself with the thought that maybe help would arrive after all.

Visions of evacuating the pigs and cows from his father's farm were vivid. Before the evacuation, Hans had no idea how sensitive to stress and disease pigs were. Although moving the animals had taken a whole day—some had left in trucks, others on the train—it had not been the most organized move in Dutch history. Many farmers had no idea where their livestock had been relocated to, the animals had no idea where they were and some recipients had no idea where their new charges came from. Other concerned citizens had graciously offered asylum for snakes, spiders, rats and other cuddly cloggy pets.

In his moments of boredom, Hans tried to envision life in one of the (free) relief camps. He had seen people interviewed on TV who reported that life was generally quite acceptable there. At one camp housing 1,300 evacuees, most thought that things were fine. *"They've thought of everything here. It's a bit like being on vacation,"* said one of the evacuees at the camp. The more enterprising inmates sifted through evacuated insurance papers, purchase receipts and bank statements, and spent their days calculating how best to capitalize on the calamity.

Yet this would not be Holland without some whinging and whining. One woman grumbled to reporters that her knitting had been left behind, and she did not want to spend money on more wool when she had some floating around in her home. To some evacuees, snoring was the main nightmare. *"The neighbour to my left snores, the guy behind me snores and the neighbour to my right coughs all night long. This is no party. Everything is well taken care of, but I can't last much longer,"* said a resident of Zaltbommel. One man staying at an antique car museum couldn't take it any longer and sought refuge in a soundproof ice cream truck. The whole concept started to sound like luxury to Hans.

The sound of a boat engine rescued the boy from his thoughts, but alas not from his situation. He peered over the top of the dike and couldn't believe his eyes. There they were, boatloads of gaping disaster-tourists. They were smiling, waving and snapping photos of him as they sailed past, having paid €3 each for the tour. As bad luck would have it, our hero could not scream for help.

Then something so extraordinary and wonderful happened that Hans ceased feeling sorry for himself for a few moments. The event happened when he noticed the day trippers gather on one side of the boat, madly waving, jumping up and down, yelling, and generally making even bigger fools of themselves. He turned to see what could cause them to act so apelike when he suddenly saw lots of TV cameras and the whole media circus swarming along the dike about a kilometre away. The next thing he knew, he saw his beloved Queen, hatless and decked in rubber boots and raincoat, stomping through the mud to survey the flood damage. It was a moment Hans would never forget. Unfortunately, the entourage was headed away from him.

Hans consoled himself by daydreaming about meeting his Queen. Later that day, a defiant environmentalist who had refused to leave the town was walking along the top of Hans' dike, allowing his dog to fertilize the cycle path in the traditional Dutch manner. The environmentalist heard our hero groaning. Expecting to rescue a small, furry animal in distress, he bent down and discovered the weak and hungry child. With disappointment, he bellowed, ***"Godverdomme! What are you doing there?"*** Hans cleared his sore throat and gave the simple, yet honest answer, *"I am keeping the water from running out, you **klootzak!**"* then added, for effect, *"Send for help. We must shore up the dike."*

"No way!" the environmentalist replied logically, *"The town is deserted now. Besides, if I do that, the authorities will come later and build all kinds of ugly new dikes and emergency water walls that cause horizon pollution. **Ja!** They might even erect some of those ugly new wind generators that don't look anything like our lovely picture-postcard windmills. That's horizon pollution!"*

"I haven't taken my morning bread yet," the boy pleaded, *"do you have any?"* *"Better than that—here,"* the environmentalist replied as he threw the boy a small bag of muesli and pointed to some dandelion leaves growing just out of reach. *"You should really consider fasting instead of eating everyday. This way you can purify your body. Well, I must leave now to kick a few dikes!"* was his parting gesture.

So there the boy remained for yet another night, thanks to his enviro-animal-rights friend. It was only the thoughts of humbly recounting his adventures on NED-2, BRT1 & 2, ZDF, BBC and CNN (and the *geld* that could be gained) that shored up our hero this second night. Where were the stampeding media hordes? If only they would pass by, he could sign autographs and perhaps even a book contract.

As daylight came the following morning, the environmentalist returned with others of his ilk, and they had heated discussions and debates about all things and theories environmental, again ignoring tired and hungry Hans. *"It is mankind and greedy politicians that are to blame for the rape of the Rhine. We have been raping nature for 40 years,"* said one of the caring crowd. *"Yes! Nature is showing us this was wrong,"* declared another. All the green guys agreed that they were being unfairly blamed for the floods, even though they were partly responsible. True, they had prevented strengthening and extending the dikes for many years with their protests, but all they wanted was to preserve the Rembrandt landscape. Now everyone was mad at them. It was unfair because the politicians were already using the floods as political fodder for elections. After some hours of debate, the environmentalists departed for more debate and *inspraakprocedures* (public enquiries), leaving Hans behind once again, and giving him the distinct impression that these floods were simply just the result of too much talk.

Then something really fantastic and unusual happened, and it cheered up Hans immensely. The sun came out! *"Ja, ja, ja! This is an important sign. Now I know I'll be saved,"* he thought.

And he was right. Later that day, he saw mobs of people dancing on the dike and returning home. Horns were blaring, but not from joy—everyone was furious at the long lines of traffic jams. Hans heard a busload of impatient inebriated locals screaming that the return home was more of a disaster than the evacuation and that they should somehow be compensated for both. He wondered why the drivers were all making a huge detour instead of taking the direct route across the bridge. Later, he learned it was to avoid paying the bridge toll again.

SPECIAAL FLOOD SECTION

Kijk in Weekeinde op pagina 3

De Telegraaf

Per exemplaar: zaterdag ƒ 1,95

Frankrijk Fr.	12,50	Madeira Esc.	310,–
Griekenl. Dr.	400,–	Marokko D.	30,–
Indon. RP	8.800,–	Ned.Ant. A./	6,–
Italië L.	2.700,–	Noorw. Kr.	17,–
Israël N. Shek	9,50	Oostenr. O.S.	26,–
Kenia KShs	120,–	Portugal Esc.	310,–
Luxemb. Fr.	51,–	Sovjet-U. SUR	3,–

No. 33,296   99ste jaargang   Hoofdredactie: Colijn R. de Wit   108 paginas   zaterdag 23 Maart, 1995

WEEKEINDE
Nog
één
avond
VRIJGEZEL

PRIVE
Rook is
ook een
mens...
pagina 33

AMERIKANEN HOUDEN ONS LACHSPIEGEL VOOR pagina TA1

"I placed my faith in a soggy Uitsmijter!"

Exclusief Verdrinker Fotos

door Laura Boucke

MAASTRICHT, zaterdag

Hans Verdrinker, the hero of last week's "high water" disaster, said yesterday that he could not have continued his ordeal without the hope of a soggy ham-and-cheese uitsmijter when he got home.

The young lad who plugged a dijk with his finger (and later lost it) was clearly moved by the attention he has been given recently.

Hans' story first came to light when he sent anonymous letters to De Telegoof, the London Times, the New York Times, Stern and the Erie Gazette. Since then he has selflessly committed to paid interviews with radio, television and the press worldwide.

Dispite some criticism from both the ME (who thought that the boy did not "obey orders") and local environmentalists (who protested his trampling of endangered weeds and mosquitos), many people agree that his controversial actions probably saved more than 2,000 cloggies from extinction.

German authorities also praised the prompt actions and hoped that in so doing, Dutch communities would be more friendly to their neighbours.

COFFEE SALES UP!

The FEDERATION OF COFFEE BREWERS & DRINKERS reports that sales of Dutch coffee have increased by 150% since The UnDutchables published a guide to how to drink the stuff.

Formerly, foreigners were just sloshing it into cups and gulping it down, without regard to how to pour and stir it.

Zie verder pag. 2 kol 1

Wat doen
DDR-BONZEN
bij
NEDERLANDSE
bedrijven?
pagina 5

VROUW
Mode
krijgt
MORAAL
pagina 19

HET WEER
RUSTIG

Veel
bewolking

Plaatselijk
mist

Zwakke tot
matige zuidenwind

ZON ONDER 18.48, MORGEN OP 10.18
ZONDAG EEN WOENSDAG
Veel bewolking en overwegend droog. In de nacht temperatuur iets boven nul en overdag circa 8 graden.
UITGEBREID WEER PAGINA 4

CARAVAN+CAMPING RAI

22 t/m 27 november
Amsterdam RAI

KLM

NOTICE

HONEYMOON
FARES & UPGRADES
DO NOT INCLUDE
MEALS OR DRINKS

NAPKIN
SHORTAGE?

RECYCLE THIS
NEWSPAPER
(ALSO GOOD FOR
USE IN TOILETS)

Our hero, a bit thinner for his ordeal, was eventually discovered by some returning farmers, who found his tale most incredible. A few minutes later, the local chapter of greenies returned to the scene, having at last found a solution to the problem of the deserted digit in the dike. Despite the experiences of the past week, the townspeople accepted the green-team dike-mender's credentials and noticeably subdued rantings about *"nature's way of objecting"* and humanity having *"no right to impose its hedonist . . . blah, blah."* With that, the farmers all wished the boy a speedy recovery and left to find their cows, pigs and chickens, and to buy more batteries for their calculators (which were sure to work overtime in the ensuing months, considering that many of the recently repatriated were protesting, filing lawsuits and making major money machinations about their flood losses). The sight of at least five zeroes lined up before the decimal point brought some to the brink of orgasm.

Then suddenly, without a word of warning or regret, the dike mender, with one swoop of his axe, divorced the boy from the barrier, close to the knuckle. In one motion, he had permanently plugged the leak, aesthetically appeased the green team, saved the son from starvation . . . and also stopped the kid from picking his nose and making his point! In future debates, when people would pontificate, *"There was no disaster, there was only high water,"* or *"The '95 floods caused inconvenience, not a disaster,"* there would be at least one hero, Hans Verdrinker, who could prove, with one hand raised, that indeed there had been a disaster, though now part of him was:

"JUST ANOTHER BRICK IN THE WAAL."

APPENDIX A
A VIEW OF THE DUTCH THROUGH THE ENGLISH LANGUAGE

beat the **Dutch**	to do something extraordinary or startling. Ex: How does he do it? It beats the Dutch.
do a **Dutch**	to desert, escape; to commit suicide
double **Dutch**	gibberish
Dutch angle	in cinematography, a shot in which the camera is tilted to intentionally distort or disorientate
Dutch auction	an auction that proceeds backwards; one in which the price is reduced until a buyer is found
Dutch bargain	bargain made and sealed while drinking
Dutch built	originally, Dutch flat-bottomed vessels; current usage attributed to: (a) male: long and lanky (b) female: see "Dutch buttocked"
Dutch buttocked	originally, a strain of Dutch cattle with large hind quarters; contemporary association is the large, pear-shaped rump of modern Dutch women, stemming from excessive Bicycle riding and dairy products

Dutch comfort	little or no comfort at all
Dutch concert	babble of noises or uproar like that made by a gathering of loud-mouths quarreling, singing, etc. in various stages of intoxication
Dutch consolation	the philosophy or attitude that, "Whatever ill befalls you, there is someone worse off than you."
Dutch courage	courage induced by alcoholic drink
Dutch defence	surrender
Dutch door	a door with upper and lower parts that can be opened independently
Dutch feast	a party where the entertainer gets drunk before his guests
Dutch generosity	penny-pinching, stinginess
Dutch gleek	heavy or excessive drinking
Dutch headache	hangover
*dutch*ing	the use of gamma rays to make spoiled food edible again
Dutch it	double-cross
Dutch light	simultaneously lighting more than one cigarette with a single match
Dutch lottery	a lottery in which tickets are drawn in certain classes or series for each of which certain prizes increasing in number and value with each class are fixed
*dutch*man	an object for hiding faulty workmanship (construction)
*Dutch*man's breeches	a toxic and narcotic flower (*dicentra cucullaria*) shaped like an old-fashioned pair of knickers
Dutch metal	a malleable alloy . . . beaten into thin leaves and used as cheap imitation of gold-leaf; also called "Dutch gold," "Dutch foil" and "Dutch leaf"

Dutch nightingale	frog
Dutch oven	a person's mouth
Dutch reckoning	guesswork; faulty reckoning
Dutch rub	using knuckles to hit or rub someone on the top of the head
Dutch talent	doing something by using one's brawn rather than one's brain
Dutch treat	a party, outing, etc. at which each participant pays for his own share (corruption of "Dutch trait")
Dutch uncle	a severe critic or counsellor
Dutch widow	prostitute
Dutch wife	artificial sex partner such as an inflatable doll
Flying *Dutch*man	a ghost ship presaging disaster
go *Dutch*	to have each person pay his own share of the bill
I'm a *Dutch*man	a phrase implying refusal or disbelief
in *Dutch*	in disfavour, disgrace or trouble
to *Dutch*	to miscalculate in placing bets so as to have a mathematical expectancy of losing rather than winning

APPENDIX B

A CHOSEN SELECTION OF DUTCH/ENGLISH HOMONYMS

ncorrect use of Dutch/English homonyms can have an interesting effect on people. At an informal get-together, a Dutch woman introduced herself to a British woman. When asked about her profession, the Dutch woman calmly replied, *"I fuck dogs."* This appendix provides some of the more potentially embarrassing cases.

Since this book was first published in 1989, many authors and websites have copied and/or expanded these lists, as well as the one in Appendix A. The intent here is to provide humorous homonym mix-ups (false cognates or *faux amis*) between the two languages. This only works with words that sound (nearly) the same in both languages to native English speakers:

Why did the salesgirl slap the customer?
Because he said, "I really like your rate."

In this example, "rate" (English) and *reet* (Dutch) sound the same, but in Dutch *reet* means "arse."

In the tables that follow, some words have more definitions than supplied (e.g. *heet* means "hot" in addition to "to be named"). Sometimes the slang translation of a word is given in addition to or instead of the ordinary translation (e.g. *doos* is slang for "vagina" and also means "box"). In short, only the relevant (humorous) definitions are included.

Dutch – English

Inoffensive Dutch word	Sounds like English word	Dutch meaning
dik	dick	fat, thick
doop	dope	baptize
douche	douche	shower
fiets	feats	bicycle
fok	fuck	breed
heet	hate	to be named
hoor	whore	hear
ijdel	idle	vain
kaak	cock (US accent)	jaw
kam	cum	comb
kijk	kike	look
kil	kill	chilly
kip	kip (sleep)	chicken
kok	cock (Brit accent)	cook
kont	cunt	buttocks
kook	coke (cocaine)	cook
kool	coal	cabbage
kou	cow	cold
krap	crap	skint, penniless, narrow
kunt	cunt	could
kus	cuss	kiss
kwik	quick	mercury
ledikant	lady can't	bed
mais	mice	corn
meet	mate	mark, measure
mes	mess	knife
natie	Nazi	nation
nevel	navel	mist, haze, nebula
peen	pain	carrot
pieper	peeper	potato
prik	prick (dick)	pop (fizzy), injection
reep	rape	rope, band, strip
rente	rent	interest
sectie	sexy	section
shag	shag (fuck)	cigarette tobacco
snoep	snoop	sweets, candy
tof	tough	"cool," great, decent
toneel	toenail	theatre, play
trap	trap	stairs
vaart	fart	travel, sail
vlaai	fly	flan
Vondel	fondle	a Dutch surname
winkel	winkle (penis)	shop

English – Dutch

Inoffensive English word	Sounds like Dutch word	Dutch meaning
back	*bek*	muzzle, snout, mouth
Bic	*bik*	eat
bill	*bil*	buttock
brill(iant)	*bril*	glasses, toilet seat
cut	*kut*	vagina, cunt
dear	*dier*	animal
dote	*dood*	dead
doze	*doos*	vagina, box
eye	*aai*	caress, stroke
fees	*vies*	dirty
flow	*vlo*	flea
flicker	*flikker*	homosexual, gay
freight	*vreet*	to eat, gorge
fry / fryin'	*vrij / vrijen*	make love, pet, neck
junk	*junk*	heroine, junkie
kicker	*kikker*	frog
kin	*kin*	chin
lid / lit	*lid*	penis, member
link	*link*	very pissed off, angry
lull	*lul*	penis
map	*mep*	smack, whack, hit
novel	*navel*	navel
pall	*paal*	hard-on, pole
paper	*peper*	pepper
pardon	*paarden*	horses
peace, piece	*pies*	piss
peel	*piel*	penis
pens	*pens*	gut, tripe
pick	*pik*	penis
pimple	*pimpel*	boozing
play	*plee*	toilet
ramp	*ramp*	disaster
rate	*reet*	backside, arse
ritz	*rits*	zipper
rod	*rot*	putrid (rot op = piss off)
sigh	*saai*	boring
slim	*slim*	clever
slip	*slip*	underpants
slope	*sloop*	wreck, pillowcase
Spain	*speen*	teat, dummy, pacifier
spin	*spin*	spider
spot	*spot*	mockery
start	*staart*	tail
steak	*steek*	stab
take	*teek*	tick (bloodsucker)
tipple	*tippel*	streetwalk (of whores)

There are, of course, many other homonyms (homophones) and lookalikes, but these are not included in cases where there is no humorous connection via an embarrassing or awkward situation by misunderstanding the meaning. Thus, homonyms such as "cake"|*keek* (looked) and "acorn"|*eekhoorn* (squirrel) as well as lookalikes such as "trots"|*trots* (proud) and "slang"|*slang* (snake, hose pipe) are not included because there is no potentially humorous or embarrassing mix-up between the homonyms.

Funny situations arise when newcomers mishear or misconstrue the meanings of near-homophones. Some English-speaking foreigners think the word *snel* sounds quite a lot like "snail" and associate *snel* with "slow" instead of "fast." One such newcomer confessed to a colleague that it had taken him a long time to figure out why the motorway is called a *snelweg*. His colleague had a think about this and a few days later reported that when she was driving on the *snelweg*, she started imagining little snails cruising down the snail*weg*, and that whenever she saw a Dutch car pulling a caravan, it evoked the image of a snail*weg*.

It's also easy for foreigners to infer the wrong meaning of some words by confusing or misspelling word parts that look or sound nearly the same. Thus a *stomerij* is not a place where idiots are made (based on the word *stom* for "stupid") but refers to a dry-cleaner's (based on the word *stoom* for "steam").

If pronunciation is discounted, another amusing avenue one could follow is that of Dutch and English expressions that look alike and that could be easily confused. A recent arrival in the Netherlands once asked if there are a lot of vegetarians in Holland. Why this question? Because so many of the Dutch people sign their letters "with friendly vegetables" (*met vriendelijke groeten*). This mix-up is based on the words *groeten* (greetings) and *groenten* (vegetables).

APPENDIX C

A VIEW OF THE NETHERLANDS THROUGH DUTCH IDIOMS

redictably, Dutch idioms obsess about the three "W's" (windmills, wooden shoes and water) as well as ditches, dikes, ships, sea, sand, flowers and Bicycles. Try using some of the phrases and words in this appendix with your Dutch colleagues, and take note of their reactions and facial expressions when you do.

In addition to the Dutch idioms, literal translations are provided for your amusement. The literal translations are listed in parentheses under the Dutch idioms.

WINDMILLS . . .

een klap van de molen gehad hebben
(to have been hit by the windmill)
to be crazy, to have a screw loose

dat is koren op zijn molen
(that is wheat on his windmill)
that's the way he likes it; that's a strong point

iemand door de molen halen
(to run someone through the mill)
to heavily scrutinize someone

met molentjes lopen
(to walk with little windmills)
to be silly

het zit in de molen (it's sitting in the windmill)	it's in the works
de ambtelijke molens (the official windmills)	the wheels of government
werken als een molenpaard (to work like a windmill horse)	to work very hard, work like a dog
in de medische mallemolen geraken (to be in the medical merry-go-round)	to be repeatedly tested and treated by doctors without satisfactory results

WOODEN SHOES . . .

blijf met de klompen van het ijs (keep the clogs off the ice)	keep out of it; mind your own business
met de klompen op het ijs komen (to come on the ice with wooden shoes)	to rush unprepared into something
nu breekt mijn klomp (now my clog breaks)	that does it, that takes the cake, what next?
op je klompen aanvoelen (to feel it with your clogs)	to be obvious
een boer op klompen (a farmer in wooden shoes)	a right peasant, an ill-mannered person

DITCHES & DIKES . . .

oude koeien uit de sloot halen (to get old cows from the ditch)	to bring up past unpleasant things that don't matter anymore
met de hakken over de sloot (with the heels over the ditch)	to make it by the skin of one's teeth
morgenrood brengt water in de sloot (morning red brings water in the ditch)	rain is in the forecast
hij loopt in geen zeven sloten tegelijk (he doesn't walk in seven ditches simultaneously)	he can look after himself
je kunt niet over twee sloten tegelijk springen	you can't have your cake and eat it too;

(you can't jump over two ditches at once) | you have to choose one or the other

iemand van de wal in de sloot helpen
(to help someone from the shore into the ditch) | to make things worse, give bad advice or poor service

van twee walletjes eten
(to eat from two shores) | to have your cake and eat it too; take advantage of two different parties

aan lager wal zijn/zitten
(to be/sit on lower shore) | to be down and out

dat raakt kant noch wal
(that touches neither bank nor shore) | that makes no sense at all; that's nonsense

van wal steken
(to go from shore) | to start, proceed, go ahead

waar de dijk het laagst is, loopt het eerst het water over
(where the dike is lowest, water overflows first) | poor people suffer first

de beste stuurlui staan aan wal
(the best steersmen are ashore) | outsiders think they know best; it's easy to give advice from afar

aan de dijk zetten
(to place by the dike) | to dismiss, fire

een dijk van een . . .
(a dike of a . . .) | a hell of a . . .

dat zet geen zoden aan de dijk
(that puts no sod by the dike) | that's of no use; that won't get us anywhere

WATER & THE SEA . . .

gevaarlijk vaarwater
(dangerous waterway) | hot water, trouble, dangerous/risky situation

in rustiger (vaar)water komen
(to come into calmer water) | to have the worst behind you, improve things

in iemands vaarwater komen/zitten
(to enter/sit in someone's waterway) | to get/be in someone's way

je moet maar uit zijn vaarwater blijven
(you need to stay out of his waterway)

you better keep out of his way

zijn geld in het water gooien
(to throw one's money in the water)

to pour one's money down the drain

de druppel die de emmer doet overlopen
(the drop that makes the bucket overflow)

the straw that broke the camel's back

bang zijn zich aan (koud) water te branden
(to be afraid to burn oneself in (cold) water)

to be overly cautious or fearful

een oplichter van het zuiverste water
(a crook of the purest water)

a crook of the first order

het water staat mij tot de lippen
(I am up to my lips in water)

I am up to my neck (in difficulties/problems)

het regent pijpenstelen
(it's raining pipe stems)

it's pouring

wanneer het op de groten regent, drupt het op de kleinen
(when it rains on the big boys, it drips on the little guys)

when the boss makes a bundle, the workers make a pittance

in het water vallen
(to fall in the water)

to fall through, be ruined

zo vlug als water
(as fast as water)

quick, sharp, bright

als water en vuur zijn
(to be like water and fire)

to be at each other's throats

water bij de wijn doen
(to pour water into the wine)

to water down, moderate or compromise

iets boven water halen
(to bring something above water)

to expose, shine a light on/dig up something

weer boven water komen
(to come above water again)

to turn up again

iets aan z'n water voelen
(to sense something using one's water)

to feel something in
one's bones

spijkers zoeken op laag water
(to look for nails at ebb tide)

to find fault, nit-pick

tussen twee waters in zwemmen
(to swim between two waters)

to work both sides to
one's advantage

water naar de zee dragen
(to carry water to the sea)

to do something useless
or futile

*dat kan al het water van de zee
niet afwassen*
(all the water in the sea can't clean that)

the shame/guilt will last
forever

recht door zee zijn/gaan
(to be/go straight through the sea)

to be straightforward/
frank/blunt

een zee van tijd
(a sea of time)

plenty of time

met iemand in zee gaan
(to go into the sea with someone)

to take one's chances
with someone

geen zee gaat hem te hoog
(no sea is too high for him)

he is game for anything

SHIPS & SAILING . . .

we zien wel waar het schip strandt
(we shall see where the ship beaches)

we'll see what happens

iemand afschepen
(to ship someone off)

to fob someone off

de schepen achter zich verbranden
(to burn the ships behind oneself)

to burn one's bridges

tussen wal en schip vallen
(to fall between shore and ship)

to fall between two stools

iemand in de boot nemen
(to take someone in the boat)

to pull someone's leg,
make fun of someone

de boot afhouden
(to hold off the boat)

to refuse, play for time,
keep one's distance

in hetzelfde schuitje zitten (to be in the same little boat)	to be in the same boat/ situation
onder zeil gaan (to go under sail)	to go to sleep
alle zeilen bijzetten (to set all sails)	to pull out all the stops
met opgestoken zeilen (with hoisted sails)	wound up, tense, angry
een oogje in het zeil houden (to keep a little eye in the sail)	to keep an eye on some- thing/someone
met hem is geen land te bezeilen (no land can be sailed with him)	he won't listen to reason
ergens verzeild raken (to be sailed somewhere)	to end up somewhere by chance
iets voor de boeg hebben (to have something in front of the bow)	to have something to do
het roer omgooien (to put the helm over)	to change course
roeien met de riemen die men heeft (to row with the oars one has)	to make do/manage
ergens het land aan hebben (to have the land on something)	to hate something
een andere koers varen (to sail another course)	to change course
alle hoop laten varen (to let all hope sail)	to abandon all hope
ergens wel bij varen (to sail well by something)	to do well out of some- thing
hoe ben je gevaren? (how did you sail?)	how did it go?
tegen de stroom ingaan (to go in against the current)	to go/swim against the tide or popular opinion
wat is er in dat kind gevaren? (what has sailed in that child?)	what has got into/ possessed that child?

er zijn kapers op de kust
(there are pirates on the coast)

there are competitors;
evil people are lurking

een man overboord is een eter minder
(a man overboard is one less eater)

what a relief to be rid of
him

kantje boord
(little edge aboard)

close call!

SAND . . .

als los zand aan elkaar hangen
(to hang together like loose sand)

to be incoherent,
disjointed

de kop in het zand steken
(to stick one's head in the sand)

to bury one's head in the
sand; hide from the truth

iemand zand in de ogen strooien
(to throw sand in someone's eyes)

to pull the wool over
someone's eyes

in het zand gelopen zijn
(to have walked in the sand)

to be ruined/spoiled

in het zand bijten
(to bite in the sand)

to die, bite the dust

zand erover
(sand on it)

to bury the hatchet;
let's forget it

zand in de machine strooien
(to throw sand in the machine)

to throw a spanner in the
works

zandloper
(sand-walker)

hourglass, egg-timer

de hakken in het zand zetten
(to put the heels in the sand)

to dig in one's heels, be
stubborn

FLOWERS . . .

de bloemetjes buiten zetten
(to put the little flowers outside)

to paint the town red, go
on a spree

de bloemen staan op de ruiten
(the flowers are standing on the
window panes)

the windows are frosted
over

iemand in de bloemetjes zetten
(to place someone in the little flowers)

to treat someone like
royalty

over de bloemetjes en de bijtjes praten
(to talk about the little flowers and the little bees)

to tell children about sex; talk about the birds and the bees

bloemlezing
(flower reading, flower lecture)

anthology

BICYCLES . . .

ga toch fietsen!
(just go cycling)

shut up; go away!

fietsen
(to ride a bike, cycle)

to have sex

fietsenrek
(bike rack)

gappy teeth

op die/zo een fiets
(on that/such a bike)

that way; now I see what you mean

doorfietsen
(to cycle through)

to flip or thumb through, hurry

ga fietsen stelen
(go steal bikes)

drop dead!

wat heb ik nu aan mijn fiets hangen?
(now what's hanging on my bike?)

what kind of mess am I in now; what's all this?

voor elkaar fietsen
(to cycle for each other)

to wrangle, manage

op een oude fiets moet je het leren
(you must learn it on an old bike)

you should learn sex from an older woman [refers to a boy having his first sexual encounter]

INDEX

The UnDutchables Birthday Calendar

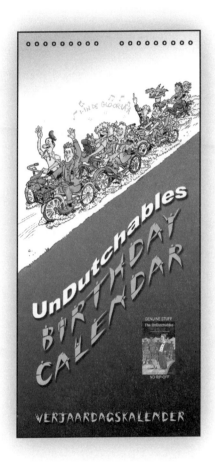

Remember all those important birthdays the Dutch way. This "perpetual calendar" allows you to identify important personal dates EVERY YEAR without making new lists or repeating diary entries. Each month is illustrated with a classic Dutch seasonal scene, all brought to you in that "UnDutchables" style. Classic.

UNDUTCHABLES BIRTHDAY CALENDAR
ISBN: 1-888580-23-2, www.white-boucke.com

a Look at the Dutch Through the eyes of a "True Brit"

BRIAN A. BRAMSON BRINGS HIS OWN FLAVOUR OF FUN TO THE DUTCH TABLE WITH THIS ONE-OF-A-KIND WORK. THE BOOK IS A COMPILATION OF PROFOUND AND HUMOROUS LETTERS FROM A BRITISH EXPATRIATE ("UNCLE BRIAN") TO HIS SHELTERED NEPHEW ("HENRY"), PREPARING THE LATTER FOR HIS IMPENDING ARRIVAL.

DEAR HENRY: LETTERS FROM THE LOWLANDS
ISBN: 1-888580-19-4, 158 pages. www.white-boucke.com

If you enjoyed this book, point your Internet browser to
The UnDutchables in the cloud.

www.undutchables.com
is a lighthearted site that focuses on *Nederlanderness*.
There are no sign-up fees, no membership fees,
no phantom "cookies," no hidden mailing list generators,
no pornography, no causes of global warming and no
racism, bigotry or child abuse.

There is, however, a free UnDutchables forum dedicated
to the open exchange of ideas and information regarding
all things Dutch.

White-Boucke Publishing, Inc.
publishes non-fiction books, video productions and
software on such diverse subjects as lifestyles, parenting,
popular music, sports and reference.

WHITE-BOUCKE PUBLISHING, INC.
PO Box 400, Lafayette, CO 80026, USA
tel: (303) 604-0661
e-mail: inquire@white-boucke.com

or visit our website at:
www.white-boucke.com